Prosper through Real Estate

Prosper through Real Estate

A Complete, Proven, Step-by-Step Guide to
Purchasing, Preparing, and Renting Real Estate

Greg Dayton and Gordon Weidle

iUniverse, Inc.
New York   Lincoln   Shanghai

Prosper through Real Estate
A Complete, Proven, Step-by-Step Guide to Purchasing, Preparing, and
Renting Real Estate

iUniverse books may be ordered through booksellers or by contacting:

iUniverse
2021 Pine Lake Road, Suite 100
Lincoln, NE 68512
www.iuniverse.com
1-800-Authors (1-800-288-4677)

Because of the dynamic nature of the Internet, any Web addresses or links contained in this book may have changed since publication and may no longer be valid.

The views expressed in this work are solely those of the author and do not necessarily reflect the views of the publisher, and the publisher hereby disclaims any responsibility for them.

ISBN: 978-0-595-45942-1 (pbk)
ISBN: 978-0-595-70377-7 (cloth)
ISBN: 978-0-595-90242-2 (ebk)

Printed in the United States of America

Dedication

Greg

For my children—Brandon, Ashley, and Zachary, for the love and happiness they bring me every time they touch my life and the reason I get up each day. From the moment you were born, and with each passing day, my love for you grows, my drive to teach and protect you strengthens, and my pride in you shines brighter. Please keep my love deep within your hearts and remember to, *"Never Quit."*

Also, to my mother, I thank you for the lessons you have passed on to me that I draw from each and every day.

Gordon

I dedicate the writing of this book to my son, Brandon Connor, who is an endless source of inspiration, joy, and unequivocal love. I am proud to be your father and cherish my time with you. You teach me to never take for granted the simple pleasures in life and to look at the world through the eyes of a child—with wonderment and possibility. May you follow your dreams and realize that all things are possible through hard work, dedication, and passion. Always remember, *"Where there is a Weidle, there is a way."* I will always love you.

To my parents, Karl and Johanna, thank you for your support and guidance over the years. You taught me the value of hard work and commitment. You were always there for me when I needed you. I love and appreciate you

Why Should I Buy This Book?

Whether you are a novice or experienced investor, this book will give you the tools you need to make your dream of financial independence and prosperity a reality. This book is written from personal experience and takes you through a detailed, step-by-step, proven process.

Buy this book and you'll learn:

- How to run a successful rental business that works and doesn't take a lot of time and money
- How money can be made
- How to turn equity into cash
- How to get started
- How to find the right properties to purchase
- How to correctly advertise the property
- How to save time and effort by identifying potential tenants over the phone
- How to find great tenants who will pay you on time
- How to find and work with trusted tradesmen
- The advantages and disadvantages of using management firms and associations
- Refinancing scenarios showing how to maximize your financial power and purchase more properties
- How to handle the accounting and taxes
- How to work with and understand legal forms and documents
- How to get out of the business when you want

Contents

Preface..ix

Introduction...xi

Chapter One   Why Invest in Real Estate.....................................1

Chapter Two   Why Aren't More People Doing This?..................14

Chapter Three   Who Can Do This?...27

Chapter Four   How the Money is Made.......................................32

Chapter Five   Retiring from the Rental Business........................38

Chapter Six   A Summary of Where the Money is Made............42

Chapter Seven   Money-How Much and Where Do I Get It?.........44

Chapter Eight   Making the Decision..57

Chapter Nine   Finding, Buying and Paying for the Property.......63

Chapter Ten   Prosper Through (The Rental) Process..................78

Chapter Eleven   A Summary on Renters..128

Chapter Twelve   Handling Calls..135

Chapter Thirteen   Working with the Tradesmen..............................138

Chapter Fourteen   Accounting For The Profit...................................141

Chapter Fifteen   The Legal Section...144

Chapter Sixteen   Associations and Management Firms...................150

Chapter Seventeen   Getting started today..155

Chapter Eighteen   Final Thoughts..158

Appendix   Real Estate Terms...161

Checklist Section...203

Preface

Thank you for purchasing our book. It may be, *should be*, **will be** the most profitable purchase you have made in a long time, if not in your life.

There is a lot of marketing materials that promise easy "get rich quick" schemes with a high ROI—return on investment. The first question that comes to most minds is; is this for real? Is anybody actually making money on the scheme other than the author who created the material in the first place, who has a flair for self promotion and marketing? Can people purchasing the material follow the methodology without a high level of frustration, humiliation, and poor results, or will the material just collect dust or end up in the garbage? How much does this cost? How much time will I need to accomplish the level of success that is being advertised? And finally, is this something that I can do and feel comfortable doing?

Remember—"It is not what you make, it is not what you keep, it is what you do with what you keep"

The key to this statement is making your money work for you regardless of the amount. If you have it stuffed in a pillowcase in your closet; you can't expect it to compound on its own when the lights dim. There are hundreds of investment vehicles where you can earn a return. We intend to clearly illustrate that investing in real estate is one of the easiest to understand and consistently provides the highest returns year after year. There are countless examples of people making and inheriting huge amounts of money and literally blowing it through senseless consumption and unwise decisions. There are also numerous examples of people with relatively meager earnings becoming financially independent based on a sound plan and making the right choices.

We will provide you with that sound plan and help you make the right choices when it comes to real estate investment. We will also focus on areas that have been routinely ignored but are key to the process—like finding and retaining good renters.

We ask that you don't put this book, or methodology, in the same category as most of the others. We can genuinely say that this methodology is real and we and others who have applied these principles have been successful in making a lot of money. You are probably thinking: "Why did they write this book? After all, it takes a lot of time, energy and determination to get a book published." After having countless requests to write a book from friends and people with whom we work, we decided that it just made sense. Those we have talked with have received so much value from our conversations and the principles we advocate. Now when the topic comes up, we can just hand them the book and save two hours. The upside of writing this book is anyone can read this and make his or her dreams of financial independence become realities. It isn't something that only a few select can achieve.

We ask that you shelf all of the bad things you hear about renting property and being a landlord. Those saying negative things fall into one of two groups of people.

1) Those who have never done it before or are getting second-hand information and are imagining the worst. They sound as if they know what they are talking about but have never gotten into renting themselves. They are thinking about how they treated their landlord or how someone they know treated their landlord. That isn't a voice of experience.

2) Those who have tried it, done it incorrectly and have been burned. They were working without the knowledge that we provide in this book, or were sloppy on how they proceeded and saw it as the easy way to make money that couldn't fail. They thought they could buy any property, rent it to anyone and get rich.

If you follow our methodology, you won't be a part of group number one, who only talk about the failures of others and you also won't do everything wrong like group number two.

Throughout this book, there are points that will be made multiple times. That isn't an accident. These are points that are the basis of our strategy and therefore need to be brought up in a number of different situations so you clearly understand the principles. Being creatures of repetition, we learn more effectively by hearing important points several times in various contexts. The points made more than once are ones to take note of by either highlighting or writing down. They are important and can mean the difference between success and failure.

Thank you again for purchasing our book. We live this system with great success which has put us on the road to financial freedom. We know that you can enjoy the same results too.

Introduction

Have you ever played Monopoly?

Most people at one point in their life have played Monopoly and have an understanding of how they either lose or win. You win by owning and controlling more property than the other players in the game. It is also apparent that if you own or control properties like Park Place then you generally do better than the others players. Properties like Park Place are situated in areas on the board that are considered high value based on their location and proximity to other high value properties. The players who acquire the most high value properties and manage their cash flow in the process don't run out of money and are successful. You land on a prospective location on the board and assess whether or not you have the cash to support the purchase. You must ensure that adequate cash reserves are in place after the purchase to cover eventualities like going to jail or picking a Chance card that demands payment. The more properties you control without putting yourself in a cash flow crisis will result in more visitors landing on your property, which enables you to purchase even more properties. The objective in the game is the same as our methodology—to make smart buying decisions based on the principles we have developed over a number of years of successful real estate investing.

We (the authors, Greg and Gordon), met while selling software for a major application firm in Chicago in the mid 90's. A strong friendship quickly developed based on our mutual interest in investing in real estate. We had a number of friends and colleagues who invested in rental properties but continually complained about the problems they were having. They were interested in knowing why our rental system seemed so much easier than theirs. After explaining our system many times, we decided that it was a process that we could share with everyone in a book format. We became more dedicated to writing this book when those who put our process to the test verified how successful and easy it really can be.

Prior to purchasing my first house, I (Greg) wanted to get into the rental business. Using the criteria that you'll read in this book, I purchased my first house (townhouse) on a quiet cul-de-sac which backed up to a nature preserve with a lake. My plan was to live there for three years and then rent it. I refinanced that first townhouse a few months prior to moving out of it and used the equity to buy my next house. Following my plan, I began buying more houses by using the equity in one to buy the next. After more than a decade of renting properties, I own a number of rental units and my tenant issues have been virtually non-existent.

Throughout my childhood I (Gordon), watched my father invest in real estate, which taught me what a sound investment real estate could be, if done properly. I acquired my first two townhouses in my early 20's while living in Canada. From that point, I became passionate about educating myself in real estate investments and property rentals. Combining this education with my own experiences and Greg's successful methodology, I have purchased additional rental real estate and have not had renter issues or problems. My experience, along with many others, is proof that our system works.

Following this process is the path to financial freedom; never worrying about paying the bills, or losing the roof over your head because of a job loss, or suffering some other financial crisis like a health issue, major accident or litigation situation.

Renting property satisfies one of the primary needs of a large and growing pool of renters who need a place to live. Renters, in turn, provide you with the equity and cash flow to acquire additional properties to ensure your own financial success.

We use the phrase **controlled** property instead of **owned** property. Owned implies writing a check for the full amount of the investment. Control means leveraging someone else's money and having someone else pay for the loan. If you simply control the properties it implies that you didn't write a check for the full-appraised value, but rather some subset of that amount. Therefore, you will be able to spread your money across more properties, which will allow you to control more property with a much higher total value.

Here's a simplified example. If you spend $100 on one investment, and the investment goes up by 5% annually, you have made $5 that year. If you use the same $100 and control 10 properties, at $10 per property, then you control $1,000 worth of property. The appreciation at 5% is now $5 x 10 or $50 per year on your $100 investment.

The key to our methodology is to use only a small amount of your own money, borrow a large amount of someone else's money (the bank), while getting someone else (the renter), to pay the monthly bill to the one who loaned you the money.

The mechanics of this process are exactly the same as when you buy a house to live in, with one additional step. That step is to find someone else to live in that house and pay you. As you will see later, this is an easy step as long as you do it the right way.

As you can see, this is a simple formula that you can duplicate every two, three, or four years to control more property without any real investment in subsequent years. This is accomplished by reinvesting the gains from the other properties through refinancing the appreciation, instead of having to fund additional purchases from saved money.

The first comment most people who hear our method make is, "I don't want to be a landlord." Being a landlord can be a tough way to make money, if done wrong. However, we will show you how to do it right. After controlling dozens of properties over the years we have yet to experience a significant renter issue that was serious enough to consider eviction or legal action. The key to success is to follow the methodology in this book to make sure that the recommended steps are taken to assess and select a potential candidate to occupy one of your properties. If you do this, your biggest concern will be having the time to deposit the rental checks.

Many people have asked us; "How do you sleep at night with all of those mortgages?" The answer is, "That is why we sleep at night." Knowing that we have an equity base that is rapidly growing and can be utilized easily to fund emergency needs gives us peace of mind.

Another reason that we sleep so well is knowing that not only ourselves, but people who are close to us can be helped in times of need or extreme loss by having those houses available. When our kids get out of school and need a place to live, we have houses available. Otherwise, they could be back home to live for an unknown number of years. Should our parent(s) have a major health issue that forces them to downsize their present accommodations, we would have options to offer. You can protect yourself too. It is extremely comforting to know that should a serious medical situation or set of circumstances at work dictate a need to downsize your accommodations, you have options available. Think of it as another form of insurance, for you and your loved ones, that is appreciating in value, while earning a return.

As we go through life, if we are to succeed, we need to think out our goals and have a plan to reach them. "A goal without a plan is just a dream." We have a plan and a methodology to make it a goal and turn that goal into a reality. We have done it and are now in a position, based on many successful years, to show you how to do it for yourself.

In this book, we explain, in an easily understood format, a very basic concept—how to control real estate and have somebody else pay for it. This idea has been around for a long time. Successful and financially independent people have found that real estate is an important component of their overall wealth portfolio. There may be a lot of people reading this book that are doing it now but their "system," or lack of system, isn't working very well. They may have high vacancy rates, collection issues, and eviction problems. Learning this business without help has proven costly and stressful. There is a better way and we plan to show it to you.

A final thought before you begin reading the book. All of us have one or two opportunities put in front of us every day.

➢ 95% of us can't recognize those opportunities.

➢ Of the 5%, who see the opportunity, 4% won't do anything about it.

➢ 1% of the population will act on the opportunity and many, if done right, will make money.

Do you see yourself as part of the 1% or part of the other 99%?

Based on our years of experience, we believe that you can be in that 1% group who is making money, if you take the first step and follow our proven methodology.

Chapter One

Why Invest in Real Estate

Here are some quick facts to think about:

➤ You control your real estate investments. In the stock and bond markets, most people will never understand market dynamics. Most people who work in the financial industry make less than the people they represent. (Ask your broker what they made last year.) Impersonal market forces control your financial destiny. Your financial future is tied to fate, luck, and market dynamics that you can neither control, nor predict. (Remember the 60% market drop of year 2000?)

➤ In real estate, there is less risk of losing any or all of your investment. Remember that real estate is an extremely liquid investment. There will always be a buyer for your property should you need the cash. The only variable is the price, which is the primary factor of finding a tenant or buyer.

➤ The trends continue to indicate rising prices for real estate appreciation and rents.

➤ With real estate, you call the shots. You are in control. You select which properties you buy, the rent you charge, the tenants to occupy your holdings, how long they lease, and the penalties of backing out of a lease commitment before it expires.

➤ The United States is the greatest country on earth. People are risking death on a daily basis to enter the country in an attempt to live the American dream. In 2004, the INS issued 946,000 green cards and naturalized 537,000 people. In addition, there are another 500,000 people who are undocumented that arrived in the same year. One constant need for all of these people is a place to live. That's what you provide. The desirability of starting a new life in America will not decrease. The population will continue to increase through immigration and childbirth. As land continues to decrease, its value continues to increase. This is a basic economic principle which will continue to drive real estate appreciation and demand.

> The baby boomers (born in years 1946–1964), impacted the housing market during the 70's and 80's as it experienced the biggest boom ever. The equity market in the 90's also took off because the Boomers had reached an age where their savings grew. Your highest annual earnings years will typically be in your early forties. It is during this time when the majority of our kids has either gone to school or is going to school. The dynamics of these factors provided an environment for an unusually high influx of money into the market. Based on market supply and demand concepts, when there is more money than product (in this case stock), then the price of that product will increase.

> Baby Boomers have driven markets since the 70's. The health and exercise craze are strong examples. They both boomed in the 90's. The GNC™s and BOWFLEX™s started their strong sales during that period. As the Boomers age, they don't want to look old and are doing everything they can to look younger. Plastic surgery is on the rise for the same reason. The Boomers will someday downsize and drive the housing market also. The upper-class homes in the late 90's and early 2000's are still being built, but we're seeing a trend that indicates that it won't be long before people will start moving out of those homes because they are getting older. They will want to downsize to smaller, but nicer, properties. Many will move to townhouses in more serene, maintenance free, locations. We recommend townhouses to be used as rental units today. This combination of demographic and property type will position you for either higher sale price or continued tenant stream in the future.

> Older couples, whose kids have grown and left their residences, are downsizing from million dollar houses to smaller ones. They no longer want to maintain larger and more expensive properties. Many couples, where both husband and wife are working, are reprioritizing their lives and putting more emphasis on family time rather than material items, such as large houses. That's why the market we are suggesting you invest in is rental townhouses. If you invest in this market today, you will be properly positioned to take advantage of this downsizing trend in the upcoming years. That trend will drive above- average, increased appreciation on townhouses that back up to golf courses, lakes, and nature preserves, as more and more individuals seek these locations.

> A sizeable majority of Americans still do not have the gross monthly income or credit necessary to purchase a home, but everyone needs a place to live. Other than food, water, and safety, there is nothing more important than a place to live.

Keep in mind that this book was written to help you understand how you can own a lot of real estate, not just purchase real estate. We are all capable of buying real estate, but very few have a good knowledge of what to do with it after the closing. We will teach you how to own it without the responsibility, or hassle, of paying for it each month.

In order to understand why investing in real estate is a good idea; you first need to understand a little about the appreciation history. Housing market appreciation in the United States has historically increased through the years. A lack of property value appreciation, or minor decrease, has only taken place a couple of times in the recent twenty-five to thirty years. In general, real estate has always increased in value and never gone down more than a few percentage points in any year. As we all know, the stock market has experienced several decreases, some substantial, in the last twenty years alone.

It is important to know that your investment in real estate, although large, is one of the safest decisions you can make. We point this out because you need to know that this investment is backed by something that you will always be able to sell in the event circumstances change in your life and you need access to that money. Housing is something that has been, and always will be, in demand because the population is growing and people will always need a place to live.

First, we'll look at some of the appreciation data in the overall U.S. housing market and also by different regions within the country.

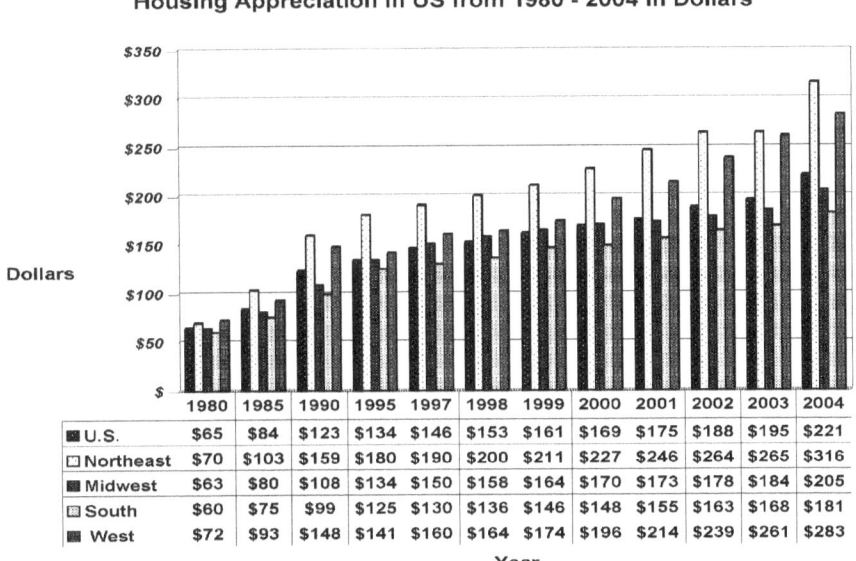

Housing Appreciation in US from 1980 - 2004 in Dollars

	1980	1985	1990	1995	1997	1998	1999	2000	2001	2002	2003	2004
U.S.	$65	$84	$123	$134	$146	$153	$161	$169	$175	$188	$195	$221
Northeast	$70	$103	$159	$180	$190	$200	$211	$227	$246	$264	$265	$316
Midwest	$63	$80	$108	$134	$150	$158	$164	$170	$173	$178	$184	$205
South	$60	$75	$99	$125	$130	$136	$146	$148	$155	$163	$168	$181
West	$72	$93	$148	$141	$160	$164	$174	$196	$214	$239	$261	$283

Year
All numbers in $000s

Chart 1

This chart shows housing prices scattered throughout the United States via census data. The data shows prices going up from 1980 through 2004 and the housing appreciation by area. The Midwest is appreciating the least with the West appreciating the most. The Northeast is second with the South following in a close third. This data shows housing prices traditionally go up, unlike most people's portfolios. The volatility in the equities market is much more extreme than nationwide housing prices.

In 1980, the average home price in the United States was $64,200, which escalated to $221,000 in 2004. That growth represents a 5.3%, year over year, compounded, appreciation rate. As we will explain later, this may sound like a smaller return than you might get in the stock market, but it is actually much higher. The Northeast has enjoyed a great appreciation, due primarily to economic growth and employment stability in New York and surrounding cities.

These numbers are actually national averages. As we saw in the chart above, these numbers are skewed slightly depending on the area of the country. In some areas they are slightly higher, and some reflect slightly lower appreciation.

To maximize your appreciation, the ideal communities are located on golf courses, lakes, forest preserves, rivers, recreational areas, schools, and transportation access areas like railway stations. You may pay a little more, but the appreciation on these homes is going to be dramatically different than homes that aren't in these settings. Undesirable locations would include buildings, highways, dumps, and shopping centers. These are not desirable from a resell standpoint, or a rental standpoint. Typically, people don't want to rent something that backs up to a shopping center. Being **close** to a shopping center can be a positive factor, but if the home's view is looking at a shopping center, that fact will limit the number of tenants you attract and the monthly rental price you can charge. The age demographics reflect renters are becoming older. Older renters are looking for peaceful and quiet settings. Don't overlook those types of properties when you are out scouting for potential purchases.

One of the factors that continue to drive appreciation is lower interest rates. As interest rates go lower, the average person can afford a bigger or more expensive house for less money. As a result of being able to borrow more money at a lower rate, the average family can pay a little more for their house, but still pay less on their monthly mortgage. In many cases, people are less likely to walk away from a house because they think it costs too much. Instead, they pay a little more knowing they won't feel the impact on their monthly mortgage. Financial lenders have also become more creative in coming up with mortgages to appeal to a wider audience of people with a wide variety of financial options.

Housing Prices Percentage Increases by Region from 1998–2004

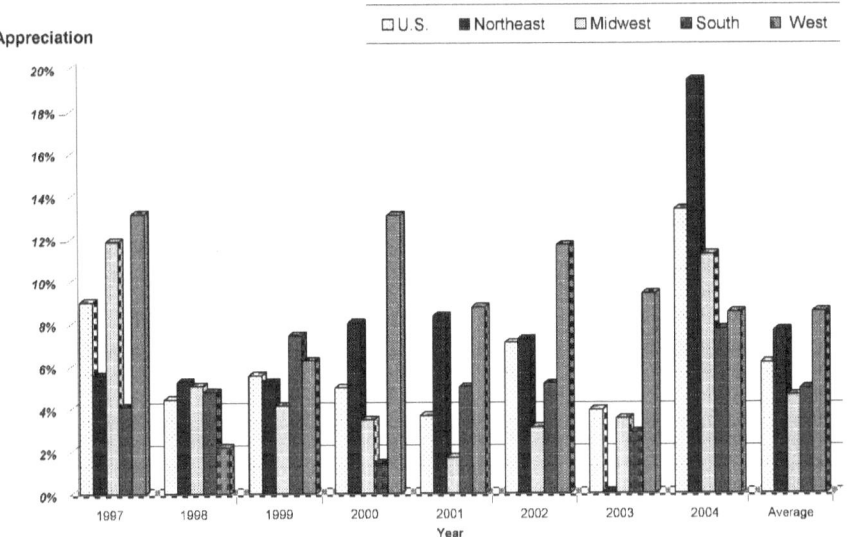

*Data gathered from U.S. Census Data

Chart 2

This chart represents housing price percentage increases annually. The United States increased an average of 6%–9% from 1998 through 2004, depending on the year. The overall average for the United States during those years was 6%, while the Northeast increased 8%, Midwest at 5%, South at 5% and the Western area increased 9%. The Northeast has had a big bump from time to time, mainly due to economic swings. The Midwest, the South, the West, and Chicago, have remained consistent, which should represent returns that won't fluctuate.

This trend doesn't look like it is going to change. Going back to census data to the early 70's, we've seen a 12% on average increase. Real estate, in general, continues to be a hot market.

So the big question is—How do we own/control real estate and have someone else pay for it? That's what we're going to show you.

Trends in the Equities Market

We just showed you some housing data that helped us understand the consistency of real estate returns. Another major investment option is the equities market. What funds do we put our money in to maximize our returns? Do you take the risk of losing a large portion of your savings like a lot of people did when their portfolios dropped substantially right after the bubble burst in April 2000? Many people lost a lot of money based on market forces they couldn't predict nor control. Many middle age investors found that the idea of retiring at age sixty two or earlier was not going to happen. These folks lost 30%–60% of their monies allocated for retirement in the 2000 bubble burst. People who experienced jumping on the perceived "easy path" to retirement have hopefully learned the volatility and uncertainty of the markets and are willing to try another path to financial independence. We are advocating that you at least consider diversification of your portfolio to include real estate.

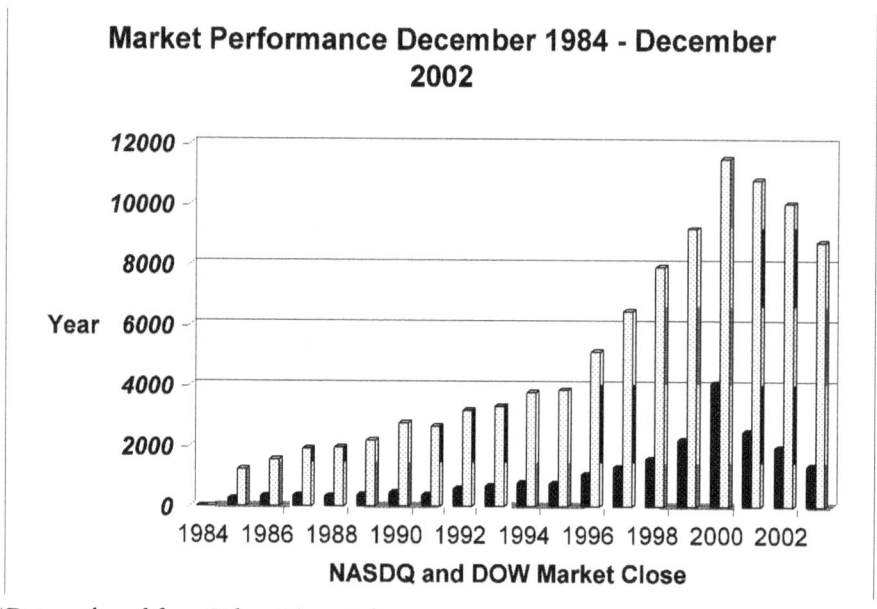

Market Performance December 1984 - December 2002

NASDQ and DOW Market Close

*Data gathered from Yahoo Financial
*Lightly colored bar represents DOW and darker bars represent NASDQ as reflected in chart 4

Chart 3

Market Performance from the Last Three Years

In general, the equities market over the past few years (AFTER the bubble burst in April 2000), has been relatively flat. Recently there has been a bit of an up tick, but overall the markets performed at the standard 9%–11% going back to 1922. On average, 9%–11% returns sound like an excellent return as compared to the 6%–7% appreciation found in real estate. But, the real return isn't found in the appreciation, but rather the return on your equity within real estate. Since your equity is initially the money you put down, or invest in the form of a down payment, your return is actually based on this number and not the overall appreciation of the asset itself.

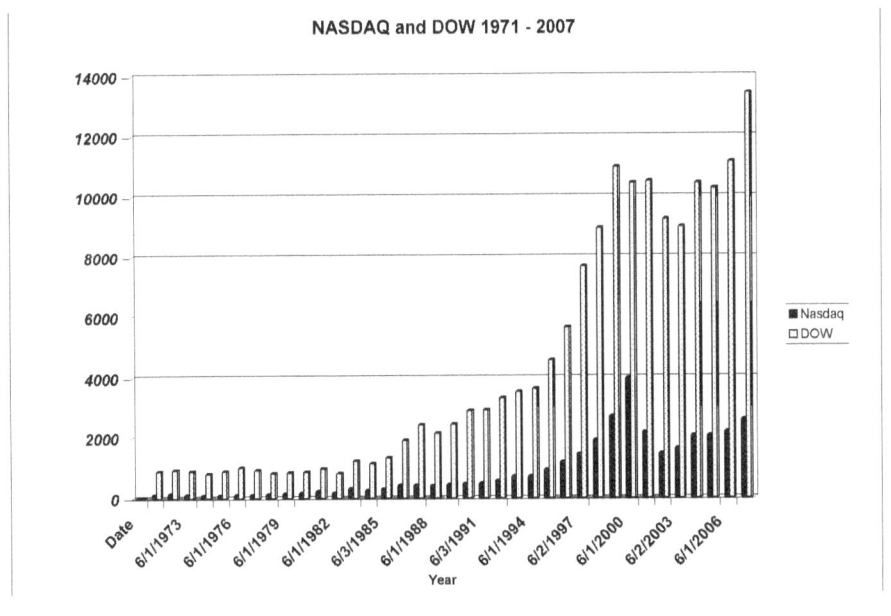

Chart 4

This chart represents stock market performance from 1971–2007 for both the NASDAQ and the DOW. The overall performance has actually declined since the bubble burst in 2000 when the markets dropped substantially. Performance is relatively flat after the huge drop. There are so many factors beyond the average individual's control that can affect the marketplace: natural disasters, the economy, government decision and policy, war and terrorism, the actions of foreign governments.

Real estate is a much safer investment without all of those inherent risks. During the period between 2000 and 2004, when the stock market was relatively flat, real estate appreciation averaged 7%–8% due to many factors, including forty year lows in interest rates. Presently, interest rates, which average 6%–7% apr., are considered to be low. When I (Greg) purchased my first home in 1991, I locked in at 10% and considered that to be a good rate.

During the five-year period from September 2001 through September 2006, the Vanguard 500 Index, a rough approximation of S&P's collection of 500 large-cap stocks, often referred to as "the market," has returned just 2.70% annually.

401(k) Investment Options

Many people today are basing their retirement on 401(k) contributions. The bulk of those contributions are used to purchase stocks and mutual funds, which are a pool of stocks, picked out by a fund manager. Over time, we contribute anywhere from 1%–15% of our bi-weekly paychecks to purchase those funds. We also know that this money is, for the most part, untouchable without severe penalties and tax consequences, with only a few exceptions. Those exceptions are education for a child, first purchase of a primary residence, or extreme medical circumstances. The penalties for removing any money for reasons not listed above are a 10% fee and standard income taxes. Your taxes are based on the bracket you are in at the time of withdrawal. Your bracket may also increase due to the amount of money being withdrawn from your 401(k).

A 401(k) is a way to save tax-deferred money, over a long period of time. The following chart illustrates the amount of money, in both tomorrow's and today's dollars, that can be saved by contributing the maximum allowed amount over a 35 year time frame.

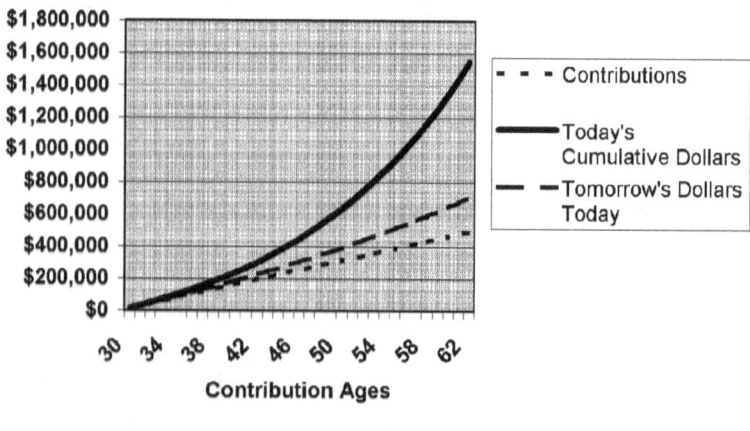

Chart 5

This chart represents that contributing to a 401(k) for thirty-five years, totaling $540,000 will have a value of $1,894,022. This is based on an annual contribution of $15,000 and a 6% annual return. The real amount of money accumulated during that period in today's dollars will be $795,422, based on a 4% rate of inflation.

We will illustrate that with a smaller, one time investment, you should achieve substantially better long term returns with less risk.

Real Estate Investment Trust Performance Since 1973

REITS (Real Estate Investment Trusts) are funds that are set up to purchase real estate. They are very similar to a stock market fund, except the fund isn't buying stocks. Real estate has become a hot investment because investors have experienced either substantial loses, or flat returns, in stocks. People have been investing in REITS since the early 70's.

Since 1972, REITs have performed at 12.5%. Even if you consider the year 2000 drop, REITs have still averaged 12.5%, while the S&P has averaged 11%. Many people are moving a lot of money to REITS because they realize that is the place to make higher returns on the investment versus stock funds. You could purchase REITS and hopefully get a 12% return, but there are other ways to get a much higher return on your money.

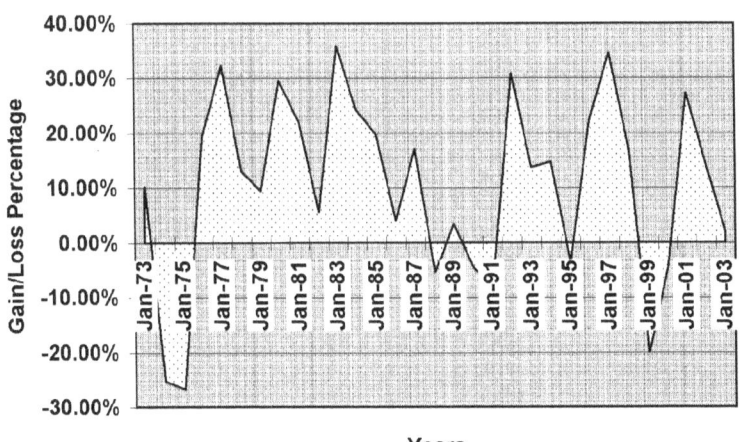

Chart 6

The Returns of Real Estate Ownership

The following example will be used to walk you through the idea of where and what the returns should be when investing in real estate. We will also use this knowledge to help you understand why renting this real estate is so profitable.

Real Estate Equity Growth

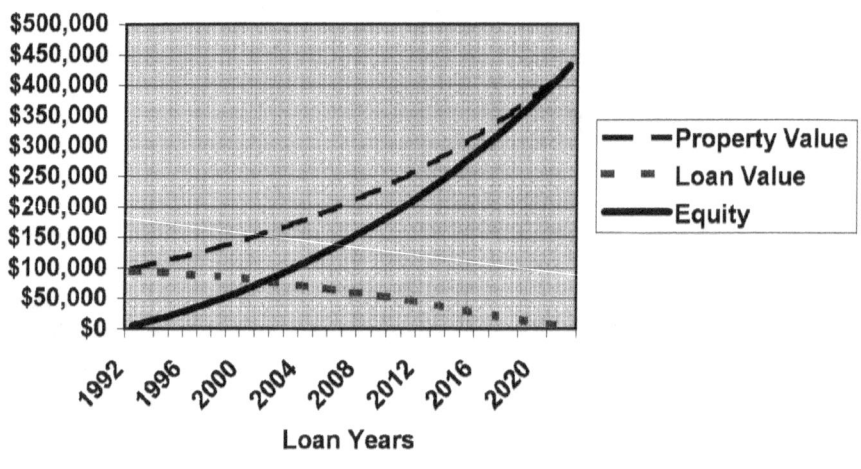

Loan Years

Chart 7

With a $5,000 down payment on a $100,000 property value, the actual equity in the property increases to $411,614 at 5% annual appreciation while the mortgage loan amount is paid off over 30 years. This represents an 8,232% of return on the original $5,000 investment.

Use this chart to think in terms of purchasing a property. Do not think in terms of renting yet, as we will discuss that shortly. There are three lines on this chart that represent the appraised value (property value), the loan value, and the amount of money you put down as the down payment. The difference in the property value and the loan value is the equity you have in the property.

When you buy a house, you will need to put an amount of money down on a piece of property worth a certain value, and take out a loan for the difference. Over time, there are monthly payments made to pay off the loan that usually range anywhere from ten to thirty years. During that time, the appraised value of the property increases. The chart above represents those three factors, and illustrates the increase, or return on investment. The three factors are appraised value of the property, loan value, and down payment or equity.

When you buy a house, you need to take out a mortgage. The amount of the mortgage will be the difference between the purchase price, and the amount of money you put down in the form of a down payment.

Fixed rate mortgages are set up so that when you make a payment, a certain amount of that payment is applied towards the principal of the loan, and the remainder of the payment is applied to paying the interest. Over time, the amount of the outstanding balance (or principal), of the loan will decrease. Inverse to the loan amount decreasing, your equity will increase, due to the rising appraised value (or appreciation), of the property.

Imagine that your appraised value did not increase, meaning that your property did not appreciate, but your loan principal was decreasing due to a part of the monthly payments being applied to the principal balance. With that scenario, the return on your money would be in direct proportion to the amount of money being applied to the principal via your monthly mortgage payment. In an interest only scenario, you would not be making any return because all of your payment goes towards interest and not buying down the principal balance.

The opposite is also true. If your appreciation was not flat, meaning your property value was going up, and you had an interest only loan, your return on your investment would come solely through the appreciation.

In the chart above, we illustrate the standard mortgage with conservative average appreciation. In this scenario, the loan value decreases as you progress through the loan due to principal payments and the appraised value increases due to appreciation. The difference between the loan value and appraised value is your real equity. That is where the real money is made.

To understand this better using some actual numbers behind the language, let's use a $100,000 property example for simplicity sake.

If you bought a property with a $100,000 value and put down a $5,000 down payment (5%), the mortgage amount you would need would be $95,000. The $5,000 initial equity will grow to $411,614 over a thirty year time period. This number represents the full-appraised value of the house after thirty years at 5% appreciation, after the mortgage is paid off. Remember, in our charts the average annual appreciation was 6%–7%, which is actually greater than the 5% we have used in this example.

The idea of taking an option on stock is similar to our real estate example above, but real estate investments don't include the inherent risks that the stock market brings. Here's a stock example. You take $1.00 of your money to control an $80 stock in the XYZ Company. If the stock goes up to $90, then the value of the $1.00 you invested to control the $80 stock will be worth $10. You took $1.00 and you're making $9 on it. You only invested $1.00, not $80, which is what the stock would actually cost on the open market. That is a big return but, as most people know, it is risky. If the stock decreases in value your $1.00 will also be lost and you could end up owing money to your broker.

Stock options are much like the mechanics of buying real estate. With real estate, you are writing a check for a down payment, which is a small percentage of the overall value of the property. You then go to a lending institution to borrow the rest of the money needed to purchase that property. Your gains are based on the appreciation of the overall value of that property, but your returns (ROI), are calculated using your actual out-of-pocket monies (your down payment).

To refer back to the example above, your out-of-pocket investment is $5,000 to own a $100,000 property. Similar to purchasing the option using $1.00 of your own money to control, or own, a stock valued at $80. When the property appreciates 5%, or $5,000 per year, your return on your original $5,000 investment is 100% annually. When most people talk about their investment return on real estate, they talk in terms of the percentage of appreciation of the overall value of the property. That is correct if you live in it and pay for it yourself because you have to factor in all of the money that you have invested. If someone else (the renter), is paying all of the monthly bills, then the investment return is based on the actual amount of money you have in the unit—your down payment, vs. the appraised amount of the unit. Remember, based on our market analysis, we are using a conservative estimate at 5%. The stock option can also increase in value, from $80 to $90. The vast majority of folks who attempt to make money using options actually lose money.

History has shown that the real estate market has neither the volatility nor the inherent risks of decreasing in value and loss of original investment.

In the example above, we provided a quick illustration of the returns that you might expect by owning real estate. Now you might understand the advantages of real estate, but you may be wondering how to actually pay for that mortgage on a month-to-month basis. After all, your returns would go down dramatically if you have to write that check every month. Renting real estate to own real estate answers that part of the equation. If you can get someone else to pay for the mortgage payment, then you can sit back and make the high returns on your initial investment without the risks of mutual funds and stocks.

To help you understand we have put together a return on investment chart that is based on a cash investment of $5,000, and an appreciation value of 5%

on a $100,000 property. We calculate the return on investment based on the return you receive on the amount of money you actually used out of your own pocket, not the overall appreciation percentage of the property. Remember, if someone else is paying all of the monthly bills, then the only money you put in is the original down payment. That is why the return is based on only that amount. Over 30 years of time, we grew it to $332,194. That translates into a 6,644% return on your original $5,000 investment.

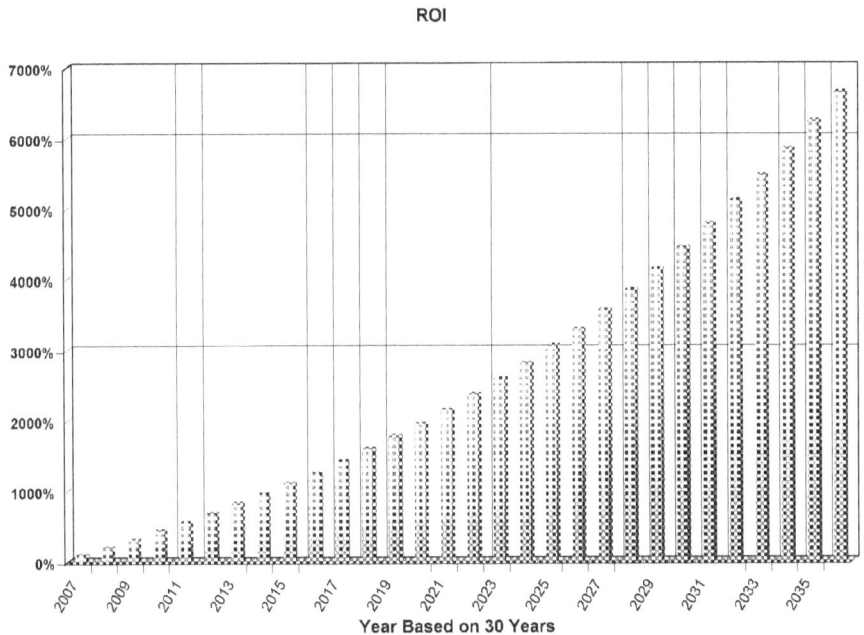

Chart 8

Chart showing $5,000 original investment to purchase a $100,000 property which grew to $332,194 through the increased appreciation of the unit

A return of 6,644% seems like a big number, but as the charts indicate, that is the return that you can get if you put down $5,000 and somebody else pays the monthly mortgage the entire term of the mortgage until it is paid off, thirty years later. At that time, the property is sold for $332,194, which means that your $5,000 initial investment grew to $332,194 or a 6,644% return. If you look at the market statistics, you're probably not going to see a 6,644% return consistently in any other investment. These returns seem unrealistic, but we have demonstrated that they are not.

Chapter Two

Why Aren't More People Doing This?

More people aren't renting real estate because they don't have a methodology, or the one they have is flawed and doesn't filter out the problems that cause headaches. This ultimately causes them to sell their rentals and get out of the market. They also aren't very clear on where the money is made because they are focused solely on positive cash flow vs. long term gains through appreciation and mortgage buydown. A lot of people want to see the money immediately so they put very little money into their properties. As you'll see in later chapters, by not making a couple of additional minor investments, such as appliances and carpet, you will end up dealing with a lot more issues.

Have you thought about the amount of money you will make, how much money you will need to save, and the amount of money you will need to pay your expenses and maintain the lifestyle you envision from ages forty through your retirement years? If so, then you know you need a sound financial strategy based on the answers to those questions.

Over the next few pages, we will help you understand some of the larger components that you need to consider as part of that sound financial strategy.

Life Expectancy Trends

Over the years, we have asked a lot of people what they think they need to live on today and in later periods of their life, from retirement through average life expectancy. Most of the answers we receive are much lower than the actual projected requirements as illustrated below. Many of these folks fall within what is termed the "Baby Boomer" age bracket. The oldest baby boomer, born in 1946, has a life expectancy of seventy-seven years. The youngest baby boomer, born in 1964, has a much longer life expectancy of eighty-four years. In 2006, the oldest of the baby boomers turned sixty years old.

Lets take a look at the amount of money that will be required, where that money will come from, and how it will need to be spent during retirement years. There are a number of factors that influence the total amounts required including prescriptions, housing, taxes, food, entertainment, automobiles, travel, and (probably the largest), medical related care.

If you retire at age sixty and you live to the average life expectancy of eighty, then you may need $1M. If you work a lot longer and retire at seventy-two, that number could go down to $750K. This number is based on spending $4,166 per month in expenses. The average income in the United States today is less than $40,000 per year. The primary difference between being able to live on your income today vs. your expenses during retirement is the money required to supplement your medical expenses. Most people today have employer based medical coverage which will be replaced by Medicare and Medicaid. These are government backed programs which cover much less and require a greater level of insured contributions.

The estimates above are based on some average minimum projected requirements. Your actual requirements may be more; based on your lifestyle and circumstances that may change as you age. Another factor that may play into this equation is the question of whether the social security program will still exist twenty years from now. If this program ends up costing the government too much and goes away, you may not have this income as part of your retirement strategy. Although it may have represented a relatively small amount (in the one thousand or so range), you will still need to find another income source to replace that money.

To help you understand what you are facing in your retirement years we will break down some of the expenses you may expect from now through your retirement years. You should be thinking not just about surviving retirement, but also being able to retire earlier than government targets, achieving financial freedom, and living in the style you have always dreamed of living.

Retirement Expenses

Most people aren't fully aware of the expenses they are going to incur during their retirement years. Most people will eventually have children, if they don't already, and there are a number of expenses related to children that will impact retirement savings. Some of those costs are cars, housing, food, and medical expenses. If you're planning on paying for college, those numbers get much bigger than the numbers we showed you earlier. The most recent trend is the propensity for college graduates to live with their parent's years after graduation.

The following chart illustrates the expenses one might expect during later working years. One of the biggest post retirement expenses, medical costs, is dramatically smaller during pre-retirement years. This is because of employer paid health care coverage during our working years and the fact that there is a direct correlation between growing older and increased medical expenses. Categories such as automobile, housing, and leisure will usually decrease during our post retirement years, after age seventy-two, due to our reduced mobility, smaller housing requirements, and less demand for our cars.

Expenses Age 40-72 By Category

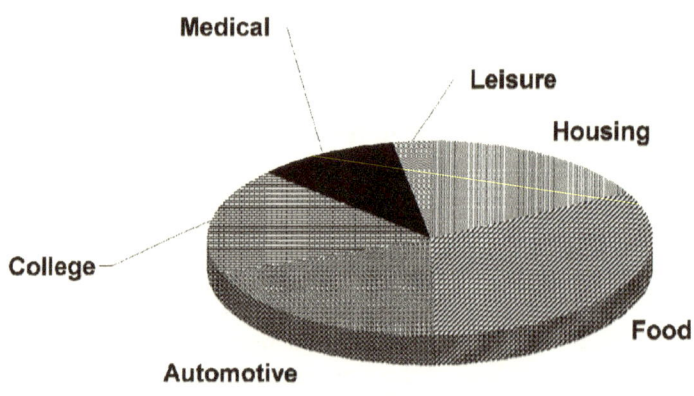

Chart 9

The following is a breakdown of the money you may need within the categories of: food/living, housing, leisure, medical, automobile, and insurance.

Medical Expenses

After retirement, most will use the government subsidized health plan commonly known as Medicare. This is a program that helps avoid catastrophic health care costs, but is usually limiting in terms of treatment options and has larger patient contributions.

In addition to increased doctor costs, the amount of money spent on prescriptions will also increase, both in the number of drugs we take, as we grow older, and in the amount of money we will pay for those drugs. Most employers offer a drug card service that allows us to fill prescriptions with only a small required co-pay amount. After retirement, we will be faced with using Medicaid—a government funded program.

Housing

The American dream is to own your own home and have it paid off by the time our retirement age goal is reached. As we plan our expenses after that date, we usually think of our house as expense free because we won't have a mortgage. We forget that we still have taxes, normal maintenance, and upkeep associated with that house. We also have expenses that will come as the house ages such as: roofing, larger appliances, siding, and foundation issues. These are usually one-time expenses, but when they do come can represent a larger expense than the mortgage payments for that year.

Leisure

During our younger years, we tend to travel more and take more vacations with our families. Some go on vacation once a year and some take multiple vacations. Depending on tastes and budget, you may spend between $1,000 and several thousand dollars for a family vacation lasting a week. Even if you choose to drive instead of fly to your vacation destination, you still have hotel and eating expenses during your stay.

In our post retirement years, if we are healthy enough to enjoy this benefit, we tend to take more lavish vacations more frequently. Many travel companies are specifically catering to the older generation by setting up less physically demanding vacation packages.

Hobbies and other leisure pursuits are expenses that have to be factored in when planning for our retirement. Unless your only hobby is watching television, this can be costly. Hobbies with our children are also usually more expensive than those without. As we age into our retirement years, we tend to have fewer hobbies.

Savings

Most of us don't think of savings as an expense, but rather an accumulation of money every month, to be used at a later time. Most also look at savings as an option each month, either choosing to save or not to save. If saving is chosen, we can feel the pinch on our monthly budgets and available spending money. Savings should be looked as an expense that must happen each month, like a mortgage payment or utility bill. When viewed in that manner, we will think of it as a true expense which must be paid each and every month.

Food/Living

During our more active ages (pre-retirement), we usually eat more and do more activities that cost more. The frequency of dining out for dinner, lunch, or breakfast with our spouse or friends, or even going to movies or plays, usually decreases after retirement. The expenses related to those events should decrease after retirement, but depending on your health, may stay constant.

College Costs

You may decide not to pay for your child's college education, which will save a lot of money that can be used for your retirement. If you do decide to pay for it, you should plan on saving a considerable amount of money. In some cases, depending on the number of children you have and where they want to go to school, that number may exceed the amount of money you need for retirement.

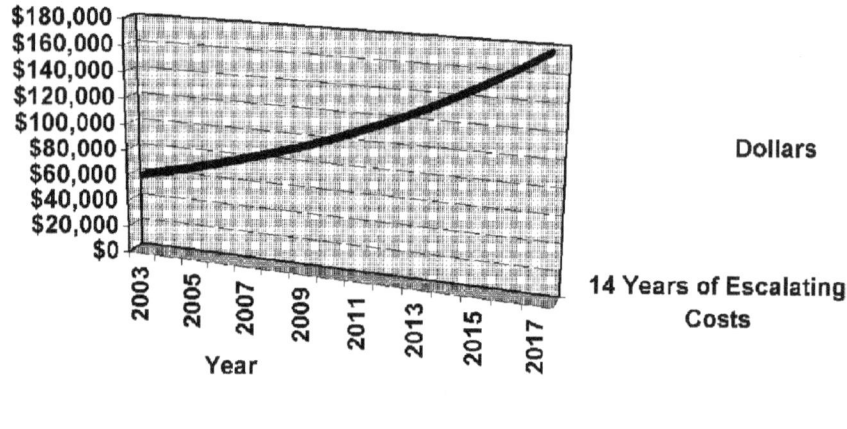

Chart 10

This chart represents putting one child through college based on $20,000 per year, which includes tuition and living expenses for four years with an annual increase of 10%. This number is also based on an in-state school with a minimal annual increase. The average household consists of two children and many have more than that number. As you can see, at over $239,000 per child for a four-year education, you will need to have a sound plan in place to pay for this expense.

Income During Retirement

There may be several sources from which we will be able to draw income during our retirement that can be used to offset the expenses. During working years, hopefully you contributed to your 401(k) plan through your employer, kept up with other savings programs, built equity through your primary residence and indirectly through social security.

401(k) Contributions

The government currently allows a maximum annual contribution of $15,000 per year to a 401(k) plan, which may be supplemented by their employer. This number has increased most years and should continue to increase. The reality is, most people don't make enough to be able to afford to contribute the maximum amount.

401K Contibutions vs. Returns

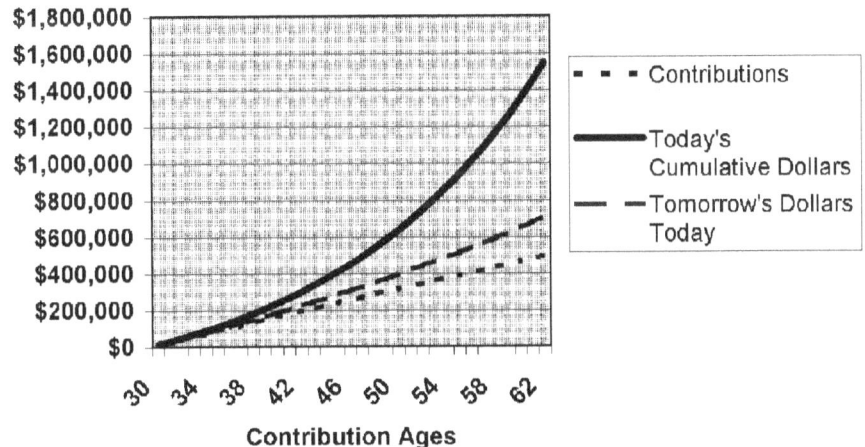

Chart 11

This chart shows 401(k) contributions over a thirty-five year period, contributing $540,000 to a 401(k). After that time, you will end up with $1.894 million dollars. After taking into account a 4% inflation rate, based on today's dollars, the real amount of money accumulated for that period would be $795,442.You would need to start contributing at age thirty and contribute the maximum every year through age sixty-five. Most people do not make enough to contribute the fully allowed amount annually.

If you make $70,000 per year, and contribute the maximum of 15%, you would only be contributing $10,000 per year. This number is still $5,000 annually less than this chart illustrates. If you can contribute the full $15,000, and receive 6% growth, based on all of the money going into the stock market, your money would grow to $1,894,022 at age sixty-five. In today's dollars that would equal close to $800,000 based on the current rate of inflation.

Home Equity

The equity in your primary home is another place that most people usually think about as a source of retirement income. The problem, however, is that you will still need a place to live when you retire.

When you're sixty-five years old, you may buy a smaller house, but you will usually end up spending the same, or a little less, on a house in a slightly nicer neighborhood. Upgrading to a nicer neighborhood will usually offset some or all of the cost difference of the smaller house, so this reduces the asset that you live in today as a major part of your retirement money.

Primary Housing Equity

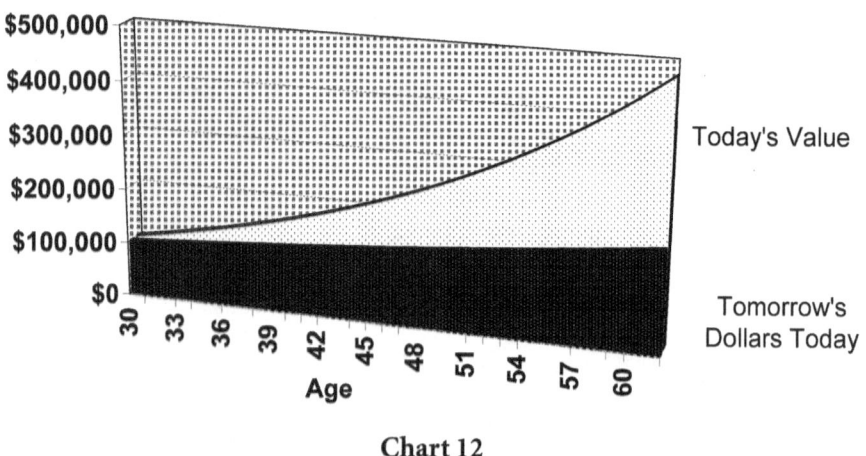

Chart 12

$100,000 home purchased at age 30 with a 6% annual increase and 4% inflation rate. Home value at age 62 is $476,494. That would be worth $188,454 in today's dollars.

To illustrate the chart above, you may currently own a three bedroom, two bathroom house and paid $100,000 for it. That house might be worth $476,494 in thirty years. Usually, people move to a slightly less expensive, smaller house, but in a more costly area or neighborhood. As a result, you don't reduce the cost of your new house by much, but you do upgrade your living style and location.

Savings

Your savings will need to make up a considerable amount of your retirement. As most of us know, it is difficult to commit to a substantial savings plan because it forces us to forfeit a part of our standard of living today. Also, most of us don't have much disposable income that could be used for future savings. The chart below shows an investment of $100/month into stock, or savings, for thirty-two years at 6% with 4% inflation. You would have accumulated a total savings of $504,000. That may seem like a lot of money but in today's dollars it would represent a nest egg of $280,000. That sum may not meet your retirement requirements over a twenty to thirty year post-retirement period.

Savings Plan For Future

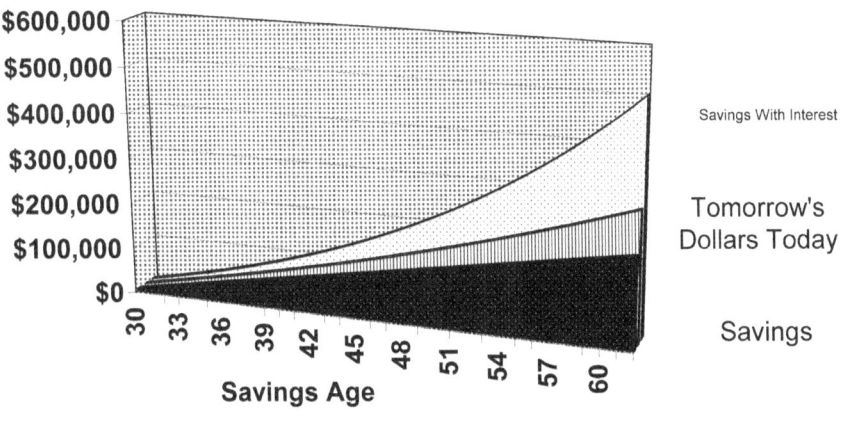

Chart 13

$100 per month for thirty-two years with 6% annual return and 4% inflation rate. Total Savings equals $504,402. In today's dollars this equals $282,067.

Social Security

Social Security is a term that we have all grown up with, being led to believe that it was established as a means of supplementing our retirement. Most people, providing they are currently contributing, should have started receiving quarterly statements which show you how much money you will be entitled to at retirement age. The following is a real example, which can be adjusted based on your income levels throughout your work life.

If you made $250,000 averaged over the last fifteen years of your work life and $100,000 twenty years prior to that, you might receive $1400/month when you reach age sixty-two. That's not enough to make it. Monthly bills will be more than that. Most people are barely making it today, which puts you in a bad position years down the road when you don't have your primary income to supplement that money.

College Savings

As we have seen, the amount of money that will be needed to put a child through four years of college is much larger that most of us realize. Due to this, we need to have a sound savings plan in place to take care of that expense so that it doesn't consume too much of our retirement savings.

There are many ways to save for this, from 529's, to monthly deductions allocated specifically for that purpose. Either way, we need to consider that expense as part of our current savings plan.

College savings plan based on an original $30,000 with a 5% annual return

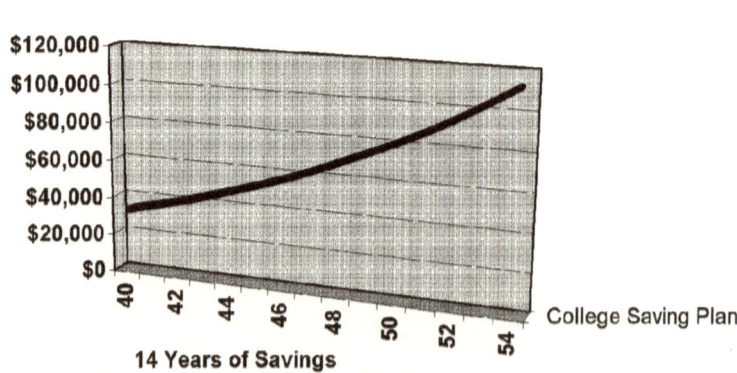

College Saving Plan

Chart 14

The chart above represents a family who puts $30,000 in an account at one time. That money grew at 5% over a fifteen year time period and was worth $60,000 at the end of that period. Most families could not afford to write a $30,000 check for the purpose of starting a college fund, much less a check for that amount for each of their children. Based on a family of five, you would need to write a $90,000 check. As we saw earlier, that amount still would not be enough to pay the projected amount required.

The example below illustrates the difference between projected college savings and projected costs. As you can see, there is a significant difference between those amounts.

College Costs vs. Savings Per Child

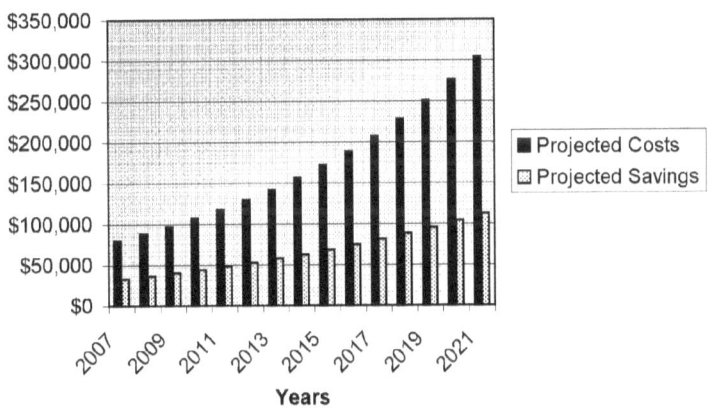

Chart 15

College Costs vs. Savings Plan Based on Original Savings of $30,000 with $100/month additional and 5% return. Compared with today's annual college costs of $20,000/year/child with annual 10% increase

This chart reflects the differences in a good savings plan and rising college costs for one child. The savings plan and college costs reflect conservative estimates from what the experts predict. The savings plan is not quite as conservative, projecting a 5% annual return, as the college cost estimates with a 10% annual increase. Many experts today suggest we may see an increase as high as 14% annually. If that happens then the average 4-year college expense may cost as much as $300,000 or more to attend a state school in eighteen years. Additionally, many college students these days are finding they require five years to complete their studies due to class scheduling conflicts.

Expense vs. Income—As We Age

During our work life, our income grows along with our expenses. At a certain point, our expenses decrease and our income continues to increase. Usually the drop in our expenses is due to our children leaving the house to attend college, or the college debt has been paid. There are many other reasons that our expenses drop also including: paying off our house, paying off a second house, or other long term debt being paid off.

Before we retire, there are a number of years when our income usually continues to grow. That allows us to contribute even more money to our retirement fund.

After we retire, we usually see our expenses level off or decrease for a period of time, until our medical expenses increase due to the aging process. As discussed earlier, Medicare doesn't pay much towards those expenses and we must purchase supplemental insurance at higher premiums.

The chart below illustrates our income and expenses as we age. The third line, expense vs. income, is the difference between those two that shows our positive, or negative, cash flow during those years. The dramatic increase in expenses starting at age fifty-six represents the first child leaving for college and the bills associated with that event. The decrease in expenses at age sixty-three represents the third and last child finishing college and the debt being paid.

As you can see, we have a negative cash flow after the retirement age of sixty-five. This represents the amount of money you will need to live on for the remainder of your life.

Expense vs. Income As We Age

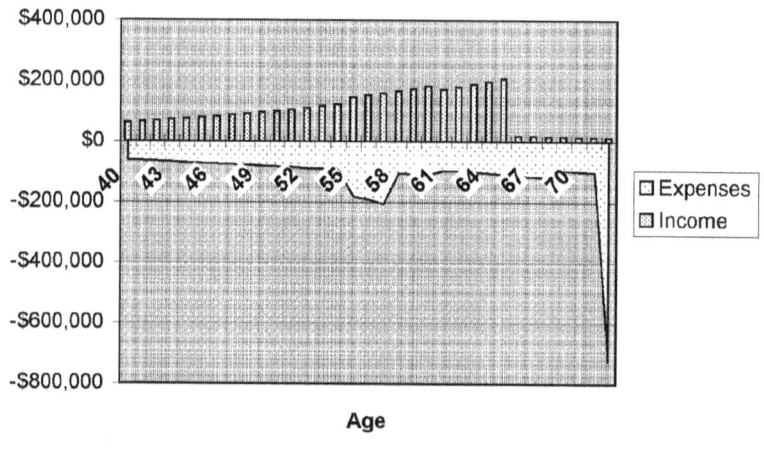

Age

Chart 16

This chart represents Expense vs. Income from age forty through age seventy-two, which includes housing, food, automotive, college, medical, and leisure expenses. This chart is shown with the expenses overlaying income to illustrate a net effect.

As we have illustrated, the type and amounts of both expenses and income will change as we age. The income represented in this chart is shown steadily increasing on the top part of the chart with some expenses represented under the center line. This represents the typical cash flow trends, although not necessarily specific dollar amounts, that most of us have or will see as we age. At age sixty-five, when we retire, our income will flatten out and substantially drop. Our expenses will also usually increase, with medical costs leading the expenses.

Expense vs Income As We Age

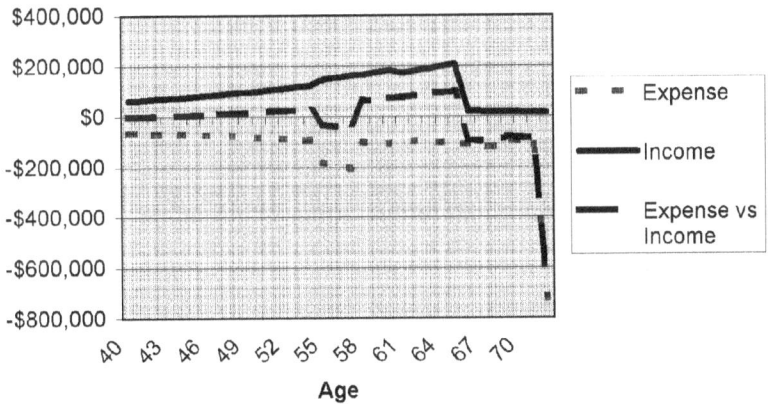

Chart 17

This chart represents Expense vs. Income from age forty through age seventy-two, which includes housing, food, automotive, college, medical, and leisure expenses. This chart is shown with the expenses separated from income. The income, the top solid line, increases until age sixty-five and then falls due to a fixed income based lifestyle.

The future is unknown for all of us. Therefore, expenses and income are equally unknown. What we do know is that we will have many of the expenses listed above and we plan on a consistent income through our working years. We also know that we will need to have a sound financial plan that encompasses most, if not all, of the variables that we have outlined, in order to be where we want to be as we age through our retirement years.

As illustrated, the expenses that we will have will probably outpace our income and savings. Having a good savings plan is no longer enough to insure a comfortable retirement, while still providing a great start for our children. We need to make our money work harder over those years. Where can we get higher returns than by using traditional methods such as stocks, mutual funds, 401(k)s, savings, and social security?

The answer is real estate investment.

Chapter Three

Who Can Do This?

Just about anyone can get into the rental business and succeed. We have found that the only qualification is the drive to get past the typical objections you hear about problem tenants. Those objections are given by people who have either never rented property or those who have gotten into the business and made major mistakes. The folks who have done it the right way only have two objections; "Why didn't I do this sooner?" and "How can I get more money to own more units?"

If you follow some simple rules, you will want to own a lot of property because this form of investment will be financially rewarding and not require a lot of effort. You can keep your full time job for the benefits, a means to support yourself and your family, and a way to generate more cash for additional properties. When you have reached your financial goals through equity and appreciation, you will be well positioned to make the decision on your retirement date and lifestyle.

Anyone can be a successful rental real estate investor. We acknowledge that some readers are better positioned than others to invest in real estate due to their schedules, skills and financial starting point.

Salespeople with a little extra time

Usually salespeople have more flexible schedules than most. There are going to be times where you might have to drop what you are doing and tend to a unit. This is rare, but it does happen. Even with the best plan and all new appliances and fixtures, you still can't totally prevent a problem from occurring due to natural wear and tear, or tenant induced repairs. Salespeople also tend to have available investment funds and typically have some negotiation skills.

Small business owners

As a small business owner, you work a lot but there is always time to slip away or turn the business temporarily over to a trusty colleague or employee. This heavily depends on the number of years you have been in business, the type of business, and what phase of your business you are in. Small business owners typically have two sources of surplus cash: funds generated by the business and Simplified Employee Pension plans (SEPs). There are ways to use SEP money to purchase rental units and dramatically increase your returns.

People with some saved money can do this.

There are people who already have the money and are just confused about what do to with that money. Perhaps they tried the stock market, lost a large amount of money, and are now reluctant to invest in anything other than a guaranteed return based investment, such as a Certificate of Deposit (CD). Real estate is a safe investment that yields higher than average returns. If you have the money, but don't have the time to manage your properties, a management firm can assume that responsibility. This is referred to as being an absentee landlord. Although you will give up some of your overall profit, these firms will alleviate the time and effort required to manage your properties effectively; and you will still get higher than market returns. More in-depth information about management firms will come in another chapter.

First-time homebuyers

As a first-time homebuyer wanting to get into the rental business, it is important to view your first home as a future rental property. The first step is to buy a property; with as little as 5% down, that can be utilized as a rental after purchasing your next property. After living there for several years, you can do an owner occupied refinance to capture the 15% to 20% equity gains to purchase your next property. Move to that one, repeat the process. Or, if your second house is the one you consider your primary residence, you can stay in that house and pull money from the first one another 2–3 years down the road to buy your next rental unit. This is a repeatable process.

Earlier, we referenced the potential to quit working in ten or so years. This would be possible if you bought one property and let it appreciate for 3–4 years, then pulled the equity and bought another property. Wait a few years and let both properties appreciate. Pull out the equity in those and buy two more properties. Now you have four houses, six or seven years down the road. Wait three more years, pull the equity out of all four, and buy four more. Now you have eight houses. As you go through this process however, never invest beyond your ability to support these properties from a time and money perspective. You want to avoid not being able to respond quickly to tenant's problems and issues. This can increase your costs in damage repairs, and increase your vacancy rates.

College students who save a little

This group is similar to the first-time homebuyer group, but they start out at a younger age with less money. When in college, we usually don't have as much disposable money as first-time homebuyers. You will need to establish a savings plan and put a little aside each month until there is enough to put down money to purchase a unit. If you cannot afford to live there yourself, you will be able to rent it out so your tenant will pay all or a portion of the mortgage. You could also use your college years to save the money so you are prepared to purchase a unit when you graduate. At that point, you can move into that unit and run your strategy as the first-time homebuyer would run theirs.

As you go through this process, you are hopefully funneling incremental money being earned through your primary profession into an account that you will be use for property acquisition. Set goals. Have a target to work towards. Understand the type of properties you're looking to acquire and the price of these properties. This will enable you to calculate the amount of down payment you will be in a position to put down (anywhere from 5%–20%). This will provide a financial target to shoot for.

People who are already doing this

Many existing investors have made mistakes, which has diminished their enthusiasm for renting properties. Common complaints heard from this group include renters who are destructive, demanding, or pay late. They also spend too much time dealing with vacant properties and the effort and expense associated with repeated showings and paying the mortgage themselves due to missed rents. Their method and lack of knowledge result in the ongoing problems they experience. Our process will help these people eliminate those issues. We don't know anyone who is following our methodology who is faced with these ongoing issues.

Negotiating Skills

Any of the groups listed above will be more successful and have higher returns based on better negotiating skills.

Negotiation is a skill that will help you be a successful real estate investor and landlord. As you follow the steps we lay out in this book, you will be better positioned to increase your profits, if you negotiate. We negotiate with everyone we deal with to maximize our returns and improve our skills. We negotiate even when we are purchasing a pair of shoes and generally come out with either a price cut, or something thrown in (like a discount on some conditioner, or polish that we needed anyway). Gain confidence in asking for things that you want.

Most people are embarrassed to ask and will not reap the benefits they may have gained had they taken a chance and asked the question. The only downside is that your request might be refused. You haven't lost anything. To quote a very famous Hockey player, "You miss 100% of the shots you do not take." Every interaction that you have with another person is a potential lesson which can be used in another situation where the stakes may be higher. You learn lessons by taking risks and making mistakes. Make mistakes in situations where the stakes are relatively minor (such as the purchase of retail items). This can teach you lessons that will enable you to be successful in situations where the stakes are higher—like dealing with renters and real estate sellers.

It is better to have a dollar in *your* wallet rather than in someone else's. A dollar that will continue to work for you is worth far more than the face value of that dollar.

Negotiation is one of the most important skills to learn. It is an activity that we are engaged in multiple times everyday with significant others, children, work colleagues, and business associates. One of the most significant criteria in your success in life and social standing is your ability to maximize your returns in any social or business interaction, while ensuring the other party walks away from the transaction satisfied that their needs were also met and they feel they would like to deal with you in the future. Never pass up an opportunity to refine your skills and try and save a couple of dollars in the process, while learning some valuable lessons and insights in dealing with people who are also motivated to maximize their own gains and position.

When negotiating, always remember that the overall objective in any transaction ends with the result of a win/win scenario. Taking advantage of another person, or cheating them, is short sighted, in addition to being considered unethical, and will lead them to resent, distrust, and harbor a negative attitude towards you. When dealing with trades people, cheating them to save a few dollars will result in sub standard work, a bare minimum deliverable, and little possibility of a future relationship—especially when you need them in an emergency situation.

"The bridge you burn today is the one you need to cross tomorrow."

Your leverage and ability to provide incentive to tradesmen is based on the desire to want to do the work and potential future business. In return, they should offer a fair price and quick response for additional services.

Negotiation is important. You can do without it, but your goal is to make more, pay less, and receive greater value from any transaction in which you are involved. Your goal is to maximize your Return on Investment (ROI).

Chapter Four

How the Money is Made

How is the money made? It is made in the following ways:

- ➤ Rental situation where you are realizing a positive cash flow situation
- ➤ Mortgage principal buydown referring to the amount of money that is applied to the outstanding loan
- ➤ Appreciation in the overall property value
- ➤ Tax write-offs, such as mortgage interest and other expenses associated with renting the property. They will help you reduce the amount of positive income you claim, thus reducing the annual tax liability owed to the IRS.

Cash-Out Refinance

The cash, or profit, is generated through the ways illustrated above, but are deposited into your account mainly via a cash-out refinance.

A cash-out refinance allows you to capture the combination of the increased equity that results from a higher appraised value, appreciation, and the difference of your old mortgage and your new mortgage amount. Your old mortgage amount is reduced as a result of the amount of money being applied to the loan amount principal through your monthly mortgage payments. Your appreciation increases due to real estate value appreciation seen in the surrounding units similar to yours in the area.

At a refinance closing, they will calculate the difference between the payoff of your old mortgage and the new appraised value of your property. The title company will then calculate the minimum loan-to-value ratio (the highest loan amount for that type of property that the bank allows), as compared to the value of the unit, and give you a check for the difference.

The following is an explanation of what loan-to-value is and why lenders have this limit. The bank sets limits on the amount, by percentage, of money that they will loan to an individual or company which is determined by the type of property that is being financed. Business properties carry a higher risk factor than a property that will be occupied by a homeowner. Lending institutions must factor in the amount of risk they assume and know that more businesses fail than individuals declare bankruptcy and can't make the payments on their homes. The lender needs to build in some additional market value; in the event they have to put it up for sale. Those sales usually are either put out as an auction or put up for a quick sale. In either case, they are usually sold at less than market value. The loan-to-value ratio helps provide the needed buffer between what they might get for that property and the loan against that property.

The following are some actual examples of refinancing closings which should clarify one way you should make money using real estate rentals.

Examples of ReFi payouts.

Example #1

We purchased a house for $132,000, put down $27,000 as a down payment, and took out a fifteen-year mortgage. Two years later, we refinanced the unit, which now appraised for $175,000, and pulled out $18,000 (a combination of appreciation and buydown), and we left 20% ($33,000) into the property. We left in more than we originally put in and we pulled out $18,000 along the way.

We did a ReFi sixteen months later and pulled out another $10,000 and left $44,000. So, by putting down $27,000, we earned $18,000 and $10,000 ($28,000), and the end result is we have $44,000 of equity, which is $17,000 more than we put down. In this case, we have gotten all of our original investment out and still have $44,000 of equity in the unit in less than two and one half years. Our total gain is $76,000 equity on a $27,000 investment in less than two and one half years.

Example #2

We purchased a townhouse for $117,000 and put down 10% ($12,000), and put it on a fifteen year loan. We ReFi'd it twice and pulled out $42,000 and $20,000, for a total of $62,000. There was a negative cash flow of about $100 per month for eighty-four months (a total negative of $8,400). We sold it for $145,000 and walked away with $28,000.

This is the value of putting down $12,000, having somebody else pay the loan the entire time, and pulling out $62,000 and $28,000 for a total of $90,000. The total investment was the original down payment of $12,000 and $8,400 negative flow through the ownership term for a total of $20,400. The net math is a $90,000 gain on a $20,400 investment. This occurred over a seven-year period.

We can show you how to do this. We'll show you how to find property, buy property, and rent it properly.

> ### *Remember—"It is not what you make, it is not what you keep, it is what you do with what you keep"*

The Formula for Success

The expense cost components of this formula are: the appraised value, purchase price, down payment, taxes, insurance, assessment, closing fees, APR of the loan (annual percentage rate), points paid on the loan to buydown the rate, and initial start up costs. We will go over the individual start up costs at a later time. The appraised value is defined as the market value of the unit, as compared to other similar properties in the area. This is usually used as a basis of determining the maximum loan amount that can be taken to pay for the unit, or "loan-to-value." These are all costs you can expect to pay as a part of buying a house. Your ongoing expenses will be mortgage payments, taxes, assessments (where applicable), and repairs that arise from time to time.

The income components consist of rent on the unit itself, garage space rental (depending on where you are located), and laundry fees. Garage fees and laundry facility fees are usually charged in large cities where this is an accepted practice.

The Eastern Culture vs. Western Culture Investment Mentality

We can learn a valuable lesson from the Asian investors who purchased a lot of commercial real estate during the 70's and early 80's. At that time, they were ridiculed because of the premium prices they paid. A short time later, we encountered one of the largest real estate booms we have ever seen. As a result of investing, with the patience and understanding that their returns wouldn't be immediate, they have been rewarded with very high returns on their real estate.

The Eastern culture is willing to wait for their money. They realize that just because they don't see positive cash flow every month, their investment could still be sound, based on accumulating appreciation and principal buydown. They have put themselves in a position where their money is working for them.

The western philosophy tends to believe that if positive cash flow isn't being seen, then they must be losing money. Positive cash flow is good to have, but may come with a cost over the long term. This is illustrated in the chart below.

One example of waiting vs. not waiting for your money is shown in the difference of a fifteen-year vs. a thirty-year mortgage. Your monthly payment will be higher on a fifteen-year mortgage (which will increase your monthly expense as compared to a thirty-year mortgage). However, as you will see, you will actually pay more in annual interest due to the higher rate on the thirty-year mortgage.

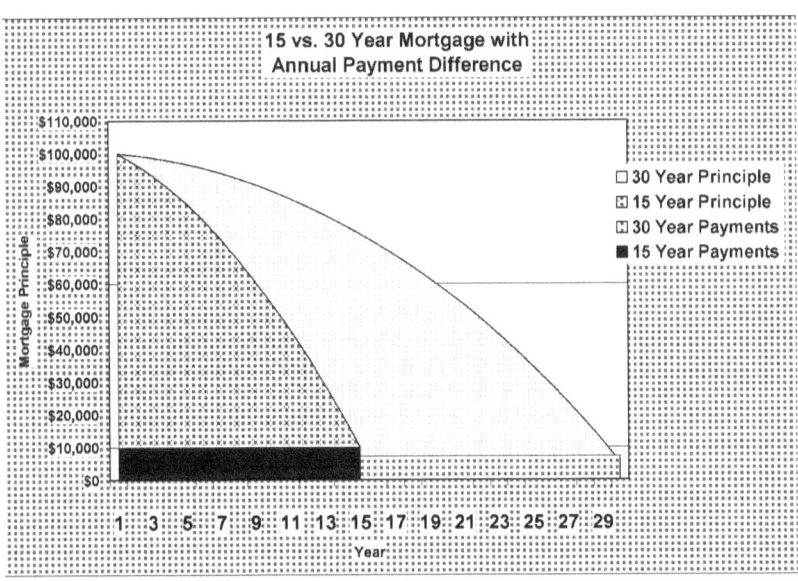

Chart 18

Chart 18 chart represents the small difference between a fifteen-year mortgage and a thirty-year mortgage. It also illustrates the difference in equity growth in the different mortgage terms.

There are many different types of loans available in the market today. Some of the more common loan types are balloons, ARMS (adjustable rate mortgages), and fixed rate terms such as fifteen year and thirty year mortgages. Many lenders also offer interest only loans, which allow you to pay only the interest with no principal buydown amount applied to the payment. The chart above compares a $100,000 mortgage that is paid off at fifteen and thirty years. The importance of this difference is the amount of money paid on your monthly mortgage vs. the total amount of money paid out over the term of the mortgage.

As you can see in the chart, the difference in your monthly payment is minimal. Your monthly payment on a fifteen year mortgage, on a $100,000 loan, at 6% APR, is $843.86. Your monthly payment for the same amount, at the same APR, on a thirty-year mortgage is $599.55. The amount of money you will pay on a fifteen-year mortgage over the life of the loan is $151,894.80 vs. $215,838 for a thirty-year mortgage. The difference, a saving you would receive, is $63,943.20. This should be looked at in terms of a monthly savings over the term of a fifteen-year mortgage of $355.24. The actual difference of the monthly payment is only $244.31 between the different terms with a savings of $110.93. This means the actual monthly savings totals $19,967.40 over the entire term of the fifteen year mortgage. Keep in mind that the savings would actually be greater than that due to a higher rate that a thirty-year mortgage would have, as opposed to the fifteen-year term. As discussed earlier, there is usually a slightly higher (between ¼ and of a percentage point), annual borrowing rate with a thirty year mortgage.

The reason this is important is you've been building equity slowly on the loan only via the buydown of the mortgage. By using a fifteen-year mortgage, it is fairly rapid. As you can see from the chart, the buydown of the fifteen-year mortgage is much faster than the thirty-year term.

Again, the choice of either the fifteen-year or the thirty-year term depends on your goals and the flexibility of your budget. If you can afford a little negative cash flow, then the fifteen-year mortgage is probably going to be better for you because you actually are making a lot more money because the buydown of the mortgage is much faster. You would pay a little more monthly, but you're making a lot more in the long run. Of course you won't actually see this money in terms of immediate cash, but the equity in the unit will grow much faster.

With a thirty year mortgage, which is what a lot of people use in this business, you may be making a little bit of money every month, or breaking even, depending on your down payment and monthly rent; but you're not building equity as fast. Also with this term, the ideas of doing ReFi's every 2–5 years will not return as much cash as you may want. Your long-term plan may be delayed if you were depending on that extra money to leverage additional units. For this reason, if you can afford it, you should try to use the shortest term possible. If you can't, that's okay too, because you're still going to have the appreciation of the house itself. You're just not going to get as much buydown appreciation as you would have with the fifteen-year note.

The nice thing about real estate is the appreciation. This is a variable that you can compare on a yearly basis to other types of returns in your investment portfolio, like the mutual funds that are in your 401(k) plan. You will see over a period of years that your real estate returns consistently out perform these other investments and you really start to realize the gains as you add properties.

Your returns are in 5–10 years but how did we get that return? The tenant pays the buy- down on a fifteen year. It is 823.73/406 through year five (average monthly buydown for years 1–5), and on a thirty year it's 599.55/115. These are monthly numbers and are based on a $100,000 mortgage at 5.5/8% on a fifteen-year mortgage and 6% on a thirty-year mortgage. The first number represents the total of the mortgage payment, principal, and interest. The second number represents the monthly principal buydown payment within your monthly payment.

In this example you can see that the difference in the payment is roughly $224 per month. The difference in the buydown is $291 month. The difference between those numbers is $67 per month. This is mainly the difference in the interest rate that you will not recover.

From a monthly cash flow standpoint, if you can afford to let the cash sit, then you can save the additional $67 per month. It may not seem like much, but over the same five-year term it is $4,020 that is yours and not the banks'. If you own five units then you are looking at $20,100 over five years. Suddenly that $67 per month seems a bit more important. Again, this is free money that comes from the difference in the interest rate.

Chapter Five

Retiring from the Rental Business

Up to this point, we've discussed our strategy surrounding purchasing the units, the value of keeping them filled, and the money that you can make in this business. There will come a time when you may want to stop doing this because you have enough money, have achieved financial freedom, or you want to retire.

You may have set some goals ahead of time that would trigger your decision to get out of the rental business or dramatically reduce the number of units that you own. As you have read, we believe in goal setting due to the fact that you can't measure success unless you have a defined set of criteria that outlines your goals. Goals are only goals if you have the criteria defined and a good plan to get there. Many folks have dreams that they call goals, because they don't have a plan.

When do I want to get out of the rental business? This is a question that only you will be able to answer for yourself. Everyone has a different idea of how much money they need versus the tradeoff of working for more. How much is enough? Is it worth working for more or can I live comfortably on what I have?

There are many options available when you are ready to get out. This is a short list that should help you identify which option would be best for you:

- ➤ Buy units where you want to retire, convert, and sell the rest
- ➤ Sell everything individually and take the cash
- ➤ Sell them as a bundled portfolio to another investor
- ➤ Pass them to your children
- ➤ 1031 Exchange

Your accountant and attorney can help you figure out a plan that works best for your individual needs and situation. They will be able to advise you on the appropriate steps to take to execute your plan from a legal and tax standpoint.

Ultimately, the personal preferences will come down to your individual needs, desires, and requirements. Make sure the advice they provide also includes some contingencies since life changes from time to time; and you will want some flexibility built into that plan. Spend some time with them well in advance of your decision to get out. Many of these options take planning to insure you get the maximum benefits from them.

Buy units where you want to retire, convert, and sell the rest

We mentioned earlier that with proper planning, you might be able to buy a unit or two in some areas where you were thinking about retiring. Think about a unit in Hawaii, or The Outer Banks of North Carolina, or any other place you've dreamed of living. The purpose of incorporating this thought into this discussion is simple. If you buy a unit now and someone else rents it from you, then when retirement day comes, you will have avoided paying the inflated costs of that current day. Simply put—buy that unit ten years prior to retirement and save half of the cost over buying it ten years later, when you are ready to retire. For those ten years, someone else will be paying the mortgage and all other costs on that unit while you save the inflated cost and build your net worth through additional appreciation. Someone else can manage the rentals and maintain it, if it is too inconvenient for you to manage. If you are using it part time, you could rent it week by week, or month by the month, so you can plan on periods throughout the year that you want to be in that special place. With proper planning, you can do this with multiple units in various locations, and spend your retirement traveling from one great location to another, spending a month or two in each.

This would also allow some flexibility on the timing of your retirement knowing that you own a place to live in your dream area and can move into that unit when you're ready. As mentioned, think about owning several units in different places so you have the ability to make retirement decisions that best suit your goals.

There are significant tax benefits to doing this; and you will get to retire in three, four or five different dream locations. You may also want to have a "primary" unit that you call home to further justify the tax advantages gained by renting the other units when you aren't living in them.

You can also convert any of the units to owner-occupied by living there for a couple of years and reclassifying that unit. There are many tax rules around this process, so check with your tax advisor.

How can you get out of one unit and into another unit safely? Or just get out of a unit all together?

Sell everything individually and take the cash

If this is the avenue you want to take, you will need to be very clear about the tax impact, prior to putting up the "for sale" sign. In some cases, depending on your tax bracket and your method of scheduling each unit, you may end up with a liability owed to Uncle Sam. You may also find yourself in a position where you have a large amount of money coming from both the sales of the units and the government in the form of a tax refund. That may be good or bad, depending on your age and your individual tax situation.

This route allows for a clean break and finalizes this chapter in your life. Once those units are sold, there isn't a clean method of turning back. Again, please talk to your tax advisor, financial planner, and attorney prior to taking this route. They may have some more ideas that might work better for your situation.

Sell them as a bundled portfolio to another investor

One method of getting out all together is to package all of your units as a bundle and sell them to an investor. You may find that you can charge a premium over what the combined market value of those units is, because they are fully rented and operational. You're offering someone an established, turnkey business that is highly profitable. In this case, there would be updated units, with tenants, and signed leases. The investor would only have to buy the package from you and start collecting the rent checks. Part of the first year's appreciation would easily pay the premium that you are asking.

In some cases, you might also be able to transfer the notes to them if your rates are better than current market rates. Your mortgage broker will be able to help you better understand if you have an "assumable" mortgage.

Pass them to your children

There are many ways of passing your assets on to your children—some are through your passing and some can be accomplished while you are still living. Vehicles, such as trusts, can be established while your children are still young and can contain provisions that pass the unit on to them when they reach certain ages or under certain conditions. Please discuss all of the pros and cons with your tax advisor, estate planner, and attorney prior to going down this road. Clear objectives are needed as trusts can be limiting and may not be reversible.

One creative idea is to use these units to pay for your children's education through a refinance just prior to them starting college. Set up properly, you might be able to pass them on to your children upon graduation to help them avoid the costly expense of buying a house as they just start out in the work-ing world. As we have discussed, the cost of real estate is continuing to increase and has done so for as far as any of us can remember. Your children can start out in a much better place than the average recent graduate and therefore get a big head start in life. There are many tax rules around this so please check with your tax advisor.

1031 Exchange

The tax rules around the next topic are somewhat complex and you will need to check with your tax advisor prior to going down this path. You want to make sure you follow the rules closely, so you don't end up with an unplanned tax liability.

In the summer of 1990, the I.R.S. finally came out with the long awaited rules on Deferred Exchanges. Section 1.1031 of the Internal Revenue Code detailed the procedure for turning a sale and purchase type transaction into an exchange.

These new rules allowed owners of certain types of like kind real and per-sonal property to sell their property and buy other like kind property with-out paying the capital gains tax. The "like kind" provision for real property is quite broad, and includes land, rental, and business property, any of which can be exchanged for the other. The like kind provision for personal property is more restrictive. This type of property must be in productive use in a busi-ness (depreciable property), and can only be exchanged for the same type of property.

Simply put, a 1031 exchange provides an avenue which enables you to take the gains and losses from one business and transfer those into a like business. In this case the business is the unit that you are renting. On the sale of one property, the money goes into an escrow, or trust, and you have a period of time (up to 180 days), to take that money out of the trust and move it into another like asset. From a tax standpoint, the end result is a transfer of all the gains/losses from one business to the other business. Again, please check with your tax advisor prior to making any moves in this area.

All of these ideas take planning and a clearly defined short- and long-term strategy. There are many life events that may disrupt your plan so it is impor-tant to have a backup plan in place. Illness, divorce, death, and change in eco-nomic status all play into your short- and long-term plan. Work out plans with your financial planner, tax advisor, attorney, and spouses so that all factors are considered before you finalize your plan.

Chapter Six

A Summary of Where the Money is Made

The simple math shows where you make money:

➢ Buydown—Whether it is fifteen or thirty year

➢ Appreciation—You get that. Percentage is all yours

➢ Cash Flow—Potentially, depending on your ratios

➢ Refinances—Cash out equity during a refinance

➢ The check at the closing

Let's assume you purchased a property ten years ago for $100,000. At that point you didn't have much money and put down 10%, or $10,000 towards the purchase. As time passed, the unit appreciated to its new value of $200,000. The annual appreciation would amount to 7% compounded annually. That is slightly higher than the stock market performance. During that time, your mortgage principal amount has been reduced from $90,000 to $75,000.

The next step is to refinance the mortgage using the new appraised value of $200,000 and the LTV ratio of 75%. (This means that you are going to take out a mortgage that equals 75% of the new appraised value.) Your new mortgage now equals $150,000. Since your old mortgage payoff was $75,000 you will receive a check at closing for the difference of your old mortgage and your new mortgage. That means you would receive a "cash out" check of $75,000 free and clear.

This easy formula looks like this:

(New appraised value x .75)

Minus (Original purchase price—down payment—buydown)

Cash out re-finance check at closing

The real math looks like this:

	($200,000 x 75%)	$150,000
Minus	($100,000 - $10,000 - $15,000)	$75,000
	Cash out re-finance check at closing	$75,000

What you have effectively done is refinanced your mortgage, which now includes your old remaining balance and some new money based on the increased appraised value. The good thing is that you have just walked away from the closing table with a $75,000 check that you don't have to pay taxes on.

The other side of this math is that you have taken your original $10,000 down payment and just ten years later, turned it into $125,000. That figure comes from the combination of the $75,000 check that you received when you re-financed, and the $50,000 in remaining 25% equity that you left in the property when you did that refinance. This works out to about a 35% return, which is also compounded annually for seven years. This return looks much better than the standard returns that you might expect to receive in the stock market.

This is just one of many real life examples:

A townhouse was purchased for $117,000 with a down payment of 10% ($12,000). This house was financed for a term of fifteen years. Two times during the next seven years, a cash-out refinance was done which resulted in checks for $42,000 and $20,000 being given back at closing. Those checks totaled $62,000. There was a negative cash flow of about $100 per month for eighty-four months for a total of a negative $8,400. Then it was sold for $145,000 and the owner walked away with $28,000. In the end, he brought home $90,000 with negative cash flow of $8,400 and a net take home of $81,600 on an original investment of $12,000. Over seven years that is a great return.

This is the value of having somebody else pay the loan while you actually own the property. This example is not one specially chosen because of the successful outcome. There are many examples of this type of return that we have both seen and experienced firsthand.

This method of making money is not like stock market returns. In the stock market, you base your returns on the amount of money you put in and the associated gains. In real estate, you base the returns on the value of the overall asset which, in large part, is mostly the bank's money. As long as someone else is paying that monthly bill, or close to that bill, then your returns are based on the amount of money you put in, compared to the overall value of the "leveraged" asset. That asset is also one that has a history of going up and not usually going down in value.

Chapter Seven

Money–How Much and Where Do I Get It?

Many homebuyers wrestle with the question of how much to put down as a down payment on the rental units. There are many differing views on this question, but you can narrow them down to a few categories.

One school of thought states that you should put down as little as possible, so you can buy as many properties as possible. By putting down less on each property, you will have more money to use to buy additional properties. Keeping with that thought, you will then be able to own more units and therefore make more money on more appreciation. That is the plus side of this method, but there is a negative side. The negative side is that your monthly costs will be higher on each unit. This puts you in a more vulnerable position in terms of vacancies and missed rents. The result is you can be left exposed during a downturn in the rental market or you may face lower rates because when more people are buying, it forces lower rents and uses up more of your obtainable credit lines. You will also need to have an excess cash source from your primary income to help with those bad times. If you have some extra money, you will not be forced to sell when you have vacancies.

Another thought is to put down as much as you can to keep your monthly costs down and insure positive cash flow. More money down also allows you to avoid certain costs, such as PMI (private mortgage insurance) and an increased rate, which would come as a result of a riskier loan-to-value position. The down side is that you would be using up more of your available cash and you wouldn't be able to purchase as much real estate.

There is a middle ground between putting almost no money down and putting down a larger percentage. That is what we refer to as the twenty percent factor. By putting twenty percent down on a unit, you avoid PMI and still preserve your cash position for other properties. In most markets, the expenses should be close to a break-even, monthly expense to income position. On some units, you will make a few dollars and lose a few dollars in others. It should be close in most markets.

PMI is known as private mortgage insurance. This is the money that is collected from homeowners monthly which is like a mini-insurance policy taken out by the PMI Corporation to underwrite your loan. This is done so that in the event that the housing market goes down in your area, or you default on the loan, the banks can make sure that that asset is covered and they are not going to lose money on the property. If you put down less than twenty points, the market could shift and it could reduce the market value of your house. This could mean that the outstanding amount of the loan is greater than the value of the house. If you put down 3% (the minimum you can put down on a house currently), and the house value decreases by 5%, the house is worth less than the value of the mortgage. The term associated with this condition is "upside down."

You will want to put down 20% or more if you can. If you put down less than 20%, you will pay an additional charge in the form of added interest and closing points and PMI, which is lost money to you and does not increase the equity in your property. The bank will be able to recover the amount of money they loaned you; in the event you default on your promise to pay them back. You never recover the PMI money or other charges that you pay. When you're trying to minimize the cost and maximize the gain, this is something to keep in mind.

You can put down less than the 20%. Five percent to 10% is what we recommend if you don't have the 20%, but the chances of you owing more on your loan than the unit is worth increases. This is that "upside down" scenario we explained earlier. There are areas in the country where housing prices drop substantially. The following lists why that may happen:

➤ Downturn of the local economy. Loss of a major employer the community depends on like a major manufacturer. We have seen this event occur a couple of times on both coasts.

➤ A major natural phenomenon such as hurricanes or flooding. Hurricane Katrina and its effects on New Orleans is one example.

➤ Changes in desirability of different areas of the country. People wanting to migrate from colder climates in the northern part of the country to areas like Florida.

How much money do you really need to put down?

The following examples are based on a unit value of $130,000, a fifteen year interest rate of 5.5%, thirty year interest rate of 6%, taxes of $1,900 per year,

PMI of $200 per month for loans of less than a 20% down payment, insurance payment of $280 per year and a monthly association fee of $125.

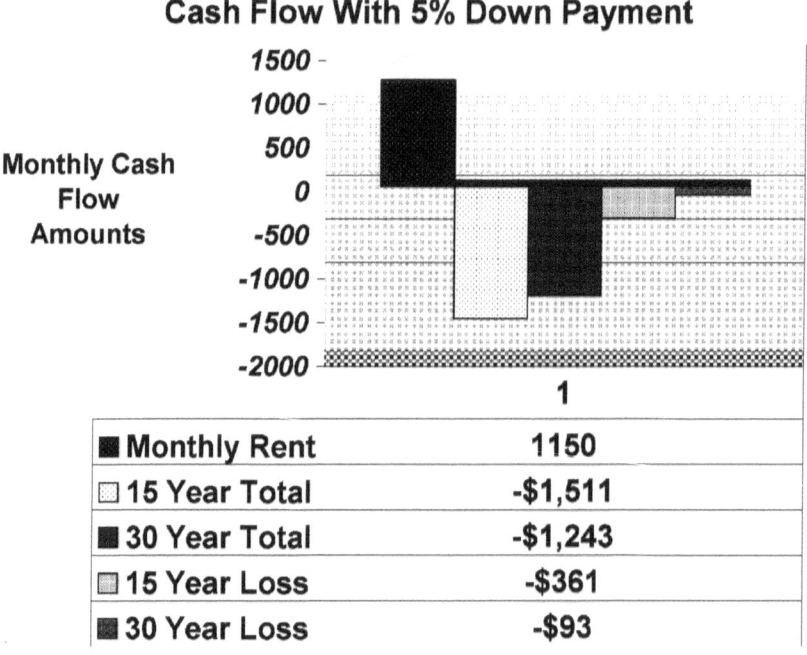

■ Monthly Rent	1150
☐ 15 Year Total	-$1,511
■ 30 Year Total	-$1,243
▨ 15 Year Loss	-$361
■ 30 Year Loss	-$93

Chart 19

As you can see from the chart, the monthly payment when your down payment is 5% is $1,005 on a fifteen-year loan, and $737 per month on a thirty-year loan of $123,500. With the other costs added in such as: tax, insurance, PMI and association dues, your costs would be $1,511 on a fifteen-year loan and $1,243 on a thirty-year loan. Compared to the monthly rent of $1,150, your loss would be $361 on a fifteen-year loan, and $93 per month on a thirty-year loan.

The next few charts show that the higher your down payment, the more secure you will be in the event of a downturn in the rental market, or during vacant periods.

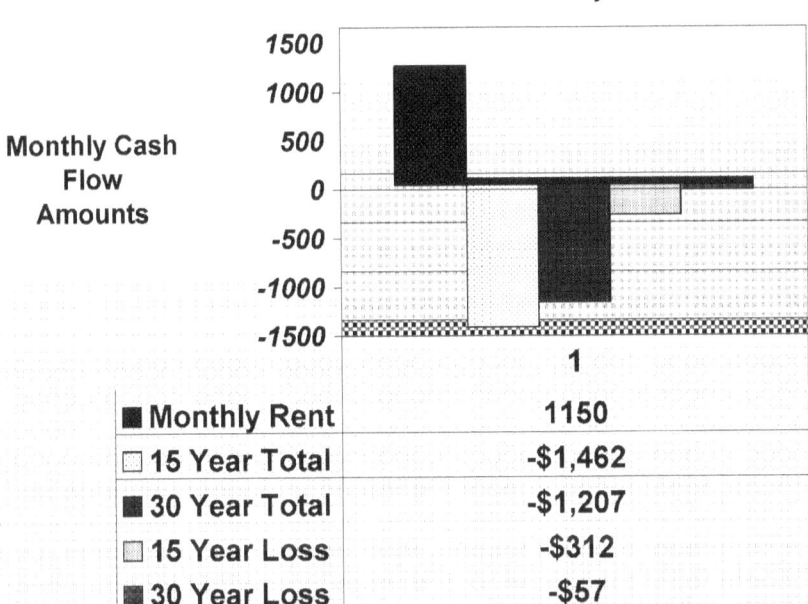

Cash Flow With 10% Down Payment

	1
■ Monthly Rent	1150
☐ 15 Year Total	-$1,462
■ 30 Year Total	-$1,207
☐ 15 Year Loss	-$312
■ 30 Year Loss	-$57

Chart 20

As you can see from the chart, the monthly payment when your down payment is 10% is $956 on a fifteen-year loan, and $701 per month on a thirty-year loan of $117,000. With the other costs added in: tax, insurance, PMI and association dues, your costs would be $1,462 on a fifteen-year loan, and $1,207 on a thirty-year loan. Compared to the monthly rent of $1,150, your loss would be $312 on a fifteen-year loan, and $57 per month on a thirty-year loan.

The difference in the total monthly expenses between your 5% and 10% down payment isn't that substantial but as illustrated, your income is closer to your expenses when you put down a higher down payment.

We want to reiterate our position that it is better to own units, even if you aren't in a position to put down more than 5% or 10%, than to sit and wait until you have more money.

The next chart that we will look at is what we refer to as the "20% Factor." We believe this is a pivotal point in terms of down payments, because there are a couple of things that happen that make a large difference.

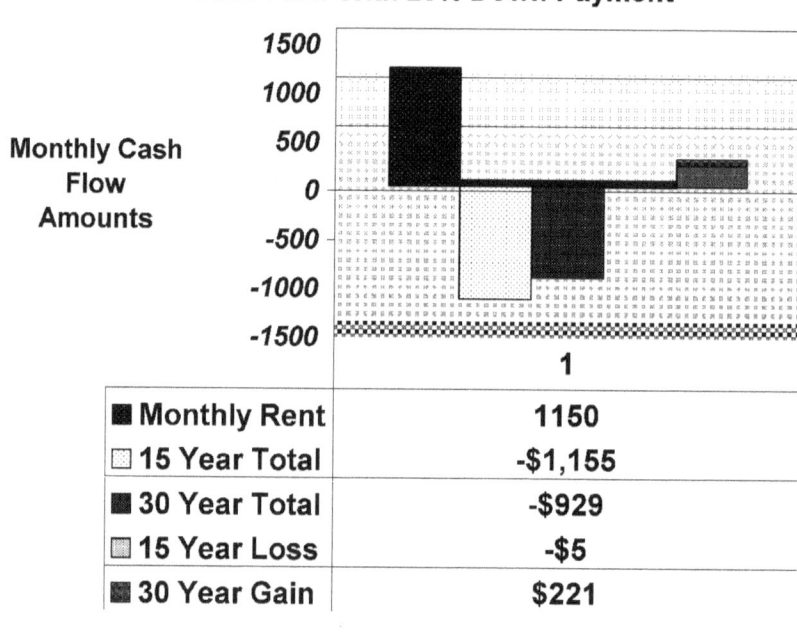

Cash Flow With 20% Down Payment

	1
■ Monthly Rent	1150
☐ 15 Year Total	-$1,155
■ 30 Year Total	-$929
▨ 15 Year Loss	-$5
■ 30 Year Gain	$221

Chart 21

The chart above shows the monthly payment when your down payment is 20%. It is $850 on a fifteen-year loan, and $624 per month on a thirty-year loan of $104,000. With the other costs added in: tax, insurance, PMI and association dues, your costs would be $1,155 on a fifteen-year loan, and $929 on a thirty-year loan. Compared to the monthly rent of $1,150, your loss would be $5 on a fifteen-year loan, and a monthly positive cash flow of $221 per month on a thirty-year loan.

Obviously, the difference of your mortgage payments is due to the difference of your down payment, but the biggest difference is the PMI. In this case, the PMI, which you avoid paying due to your down payment of 20% or more, is $200 per month. As we mentioned earlier, PMI is money that you will never get back and doesn't pay for anything you need or help you in any way. It is similar to an insurance policy that helps the bank in the event you default on your mortgage.

The monthly mortgage principal and interest payment difference between a 5% and 20% down payment is $155 a month on a fifteen year loan, and $114 a month on a thirty year loan. The monthly mortgage principal and interest payment difference between a 10% and a 20% down payment is $106 on a fifteen year loan, and $78 a month on a thirty year loan. As you can clearly see, the primary factor that causes the biggest difference in your monthly cash flow is PMI. By dropping the PMI, you save an additional $200 per month.

Types of Loans

There are a variety of loan structures available today that you can use to purchase your units. Depending on your cash position, type of property, overall goal, current situation, and the down payment being applied, you can find one that fits your budget and plans. Your mortgage broker or banker should be able to walk you through the different types, and the monthly numbers associated with each loan.

The following are some of the choices available today:

Fixed conventional—This type of loan has a starting and ending date determined by the actual term of the loan. They are usually referred to as ten-year, fifteen-year, twenty-year and thirty-year fixed loans. They have payment structures that apply part of your monthly payment to the principal balance (outstanding loan amount), with the other part being applied to interest on the loan. In the earlier years of this type of loan, a large majority of your payment is applied to interest and a small part is applied to your principal. In the case of a thirty-year mortgage, the majority of your payment is applied to interest throughout more than half of the mortgage term. You will usually end up paying about the same amount in interest as the original loan amount, throughout the life of the loan. This type of loan is usually used when you need to count on a fixed monthly amount, and want to build equity through both appreciation and principal buydown.

Interest Only—These loans are set up so that you pay only the monthly interest on the money that you are borrowing. None of the monthly payment will be applied towards the principal loan amount. What this means to you is that after a ten year period, the original loan amount will be the same as it was the day you borrowed the money. These loans are usually used when it is imperative to have positive monthly cash flow, or in areas of high appreciation over a short term. These loans will usually fluctuate with one of the government published interest rate indicators, or money funds.

There are other types of loans that you might want to use like lines of credit and forty-year notes, often referred to as negative amortization loans. Check with your banker or broker to determine if some of the other choices might be better for your situation.

The loans shown below represent just some of the most common ways to finance property and different monthly payment amounts for each. You can see that as the number of years on the loan increase, the amount of principal that is paid from your monthly payment decreases. The monthly payments do increase, but when calculated out, the extra monthly amount is much less than the actual decrease of the principal impact.

Mortgage Term	10 Year	15 Year	20 Year	30 Year	Interest Only
Loan amount	$ 100,000	$ 100,000	$ 100,000	$ 100,000	$ 100,000
Annual interest rate	6.000%	6.000%	6.000%	6.000%	0.000%
Loan period in years	10	15	20	30	10*
Scheduled monthly payment	$1,110	$844	$844	$600	$500
Scheduled number of payments	$120	$180	$240	$360	$180
Total interest	$33,225	$51,894	$71,943	$115,838	6000/Year

Principal Buydown

Ending Balance After 5 Years	$58,245	$76,471	$85,190	$93,188	$100,000
Principal Paid After 5 Years	$41,755	$23,529	$14,810	$6,812	$0
Ending Balance After 10 Years	$0	$44,271	$64,923	$83,866	$100,000
Principal Paid After 10 Years	$100,000	$55,729	$35,077	$16,134	

Chart 22

As the chart shows, with a shorter term, more principal is paid throughout the term of the loan. Also, with a shorter term, the amount of the monthly payment increases. This is why it is important to have a clear understanding of just how much monthly cash flow you can afford to put in to your properties. It also helps with planning what your investment goals are when thinking about getting into this business. Things can and will change, but if you are clear in your direction, your outcome will be better.

"Goals without a plan are just dreams"

We have shown a $100,000 loan broken out by different terms. The most common terms are ten-year, fifteen-year, twenty-year, thirty-year, and interest only loans. Interest only notes are those where none of your monthly payment goes to principal buydown. Since you are only paying the interest, your payment is much less than a thirty-year mortgage. These notes usually have a term cap on them, which means they must be paid off in that defined term. The more common terms are seven and ten year terms. That doesn't mean you have to suddenly have a check for that amount on the last day of the term, but that the note has to be satisfied. You will either sell the unit, or take out another note to pay off the first one, and potentially, another interest only or standard term P&I (principal and interest) note.

Principal and Interest are the two primary parts of most notes, other than a straight interest only note. The principal is the amount of the payment that goes towards the actual loan amount. That is the dollar figure you actually borrowed from the bank. The interest part is the finance charge, or the money you are paying the banking institution for loaning you the money.

The other parts of the monthly loan payment are:

➤ -PMI

➤ -Insurance

➤ -Assessment Fees

➤ -Escrow

This is a good time to reinforce the idea of knowing what your monthly payments will be, prior to moving forward and laying out your plan. You don't need to calculate this within a penny, but you can calculate those numbers accurately enough so that you won't find yourself overextended after the property is purchased. This should also provide some understanding of your cash flow position, based on the current rental rates seen in the area of your property. In the event your monthly rental cash flow position is negative, you should be clear about your ability to carry the loss. Remember, the market will set the rental price and not the total of your monthly bills against that property. If your monthly bills exceed the rental market monthly prices, you will need to accept that and do what you can to keep it occupied. As illustrated earlier, if your unit is vacant for a month, your overall returns drop dramatically.

PMI

PMI (private mortgage insurance), is based on the percentage amount that you put down as your down payment. When your down payment is 20% or above, you can avoid PMI. Less than 20%, you will pay PMI with your monthly payment.

Insurance

Your homeowner's insurance can also be escrowed along with your taxes. This is usually done for convenience purposes so you don't have to remember to make those payments. When dealing with investment properties, this may also be a good alternative.

Assessment Fees

Assessment fees are usually made directly to the homeowners association of the development where your rental unit sits.

Escrow

Another benefit to putting 20% or more down, is your choice to escrow your property taxes or not. When you put down less than 20%, the lending institution will automatically include property taxes as part of your monthly payment. This allows the bank to use your money throughout the year without paying interest. They will also be responsible for making sure those taxes are paid when they are due, and pay any penalties in the event the taxes are paid late. The lender is also allowed to "over escrow" by collecting more than the projected amount owed at the end of the year. The lender will perform an annual escrow analysis after the final tax payment has been sent to the county, at the end of the year. Most of the time, this will illustrate that they have collected too much, and they will send a check to you for the overpayment.

In newer subdivisions, the lender will usually underestimate the taxes for your first year after the house is built. The initial tax assessment is based on the land value without the added value of the house or townhouse. This sets up a situation where your monthly mortgage payment can dramatically increase. The second year, the lender will need to add the underpaid amount from the first year to the monthly payment. They will have a better idea of the correct tax for the second year and make the adjustment as an added increase to the monthly payment. They will also include some additional money to cover any increase in taxes for the current year. County taxes are paid a year late, and can increase between the time you make your final payment and when you receive your tax bill for the following year. As a result of these increases, your monthly payment could increase hundreds to thousands of dollars each month.

All of these items can be put into an escrow account, if you would like to have the bank handle the payments of these costs for you. The decision to have the banking institution collect and pay the money in each category is a personal one, provided you have put more than 20% down as your down payment. Many do it out of convenience so they do not have to think about it, thus avoiding the exposure of missing one of those payments. It also makes it easy to see what you take in (rents), and what goes out in a single line.

The obvious drawback of setting up an escrow with your bank is that you are essentially setting up a non-interest bearing account. The bank will not pay you interest for this type of account. The justification for this is they are providing a service to you by having the record keeping responsibility and cutting checks against that money. They also have to deal with the creditors who will receive that money.

What Other Factors Determine the Type of Loan

The decision on what type of loan you will want on each unit will depend on a number of data points. There isn't a "one size fits all" methodology for determining what loan you will need. You need to first answer the biggest question—what is your overall plan?

Do you have a full time job with limited time?
Do you have a limited amount of money to start?
Do you have additional money so that you can afford some monthly negative cash flow without it dramatically affecting your standard of living and ability to cover your other costs on a monthly basis?
How much do you want Real Estate to contribute to your monthly revenue/asset stream?
How fast do you want to get in and out of controlling properties?
Is this going to represent ongoing cash flow for retirement?
Do you want to make enough and work harder now, so that you won't do this during your retirement?

These are just some of the questions you will need to ask yourself in order to keep your loans in line with your long term plan. To reiterate an earlier point, do not overextend yourself financially. If you are continually worried about meeting your monthly expenses, then you may want to determine how you can increase your equity while reducing your expenses via increased cash flow.

There are a number of questions you have to ask yourself in determining how you want to structure this business for both the long-term and short-term. We have provided some of those, but there will be more, depending on your individual situation, current cash flow, present and future cash requirements, overall "handyman" competency, and the amount of time you can devote to running this business.

If your plan is to buy as many properties as you can manage, and you do not have a lot of extra monthly cash, then you will need to do longer term loans or interest only notes.

Now that we have determined what type of investor fits the personal criteria and circumstances we've described, we can look at the type of loan you will need to fulfill the requirements.

Where Can I Get the Money?

The difficulty that a lot of people have with this plan is trying to find out where to get the money. We need to illustrate that there are non-traditional and traditional ways to get this money.

The first rule in financial planning is to not take money from somewhere that you might need in the event of unforeseen circumstances. As with any good financial plan, you need access to short term, liquid, money to get you through untimely events that may come up. Having at least two months of salary in an interest bearing bank account, stock, or short term CD that can be accessed and liquidated quickly without major penalty, is prudent. When you invest in a rental unit, you should plan on that money representing your second or third tier of savings. That means this is money that you will not have immediate access to and you may have to wait until either you sell the unit or do a refinance. Either way, you may wait 30–120+ days to be able to get that cash out.

Savings

A savings account is an obvious place from which to pull money in order to finance your first real estate investment. Research the market to determine the value of the house that you want to purchase. Take 20% of that value (for the down payment), plus an additional 5% in costs, closing, legal and insurance. Now you have a financial target to save. Assess how much you can contribute on a monthly basis, and the time it will take you to achieve the target, to see if this approach is viable. If you're looking at saving $50,000 (25% of a $200,000 property), and you can only contribute $50 a month, then based on the period of time, this may not be a feasible plan and you might have to make some adjustments to your strategy. Either lower the value of the property you are intending to buy, or figure out a way to increase the amount that you save on a monthly basis, or a combination of the two.

The first property will always be the hardest in many ways. You have to take that first step and find the money to purchase it, plus all of the costs associated with making it rentable. Your second property will be much easier due to experience, the ability to use the first property as an asset through positive cash flow, and refinanced equity to fund the second property.

401(k)s and IRAs

Many people have 401(k)s and IRAs. The average financial broker will tell you that because of the tax penalties involved in IRAs, that isn't a place to grab money. But as you have seen, the amount of return is so great, it should far exceed the taxes and penalties. Even though you have to pay taxes and a penalty on April 15th, when you file your taxes, the amount of money you'll make in the first year should be exponentially larger than the 10% you paid to get the money. Your accountant and others will advise against using this money, but when you run the numbers, you'll see that the penalty number is nothing compared to your return.

Another use of your 401(k) is to borrow against that money. There are two primary benefits to using this approach. The first is you are borrowing from yourself and not a bank, and therefore pay yourself interest. The second benefit is you are avoiding the penalties and income taxes associated with making an actual withdrawal. You are still setting up a loan, and therefore will still have a payment associated with using this money. There are also rules that can make that money due immediately—if you borrow from an account that is established with your current employer and you are terminated, or choose to leave that employer.

SEPs

SEPs are self employed pension plans for small business owners. Small business owners set up the equivalent of a 401(k) for themselves and contribute money to an account, which is tax deferred and tax deductible. They are allowed to contribute up to $40,000/year, which can be used for investments such as stocks, CDs, or investments such as rental properties. In June 2003, The Wall Street Journal published an article about the growing number of business owners looking for places to invest their SEP funds. It specifically named rental real estate properties as an option for SEP funds.

Current House Equity

Many people who get into this business use some equity from their existing property to fund the down payment to purchase their first rental property. Real estate appreciates every year. After you have been in your home three or more years, you've probably built up a fair amount of equity.

Some people plan ahead and purchase a house to first live in, with the objective to rent it later. This is a great way to start in the rental business. If you plan right, you can refinance your primary residence, find another house that you would like to move into, and use the money you received from the cash out refinance to purchase that next primary residence. At that point, you rent to someone else the house you just came from. The biggest benefit of doing it this way is that refinancing will allow the mortgage to be done as an "owner occupied" loan, which provides lower interest rates. "Investment property" is usually done at a ½ to ¾ point increased interest rates. This difference is put in your rate as a risk factor, because you are not personally living in the unit.

Brokerage Accounts

Brokerage accounts containing stock can also be used to purchase additional properties. This decision will come down to a matter of return on your money. As we have illustrated, the returns from renting properties should be much higher, with much less risk, than the returns historically seen in the stock market. The stock market is also more volatile than traditional real estate valuations.

Chapter Eight

Making the Decision

The commitment question is one that we all have to make in every aspect of our lives. Many required commitments are delayed in favor of a "better time." With most delayed decisions, there isn't a real cost for that delay, but simply the delay itself. In those cases, it is okay to put things off to another day or time because the only impact is the fun you might have had doing that activity, or the restaurant you didn't go to that night. In some cases, where a decision must be made but is put off, there is a penalty in the form of a fee or some other impact to your life. This can be as simple as a late fee on a bill you have, or a penalty for renewing your license plates too late. This can also impact your credit, if you are late in paying something and they report negative information to the credit agencies.

Some decisions are classified as emergencies and need to be done immediately. Most people don't have a difficult time making the decision to move forward with those because our inner fight/flight response takes over and forces us to take action. Those, in a sense, are made for us rather than by us.

Making, or not making, the decision to invest in real estate as we propose is what we refer to as a missed opportunity decision. Unlike the others, there isn't a penalty or something as simple as a loss of fun that comes from not making this decision. The opportunity decision you don't make will cost you some of the highest returns on your money that you will probably ever experience. You won't have a penalty, and putting it off will only mean that you end up with less money. This decision is the difference of simply parking your money in some vehicle that will have significantly lower returns, or taking a step that will change your life and provide financial independence.

To commit or not commit? When making the decision to commit to anything, you will need to evaluate the following:

Short and long term goals

You will need clear short- and long-term goals in order to decide if this is something to pursue. If you have a partner or spouse, they will need to be part of that discussion, as their cooperation will be helpful in order for you to achieve the level of success defined in your plan.

We have listed goals as the first area to consider in making this decision. We feel that you need to be somewhat goal oriented—meaning you have some goals defined in your mind, or you wouldn't be thinking about making additional money in the first place. Goals are an important part of life. It is hard to accomplish anything, short- or long-term, without having first defined a goal and planned a path to accomplish that goal. Without that path, they can become just dreams that never become realities.

If one of your goals is to retire early, have more money, be financially free, find a way to pay for your children's college, or any other money based goal, then you need to assess the urgency behind that goal. If you have a goal that can be accomplished in five years or thirty years, then it may not matter what path you choose because you may have the time to take a more traditional route. If your goal is more time sensitive, you need to do something more, like renting real estate, to accelerate your plan so it is more aligned with that goal.

Gains vs. exposures of possible risks

There is some risk associated with this type of investment, which primarily comes in two forms. The first is making sure you follow the credit rule to insure that the tenants you choose will pay the rent and not damage your units. The other risk is making sure the units are occupied. If they aren't occupied, then you are the tenant who pays the rent. That isn't a great way to increase your returns on your investment. If you have to make one or several additional mortgage payments every month, and have no rent to offset those obligations, this could put your financial situation in jeopardy. If you believe our system works, we encourage you to commit to the rules we have laid out so your units stay occupied by the right people.

You will also need to look at the gains and evaluate the amount of exposure, or risk, that is associated with your ROI. Nothing in life is free. Everything comes at a cost. As with any investment, there is usually a down side that can either eat into your profits or, in some cases, take you down with that investment. The good thing about this investment is the exposure is limited. Most people would think that since you are dealing in bigger dollars (buying houses is usually the largest purchase any of us ever make), the risk is greater.

Our earlier graphs showed that real estate goes up most of the time. Let's say that you buy the unit and a year later you find yourself in an uncomfortable financial spot and need that money. At that point, you would sell the property and get your money out. Since real estate appreciation has averaged around six percent, you should be able to pay the real estate agent and still come close to breaking even. Keep in mind that this process isn't like putting money in a bank because you can't just pull it out when you want or need that money. Another option would be to refinance that unit and pull out some cash, or take a line against that unit to cover some short-term financial needs. The bottom line is, you probably won't lose like you can in the market, and the gains are usually higher.

Renting real estate can provide a drastic improvement in returns over the traditional methods such as buying stocks or bank accounts. As illustrated earlier in this book, the market performance has not been able to come close to the returns that you should see if your follow our methodology. We do need to tell you that there are a lot of variables and, like anything you invest in, there are no guarantees around the returns that you should see in the rental market.

Your cash position, earning potential and credit rating

Cash position, earning potential and credit rating are things that may delay, make more difficult, cut into your returns, or altogether stop you from getting into this business.

A proper evaluation of your credit rating, current cash position and earnings potential is important. In terms of your credit rating, you will need to make sure your rating can support applying for additional mortgages. If you have a poor credit rating and you can't get a loan for your first rental unit, then you can't get into this business.

If you don't have any money for down payments on your first unit, or maybe won't have it for a couple of years, then you will need to work that into your overall plan. There are a lot of people on television and writing books that will tell you the twenty ways you can buy real estate without using any of your own money. We agree that there are a couple of ways (certainly not twenty realistic ways), but would also agree that you will be totally upside down in your monthly calculations if you use them. In our methodology, you will need some of your own money in order to make this work. It can be done with less—but you will need different loan structures and will need to depend more on your regular income to shore up your monthly totals. As mentioned earlier, we encourage twenty percent down payments because there are a lot of benefits. Monthly cash flows, PMI, and getting your mortgage approved are just a few.

Your credit rating influences your ability to get money, and how much, when you need to make a move. You should run your credit report once every year or so in order to understand what is on it and how that might negatively affect you when applying for a loan. We cannot stress this enough. You don't want to find the unit, negotiate the buying price, and start to run the rental ad, just to find out you aren't going to be approved for the loan because you either have bad credit or are stretched to your limit. In the world of credit, the more you owe, the type of loans you owe on and pay for on time, the better your credit usually looks. There are limits to that rule, but generally speaking you can get more, if you spend more, and make the payments on those loans.

Earning potential is also a big limiter. Paying on loans is a part of your credit rating and you can't pay them unless you earn enough. This is why you need to balance your monthly cash flows with your ability to manage your units. Some people have a lot of time and could deal with a large number of units, but don't have enough money to buy that many. Others have a lot of money, but don't have the time to manage any more than a couple of units. Your earnings will also have to be evaluated very carefully. If you are living check to check, it will put you in a tight financial spot if you have a lapse in incoming rent payments. Selling a unit or missing a mortgage payment can be the result of not being able to go a month without that rent check. This isn't to say that you have to have six months of mortgage payments in the bank in order to get into this business, but you should be able to withstand a short term (a month or so), in the event something goes wrong. Investors pick up great buys every day from someone who didn't plan and found himself or herself in a position where they had to liquidate in a short time frame. That person wasn't in a position where they could negotiate and ended up taking a loss on their investment.

Amount of excess time vs. the amount of work involved

The time you have to devote will be an important decision. As we have stated, there isn't a lot of time required, after you have purchased and filled the units. There may be from time to time, something that comes up that you will have to deal with immediately. This is rare, but if it happens, either you or your partner will need to take care of the issue. This will involve a block of time from your schedule. We have found that initially, there can be about twenty hours per house to find, buy, and prepare the property. This time is a one time, up front investment. We usually spend four to six hours a year, per unit. Believe it or not, about half of that time is spent on meeting new renters for the first time, signing the new lease, and going over the first day walk through with them. You would spend more time than that with your broker or banker. We don't use management companies to save time because they usually charge 8%–12% of annual rent. We haven't found that there is anything for them to do that justifies their charges.

The amount of time you have will greatly affect the way you go about running your rental business. You can go the route of buying those so called "fixer uppers" and doing a lot of work on the front end; or you can buy the turn key units that have associations and all of the work done for you. Both of those scenarios come with a price tag.

The idea of doing a lot more because you have the time will work for some and save some money. Buying a unit that does not have an association, which will do more of the work for you, will force you to do more of the work. Things like landscaping, exterior painting, roofing, siding maintenance, and snow removal require a lot of hours to complete. If you have the time, you might want to go this route. Just remember that time spent on one unit is time you don't have to spend on finding another potential unit.

If you have limited time, you will want to buy units that are more "self maintained." The association does most of the upkeep in these units and you just write a monthly check to pay the association dues. Dues are collected from all of the units in that development and are pooled to pay for some of the items listed above. This will leave more time for your full time job, but also means that it costs you more and eats into your profits. You need to weigh this cost against the amount of time spent away from your regular job.

The type of work required

Please don't interpret the last statement as us stating that there isn't any work to be done and you will make lots of money by simply cashing the check every month. There is some work, but if done correctly, most of it is on the front end. This work comes in the form of picking the unit out, setting up contracts, showing the property, and getting the property ready the first time. From time to time there may be a repair that needs to be done, but usually that is an appliance or furnace, which will be done by someone else. You will place the call but probably won't do the work yourself. As we mentioned earlier, when repairs are needed you will need to stop what you are doing and make the call to get someone there, depending on the severity of the issue. A call to a tradesman may not represent a lot of time, but may have to be done at an inconvenient time.

Some work needing to be done in your units can be done by just about anyone (like painting or replacing a lock). Other work, such as repairing a broken pipe, a hole in a wall, or replacing a ceiling fan, can be a bit tougher. You will need to assess your level of skill and decide what you will be willing to take on vs. what you will need help with. Most tasks can be learned and can be mastered after you have been doing this for a while. Some items will be ones that you will never want to take on yourself. You can save money doing more yourself, but in the end, if you can't finish the job, then you will need to call someone to clean up your mess. That comes at a higher cost and a costly delay to the tenant. Neither is going to help your business.

The points that we have discussed will need to be considered and decided upon when you are planning out your rental business. All of them will impact your level of success and either increase or decrease your profits. There are many, many more that you will have to consider. Since most of them deal with personal goals and objectives, you will have to make them independent of most outside advice. Obviously, we would advise you to get into this business or we wouldn't have written this book. Only you will know what else might affect your ability to run your business smoothly.

Chapter Nine

Finding, Buying and Paying for the Property

How Do I Find the Right Property?

Finding the right property will probably prove to be the second most important decision you will make in this process. The first being making sure the tenant is credit worthy. The priceless question is, of course, what makes one property better than another?

Our methodology is to rent out premium properties. Most properties are average looking, in average locations, with average floor plans. Don't get us wrong, you can rent out almost any property because ultimately everything will rent at a price. The question is, are you going to make any money when it does rent and how much time will you spend trying to rent that property? You want to make sure you're making money in this process and not spending more time than your full time job.

The qualities of the ideal property include an area with high appreciation. Look for properties that are three to eight miles from large business centers and easily accessible to trains. There are a lot of these areas out there. Places with high concentrations of business are also prime targets. You don't want to be next to those businesses, but rather on the outskirts of those locations, so your tenants have quick access to them but don't have to directly look at them from their windows.

What the unit is looking at is very important. Location, location, location is so overused, but so accurate. You don't want to be looking at the back of a store, huge office buildings, a garbage dump, other houses, or apartment buildings. If you can avoid looking at the back of a house, or large retail or office space, it will help with both appreciation and your ability to keep it occupied. Your unit should be looking at something like a golf course, a lakefront, a nature preserve, a school playground, or something peaceful and serene. Remember that your tenants go to work in big office buildings, retail locations, or commercial structures. They want to come home and look at something nice and peaceful.

Do you remember what we said about the Baby Boomers? This is very important. What has happened with the Boomers, and what is going to happen with them, and the changes they go through as they age—all of these have an impact on their choice of housing and your rental business. The older boomers have already begun to make some of these changes including: downsizing their house, moving to places that are more convenient to local commerce, and moving near friends who they can rely on in the event of an emergency.

They are also moving to places that are more serene and peaceful than where they have lived during their working life. They have worked hard and want to relax. They want to sit on their porch and look at something calm and serene such as golf courses, lakefronts, nature preserves, schools, and parks. So logically, if you own those types of units now, in ten years, twelve years, fifteen years, when all those people are migrating down to those locations, it will put excess demand on houses in those locations. That is your target market for both the short- and long-term. Work with this knowledge as part of your overall plan.

Time is money and opportunity; don't waste it. The bottom line is, if you can reduce the hassle, the risk, the number of trips you have to make to each unit due to repairs and maintenance—then your ability to replicate the model with more units goes up dramatically. If you can reduce your overall effort, then the majority of your job on that unit will be cashing the monthly rent check and resigning the lease.

Townhouses vs. Condos and Single Family

Condos are effectively apartments with titles, with some tax advantages. That's not a negative if you want to rent an apartment. What is the difference between renting an apartment and a condo? When it comes to resale time, the appreciation on a condo will probably not be as much as on a townhouse. Condos aren't as desirable from a privacy and shared ownership standpoint. A lot of people aren't going to pay top rent for a condo either, even though you may have paid a premium on the purchase. Keep in mind your rental target market.

Condos are less expensive to purchase than townhouses, but keep in mind resale value and the ability to rent it. The easier it is to rent, the less likely it will be that you have to deal with vacancies, which can make or break your success quicker than any other factor. With condos, you are competing with apartments. There are apartment buildings on every corner. You would be competing for the same renters and therefore your ability to get your asking rental price drops.

With single family homes, you have a very limited market. As far as potential clients, there aren't too many people who will rent a single family home for reasons such as lawn upkeep and general maintenance. Single family homes are rentable, but you have fewer people in that market wanting to rent. The end result might mean having to reduce your price and not making as much money.

Your goal is to find a housing option for the largest pool of potential renters in the marketplace. The option that is between a condo and a house is the townhouse. This is why we've targeted townhouses. It is set up like a house, except it is maintenance free. There is usually an association involved and you don't have to deal with upkeep. Renters don't like to cut their lawns, but they'll have to in the single family home. In terms of space, most townhouses are two to three bedrooms. This is the size most renters are interested in. They are small enough for someone that is single, but also adequate for a small family.

Rental rates between townhouses and apartments are comparable. Your ability to price a townhouse for slightly more is due to the fact that they are more desirable. Townhouses generally offer amenities that aren't found in apartments such as: garages, additional space, and privacy. They can also offer nicer views and less interaction with your neighbors. People usually perceive a townhouse as a step up, or an upgrade, from apartment living.

Age of the Building

Another qualifier to consider is the age of the building. The ideal age is in the ten to twenty year time span. You can purchase something that is a bit older, up to twenty-five years or so, but buying a newer unit is an advantage. A new unit means fewer things are broken, or will break, and require repair and/or replacement that cost time and money. Units that are ten to twenty years old should provide years of trouble free renting and allow you to keep this investment to a part time occupation.

We've been asked about buying younger units, such as new construction, or recently constructed. From a maintenance standpoint, younger units are great, but from an appreciation standpoint, they don't help your ROI. Too many people seem to buy, build, and then move. In the beginning, this will keep your appreciation low because many people will sell at any price to get out, instead of waiting for their price. If too many people do this, then you are looking at appraisal comparisons that are based on other people in the neighborhood dumping their units. The next section gets into this in greater detail.

Existing vs. New Construction

A lot of people say, "You know, the trailer just went up, I'll go buy and get pre-construction prices." The problem is, traditionally you are not going to get the desired return. If the house gets built in a community of one hundred others, within the first year, in excess of 10% will have a "for sale" sign up. Those trying to sell are competing with the brand new house. In order to sell their house they will usually dramatically lower their price. The difference of a few thousand dollars between buying a new unit and buying a "used" unit can be a few dollars a month impact on the monthly mortgage. Most people like picking out all of their own options on a new house.

This is an example of what normally happens:

You're going to either buy a new unit or you're going to buy an existing unit. If you own a unit, the value of your unit isn't really going up, even though the model is going up in price. The value of your unit isn't going up because, if you had to sell it, you would be competing with the builder's new unit. When the appraiser determines a value of your unit, they use, as comparisons, similar units in the area that have recently sold. These are called "comps." If five units sold in the past month or two for $10,000 under what the people selling the units paid, which is $15,000 less than the new one, then the appraised value of the used units is going to be in line with those houses sold at a reduced price. This means your appraisal just went down by the same amount.

As a result, your refinance, or ReFi, capabilities decrease due to lower "comps." You're probably not going to ReFi for years. The effect of this usually takes about five years to work itself out so that the appreciation begins to be more in line with what you would expect. That's a long time to wait for your money. New construction discounts may seem to be a good deal. They really aren't.

Existing Construction

After units have been there for five to ten years, the appreciation usually evens out and becomes consistent. After that five-year curve of new construction, things work themselves out and, for the most part, people stop moving in and out as rapidly. The trailer has been gone a few years and housing prices are allowed to rise. They usually rise up within the same neighborhood at about the same rate of appreciation. People will always have a reason to want to, or need to, sell their house.

That isn't to say all neighborhoods appreciate well. Some areas, such as those in bad school districts or run down areas, don't appreciate very well at all. This is referred to as flat appreciation and would be a bad investment.

Finding the Right Properties

There are many ways to look for properties, and some are more effective than others. Most people will use real estate agents who search through the MLS (multiple listing service). They also have the ability to send out mailers to neighborhoods that you are targeting. You can also look at the appreciation trends, cruise the neighborhoods, and look for "For Sale by Owner," commonly referred to as FSBOs, (pronounced "fisbos").

If you already own units, one of the things we have done that has been highly successful is to have our renters look for other units. If we have a good unit in a specific area, and we're making money on it, we want another one in the same neighborhood. How do we find another one? We're not in those neighborhoods all day long. When a "For Sale" sign goes up on a house in that neighborhood, we want to know about it within an hour of that sign going up. We have a technique we've used for years that has saved us a lot of money.

We have a deal with all of our tenants. If they let us know about a unit that we go on to buy, we give them $1,000. It provides a little incentive for them and we usually end up saving thousands of dollars on the purchase price. We have written several checks actually. Or we offer a free month's rent to our tenants. We get a phone call within an hour or two of that "For Sale" sign going up. We're the first to inquire about the unit, and because we know the units, the neighborhood, and what they are worth, we can make a quick decision. This allows us to get the unit off the market before the sellers have an open house, avoiding a bidding war with three other potential buyers.

This is where negotiation can benefit you greatly. If a person is selling their house on their own, they might not know what the house is really worth. They usually base the sale price on the last price they heard their neighbor received when selling their house. Because we own other units in the same neighborhood, we have them appraised all the time and know what that house is worth. We know when they are absolutely out of line with too high of a price, in which case we will offer them less. If they don't take it, they continue to try to sell it to someone else. Eventually, they may realize it would be wise to accept our offer because if they don't find a buyer, they may be forced to have a realtor assist them. The realtor will take six points and they would have to inflate the price another fifteen points to break even with what we would have paid them. They come to realize that isn't a financially smart move.

Generally, if the asking price is close to what we think it is worth, and we have to pay a few thousand dollars more on a mortgage, it is okay. Because of the rental model, we're not paying the mortgage anyway, someone else is. Ultimately, if it's a good asset, we'll pay a little bit more, or have one of our tenants pay a little bit more, for the availability of having that equity in a few years. Our purchase takes the unit off the market. We give the seller what they want (generally, because it's a FSBO, they are under-priced) and they are happy because they sold their unit in two hours. They happily sign the contract and we get moving.

The renters are really happy because as you will see later, they are the ones who are the rental agents in our formula. They rent the house for us. We don't even need to go to the houses anymore. We just pick up the phone and send the potential renter over to the unit. They meet the current renter, who sells the potential renter for us. Part of the reason they are so willing to show the unit, and effectively "sell" the rental, is because we have treated them so well. It could be a renter who got $1000 from us a couple months ago. They are pretty happy to brag about their landlord, which makes the unit a lot easier to rent. Everything you can do to make your renters happy will improve their attitude about you and your unit when they are showing the unit.

When to Find the Property

When do most people move? In Chicago, and most Northern areas, it is May 31–August 31. Before May 31, you can't count on the weather. No one wants to move when it is twenty degrees outside. After August 31, it could be raining, or there could be four inches of snow on the ground. Eighty percent of the people in Chicago move during June, July and August. That can make it difficult to find a rental truck or rent a unit. When consider buying a house, think about aligning that rental to the season. We call it the rental season. Buying outside of this season is still okay, but you will need to adjust your lease to end at a time that aligns with the start of the next rental season. We get into more detail about the rental season later in this book.

Buying the House

There are a number of ways to find a house including open houses, MLS, FSBOs, and word of mouth. Each will have some good things and bad things to know in order to negotiate the best possible deal on that unit. Keep in mind the best deal doesn't always mean just price. It could also mean the flexibility of when you take possession of that unit to work around the rental season. It could also relate to what is staying in the unit that will save you money when you are preparing the unit.

Open houses are probably one of the more common ways to find a unit. They are easy but have one major drawback. The fact that there is a realtor involved means there is additional money built into the price to pay that realtor. You end up paying for it because it raises the lowest amount the seller is willing to take for that unit. The other drawback—if it's in a hot area and you have an open house, especially in the townhouse arena, you'll have ten people at the end of the day offering a lot more than the house's listing price.

Again, why buy FSBOs? Why do you get there two hours after the sign has gone up? You don't want to be at the back of the line, bidding $10,000–$20,000 more than the listed price of that house. You want to be there, giving them the price they are asking. Most people won't argue with that.

This idea is also based on the assumption that your existing unit is in a hot area, and you have been successful in keeping it occupied at a good monthly rate. If that is the case, then buying another one in that same neighborhood will also help you keep your rental business simple. Why travel to different neighborhoods, with different location factors, if something works? Keep it simple and keep making money.

Using a Realtor

Using a realtor to work for you is a good idea—but that person has to get paid. The realtor is probably not looking at FSBOs. They are probably only looking at listed properties with higher prices. Listed properties are generally more expensive because the realtor has to get paid. So even though you're not paying a realtor, your realtor is only looking at properties listed by realtors, which are inflated.

Pitfalls of Houses That Are Listed

To buy a listed house, brokers know what the house should sell for. You will pay too much. FSBOs usually don't understand the real market value of their properties. You need to be in a position where you understand it better than they do.

Negotiating the Purchase

When you are an investor, you have a lot more negotiating power. A powerful negotiation tool is to find out why they are selling. You can use this information. If there are health issues, a job transfer, major financial changes, retirement, changes with children either moving in or moving out, or the seller is getting married, you can keep this reason in mind.

If they are getting a divorce, usually, neither person cares as much about how much they get for this house. They just want out because they don't want to have to neither deal with the other person ever again, nor be reminded of the property that they shared as a couple. We have negotiated under market prices on houses because of this issue.

Was there a death in the family? It could be that mom or dad just passed away and it was their house. The kids have estate money coming and they don't really care how much they get for the house, because split three ways that might not end up being much. They have no equity in that house and therefore they'll think anything is better than waiting a long time to get that money.

In the case of the elderly, they might be at the time in their life where they are moving in with one of the kid's at their house. When that is the case, you can do certain things that won't cost you much money to increase your position. One thing we have used is to pay a service to come in and pack up for them. This would be about $1000–$2000, depending on the size of the house. This isn't a lot of money relative to the purchase price, but it means a lot to that elderly person who won't have to do it themselves. You can simply say, "I'll even give you $1000 in packing expenses." You have now given them the possibility of forgoing having to sit there, bend over, and pack a box a day because that is all they can do. Many elderly people don't have the strength to do all of that packing. It is a big point of negotiation vs. the next guy who isn't going to do it.

Urgency can be a big motivator. If the seller needs to sell quickly, it is better for you, the purchaser. A seller with no urgency is going to be willing to sit and wait until that money comes, whatever price they are asking. You will benefit if you know answers to questions like: Do they need to sell because they have a contingency on another house? That's a big motivator. Will they lose their dream house because they can't sell this unit? They have to take less money for this one. Again, it's a mortgage with monthly payments that won't change much by getting a few thousand dollars less for the unit that they are selling. They won't care about a few additional dollars per month on their new mortgage, if it means they can buy their dream house.

The idea of negotiating any purchase is to find out as much as you can about their situation with the hope of using some of that information to lower your price or increase your negotiating position. The exception to this is if the seller is under water on the mortgage due to the realtor commission they will have to pay. In that case, they will have a minimum selling price that they will have to get.

Try to find out what the main loan on their property is. You can do this by some searches to find out the last time this house was purchased or sold. That information is a matter of public record and you'll be able to find out what they paid for the unit. This is important because it will tell you a lot about their flexibility when it comes to negotiating the final price.

Items to include in the contract

When writing the contract, there are a number of terms and conditions that you will want to include. Most of these will revolve around your ability to show the unit prior to close, rent backs, and taking possession of the unit. These clauses will accommodate both you and the seller and should be presented as a win-win for both.

The first topic we will cover is the ability to show the unit prior to closing. It is important to be able to "pre-market" the unit so that it is rented within a couple of days of closing, so that you begin making money as soon as possible. It will only take a couple of days to prepare the unit after closing and if you have a signed lease, you can make money from the first day.

The people who are selling the unit to you usually won't mind doing this, but you will need to make sure you negotiate this into the contract since you might not be able to get them to agree to it after the paper is signed. As part of selling their unit, most sellers will agree to some extras that they might not agree to after it is sold.

The next topic is the idea of being able to rent the unit back, commonly referred to as a "rent back," to the seller after you close on the unit. If the timing doesn't look like it will work, you might be able to propose a "rent back" to the current owner. You would use this in the event you purchased the unit out of "rental season." This is usually attractive to the seller because it allows them some additional flexibility in terms of when they can, or have to, move in to their newly purchased property. In many cases sellers have contingencies written into the purchase contract of their new property that allows them to be released from the contract in the event they fail to sell their existing unit. From a seller's standpoint, this might eliminate the prospective buyer from the bidding process all together. This may mean that the person who is selling their unit to you might not get the unit they are trying to buy due to that contingency.

This will also allow them the flexibility to be able to close on their new unit while staying in the unit that they have lived in and are comfortable with, and provide additional time to prepare the new unit so that it is ready when they want to move in. This could include: painting, new carpeting, sanding the floors, drapes or even redoing kitchens. Many people simply close on one unit and move into the new unit in a matter of a couple of days. At that point, they try to do the necessary painting and repairs while all of their belongings surround them. In the case of sanding floors, this could mean they have to live with all of the dust, stain and topcoat smells for the first couple of weeks in their new unit. Even more traumatic is a family who is forced to move into a temporary location or with relatives while they wait until they can take possession of their new unit. In this case, they would end up moving twice, which is extremely stressful.

As an investor, instead of a homeowner needing a place to live, you have some unique negotiating leverage that can mean the difference between getting the unit or being outbid. This needs to be presented as a win-win for both the seller and you, the buyer.

Possession is another important aspect of negotiating the contract when you purchase the unit. It is best to try to time the date of possession around your "rental season" in order to reduce possible vacancies. As you may recall, many areas, such as colder climates, have periods when people tend to move more than other months. Summer months are big move months, due to the weather being more favorable and the kids being out of school. The term we use for the more active moving months is "rental season". For example, if you live in a colder climate and you purchase the unit in February, you might want to negotiate the possession date to be extended to the end of April or May. Many sellers will welcome the opportunity to stay in their existing home longer to prepare for the move to their home. You can use a combination of a rent back and simply extend the possession date to gain several months, if you are too far out of your "rental season."

Also, if possible, you want to take possession about one week before the end of the month so you can time your mortgage payments and lessen the amount of money you will need at closing.

Negotiable Items

The right to do a home inspection on the property will always be in the contract, unless you are buying a new unit. This is an item your attorney will take care of and insure is in the contract. A home inspection should be done by a qualified and licensed home inspector. That person will go through the house and provide a full report on any items that are broken, in need of repair, constructed improperly, or involves wiring issues. Items noted on the report can be used during the negotiation to either have them repaired, or reduce the purchase cost.

Window treatments, garbage disposals, air conditioning units, and things that are attached to the house itself will be included in the contract and usually stay with the unit. If the appliances aren't new, or are only a couple of years old, negotiate them out of the contract. This means you request that the sellers have them removed or take them. Most sellers don't want the old appliances and will be inclined to reduce the price so they can leave them with the unit. In many cases, the sellers will be buying a house that already has appliances that fit the new house or want all new appliances anyway. As stated earlier, you will replace all of the appliances just after you take possession, so you won't want to "pay twice" for the same appliances.

Ask About and Beware

Special assessments are something most buyers fail to ask about and isn't information that the seller will usually volunteer. Special assessments are payments, usually in lump sums, made by the members of the home owner association, that pay for larger items that weren't planned, or budgeted for, by the association. The normal association dues cover normal maintenance throughout the year, but when something large comes up, the expense will be covered with a special assessment. If a balcony project is being done, for example, it may be outside the scope of what the normal assessments would cover. These can be a small amount, such as a few hundred dollars, but can get up into the thousands with larger projects, such as roofs and porches. The association will solicit bids from outside firms and then award the contract for the work to one of those firms. They will then divide the cost of those special projects by the number of units participating in the work, and assess the proportioned amount to each unit.

As an example, a chimney project needs to be done due to the large number of chimneys that are beginning to show rot around the bases. The association will want all of these chimneys to be replaced so the work is uniform and surrounding common walls of the units aren't destroyed. If the work is left up to the individual unit owners, it may not be done by qualified tradesmen, done in a uniform fashion, or done at all due to the financial circumstances of the unit owner. If this work isn't performed, the association may end up replacing much of the adjoining wall due to the damage caused by the rotting chimney. This would end up being more costly than they anticipated. The result would be another special assessment, larger than the original chimney special assessment.

If there are twenty units in the association and the total expense of the chimney replacement is $100,000, then each unit would owe $5,000. If you didn't ask the question, and get it in writing, this would be a charge that you would not have planned for and would not have used it in the negotiation. You would end up writing this check shortly after you closed on your unit.

This same example could apply to a siding project, balcony project, driveways, windows, or roof projects. The main point is, ask about special assessments in any community that has an association in place where monthly dues are collected. Also, make sure their answer is in writing as part of your contract. You may also ask your attorney to write a letter to the association, asking if there are any special assessments planned for the near future.

Getting Financed and Credit

Getting financed, and the impact that your credit will have on getting financed, is extremely important. If using other people's money, and a lot of it, lenders want to make sure that you are credit worthy. Most people think they have good credit because they don't understand what bad credit is, or don't want to take the time to find out if it is bad. They think if they miss a bill every once in awhile, it won't have an impact to their overall credit score. They don't understand the actual impact on their credit and what that means in terms of borrowing power.

Good credit vs. Bad credit. Your credit score should be in the 650+ range to make borrowing to acquire properties easier. This means you will expand your borrowing power and ultimately be able to buy more properties based on your credit worthiness. Most realize there is a scoring system that means something. Usually a loan is needed when buying a car or a first house. A credit report is ran, and if the rating is good, buyers are approved for their purchase. But your credit score affects more than just loans. Did you know your car insurance and homeowners insurance are based on your credit score? Simply put, people with good credit are more responsible, pay their bills, and overall cost less to do business with. They get better rates and access to more credit. To a lending institution, a good credit score minimizes risk, exposure, and the likelihood of a defaulted loan.

If you don't know your credit score you will need to run a full report. When you go to the "free credit" reporting sites on the web, you will be given a score but not the details behind the score, unless you pay to get that detail. This is not an area that you want to save money on because you will need to know who is reporting your credit, what they are saying, and the information to clean it up if there are negative entries.

You can also ask your broker/banker to provide that information when you go for pre-approvals prior to your first investment purchase. If you have a current relationship with those folks, go back to them and ask them for a copy. If you've never seen a credit report before, it can be overwhelming and will need explanation. If you don't understand what it contains, ask for help in deciphering the "code". Since you will be doing business with this person in the future, it is okay for you to ask them to run this for you at no charge. If they won't do it for you, find another contact. You will be doing business with them in the future so you need someone who values the business relationship. Those who are good business contacts realize it is about the relationship, long term, and not just about the immediate transaction where they are making money now.

They are willing to do things for their clients, regardless of whether they are making money on every task or not.

Fraud protection insurance can also be taken out to limit your liability and provides you with legal support to reestablish your credit in the event of identity theft. Most major credit cards have offerings around fraud protection and services to identify charges that appear outside of your normal spending patterns, or purchases that suddenly take place that are unusual in locations that are far from where you reside. Identify theft is a very common problem and everyone will likely experience it. Protect yourself. Protect your credit rating. We can't emphasize this enough.

By putting down 20% or more on the unit, the requirements change in terms of your borrowing power because it limits the lender's exposure to the amount of the loan on the property vs. the actual value of the property. If you were to not pay your mortgage and the lender had to repossess it to sell that unit, then they would not be as concerned with a higher selling price of that unit. They could sell it quickly, get it off of their books, and get their money back out of the property. This would protect them from showing a loss on that property.

There is also a process referred to as a "no doc loan" that you can use if your down payment is 20% or more. This loan type can cost a bit more, but provides a way to obtain a mortgage if your credit is marginal, or sub par, without having to "fix" it first. That's why it is best if your score is 650 or better. In contrast, a credit score of 720 to 740, depending on the lender, is considered premium credit.

It also helps to do business with a mortgage broker who specializes in investment properties. They seem to be able to get the mortgage paperwork through the process while eliminating some of the additional paperwork that standard lenders require on investment properties.

There are three major credit bureaus in the United States that lenders draw from: Trans Union, Experian, and Equifax. They act as repositories where the creditors "deposit" your individual pay history every month or two.

What do you need to obtain a loan?

- ➤ Three months of bank statements
- ➤ One month of pay stubs
- ➤ Two years of W-2s
- ➤ Broker statements
- ➤ 401(k) statements
- ➤ Down payment money in an account

The lender will want to see the documentation listed above because they want to validate that you can pay for the mortgage. The bank statements will illustrate any money that you make on a monthly basis and validate your pay stubs. The lender will also want to validate where the down payment will be drawn from. They do this by looking at your bank statements, broker statements, or your 401(k) (if this is your first house and will be using that money).

If you are using your 401(k), then you can withdraw the money anytime, but will pay a capital gains penalty and have to pay the taxes on that money. As mentioned before, you can also use it to withdraw the money and only pay the taxes, not the penalty, if it is your first home. You can also borrow from your 401(k) but you will have to set up a payment schedule with your employer, which will be automatically deducted from your check on a monthly basis. The lender will need to know if this is the case, since it will reduce your available monthly income.

A lender wants to make sure that they are going through the loan approval process and that you will have the down payment money when you get to closing.

Owner Occupied vs. Rental

There is a difference in loans for an owner occupied (a place you live in), and non-owner occupied. In banking terms, there is more risk associated with a dwelling that is not occupied by the person whose name is on the mortgage. A unit that is being rented out carries more risk because the person who is paying for the mortgage sometimes can't make the payment if they aren't getting paid by the renter. If there is more risk to a loan, the bank wants to receive more money to assume that risk or exposure. In banking terms, this means that you will end up paying a higher interest rate. The bank wants to be paid for the additional risk of having to count on your ability to choose the right renter who will pay you on time and will not destroy the unit.

The typical rate difference between the owner occupied and non-owner occupied types of loans is between   and ½ of a point higher. If your rate on a thirty year is 6%, if could be as much as 6.5%. When you calculate your returns and costs at the front end, you will need to take this in to account. It will definitely change your monthly costs.

This is also a great time to mention another strategy that we have used. You might want to rent the place that you are living in currently. Most want to upgrade as part of their overall life plan and move to a larger house in a potentially better neighborhood. If you buy your first property and live in it for a few years and then rent it, you will be able to take your equity out of that unit and apply it to your next property, while still owning the unit you are moving out of.

The mechanics work like this:

Find another house, your "upgrade," and take the loan for it as an owner-occupied house. Close on the new mortgage for the unit that you will be moving out of, and then place the ad to rent that unit. This will save you, on a one-time basis, the additional one-half percent APR on a rental unit. There is not a requirement to go back to the bank and convert that loan to an investment note. This will save you a little money over the short term, and a lot of money over the long term.

The Closing

The number one rule of closing is to make sure you show up with the money. You also want to make sure to have a good attorney, be on time, and have your driver's license. There will be things that come up during closing that need to be discussed and agreed upon. People are more willing to compromise when they haven't been waiting for you to get there. Many forget their driver's license. If it is forgotten, you won't be able to close that day. It serves as proof of identity with a photo ID. The bank wants to make sure they are loaning money to the person whose name is on their documentation, and the name and face on the driver's license matches that name. These may seem like obvious points, but there are a lot of folks who don't do one or more of these things and end up not being able to close on the unit.

Chapter Ten

Prosper Through (The Rental) Process

There are five rules that we have found should be followed to help you succeed in the rental business. The following is a brief summary of these rules that you should be able to remember easily. We will go into more detail later in this chapter to provide more reasons as to why these are the most important, and why you should never break them.

1) **Credit is everything.** A person who pays everyone else will usually also pay you. The reverse is also true. If they don't pay anyone else, or tend to be late with others, the same pattern will eventually exist with you. A credit check is the best place to gain insight into their past payment history.

2) **Location, location, location.** Renters want to be in scenic locations and as well as those that meet their functional needs. Being close to goods and services they need on a weekly/bi-weekly basis, recreational opportunities, family, and friends are strong selling points when potential renters are assessing their next possible "home."

3) **Your costs have nothing to do with what you charge for monthly rents.** The rule in the free market is that the market sets the price, not the amount of money it costs to produce the product. This means you will need to set your price based on the asking price of other comparable units around the unit you will be renting. Your monthly costs should not be your primary guide for setting the monthly rent. Factors such as paying too much for the unit, not putting enough down, or structuring the loan incorrectly can have a negative impact on your overall monthly costs and need to be considered when buying your unit. Raising the rent to cover up mistakes made on the front end can lead to vacancies.

4) **Appearance can make the difference between renting and another showing.** Make the inside of the unit look better than the other avail-

able units. The first impression a potential renter has of your unit usually means the difference between signing a lease with them and showing it again. Appliances, blinds, carpet, and paint need to be kept up in order to provide the impression that your unit is better than the last unit they looked at.

5) **Fix it now.** Treat your renters like you would want to be treated. If something breaks, fix it now and fix it right. Delays in your response will not leave a good impression with your renter and might force them to move once the lease is up. You will also need their endorsement of their landlord when they are showing your unit the next time you need to rent it to someone else.

Preparing the Property

Think back to the first time you went looking for a place to live and went to several places until you found just the right place. Whether you were thinking about it or not, at least part of your decision was based on the overall appearance of the property, both inside and out. Hopefully, the owners of that property took some time before they started to show it to prepare the property for showing. If they didn't, your first impression was not likely a favorable one and you selected another unit. You have probably looked at some units that weren't cleaned from the last renter, or since the landlord purchased the unit, and you couldn't imagine yourself staying one night there. Saving a little time or money before you rent it will cost you a lot, if you have to show it multiple times or end up missing a month of rent.

There are a number of things you must do in order to give it that "curb" appeal, even if the "curb" is in view from standing in the kitchen. The attraction of any rental is seen from both the outside and the inside. What is viewed from the inside becomes very important.

What would you do to your own place? Paint? Carpet? Appliances? Fixtures? Lighting? Bathroom sinks? Toilets? Showers? Would you also take care of bad looking floors? Believe it or not, if any of these are not presentable, a potential renter may go elsewhere to do their renting. The last place they looked at may have had all of those things taken care of. The decision is more than just a potential renter wanting to move into a place that is clean and perceived to be maintenance free. The decision to rent is also based on a landlord who will be responsive when there is a problem. Someone who will be proactive in making repairs and improvements before a crisis occurs. Other than the price, one of the primary motivators for a renter is to not have to constantly deal with repairs and maintenance on a place they do not own. They are also looking for a place where they will be proud to bring their friends and family.

Don't be fooled into thinking that if it isn't done, you can just tell them it will be taken care of before they move in. Most renters will say okay, but it will become a concern, an inadequacy in the property, or a reflection on the type of landlord you are. We have all had an experience at one time or another where we were told, "Don't worry, I'll take care of that before….". Although most of the issues do eventually get taken care of, in many cases, it takes a huge effort to get that person to keep their promise. You don't want to be seen as that person before, or after, you actually rent the unit.

Here are a few items you will need to take care of before you start to show the property. These will need to be done in every situation, but the timing is different for a newly purchased property than a property that you are re-renting. We'll cover the newly purchased property first.

You have found your unit, negotiated it, closed on it, and now you have to prepare it so you can show the unit to prospective renters. The easiest way to remember the steps is to walk through the property as if you were looking at it for the first time.

When the door swings open, one of the first things you see is the carpet. If it is very old, has multiple wear patterns, or stains, you should replace it. This does cost money, but in both the long run as well as the short run, it is worth it. Consider the cost of the carpet vs. having the unit empty for two months because the potential renters could not get past the carpet in its present condition. If it is good condition, then it will need to be cleaned. Carpet cleaning is one area where people can make some mistakes pretty quickly. Most will either, go out and rent a portable rug cleaner and clean it themselves, or try to have carpet cleaned that should have been replaced ten years ago. So, what is wrong with renting a portable rug shampoo machine and doing it yourself? These machines are not powerful enough and most stains will not come out. If there are stains, and the carpet is in otherwise good condition, the best way to get them out is by a professional who uses special chemicals to clean specific stains.

Remember, lost rents come in many forms—not just a lack of interest. You can show a unit many times and you may be facing an issue as simple as a poor showing. Most people who rent don't want to be reminded of the fact that they are renting, as opposed to owning the unit, every time they walk through the door. Carpet that is worn and stained serves as a great reminder of a home that they do not own themselves.

As you continue to walk through the unit, the next thing you notice is usually the paint. Does the unit look like it has been recently painted? Are there holes in the walls from picture hanging nails that have been pulled out? When you walk across the room, does it look like the walls were painted only in "spots that needed it" instead of all of the walls looking the same? Does the base trim have marks on it, or is it all the same color? These are all things your renters will be looking at as they walk through your unit. It is important to pick one color, usually a color that is fairly neutral, such as off white, and paint the entire unit. This presents a uniform look that gives the appearance of newness. Usually the ceilings get painted only when you make a color change and are usually always white. White ceilings add the illusion of additional depth, making the rooms look bigger.

Many people have asked about painting the closets and laundry rooms. Usually, those don't need painting from renter to renter because they aren't seen. Most people who own their own home don't paint them either. Once clothes are hung in a closet, you can't see the walls. Doors to the closet are generally closed, if you aren't going in them. They are also usually dark places that don't show dings and scrapes, so you won't see the imperfections like you would in a hallway or living room. If there were holes in the closet wall, or a raw piece of drywall that had to be replaced, we would definitely paint. Take a look at these areas after each renter and make the decision. The good thing is they are small and don't take long to paint and because it is out of view, you don't have to be exact.

In all the time we have been renting, there has only been one renter that asked about painting the closets. We explained our philosophy about it and told them if they wanted to paint them we would pay for the paint. To date, they have not been painted.

This seems straight forward, but so many people want to save money by not painting at all. If you want to save money, do it yourself and don't hire someone to do it for you. Don't try to save money by not painting at all. This will cost you money in lost rents. Touch-ups completed by someone who doesn't know how to paint will be obvious and likely have to be redone. That is a waste of time and money.

The next areas of the unit you will need to look at are the kitchen, laundry area, and bathrooms. Kitchen or laundry rooms are places where you can easily make a good impression or a bad impression. Generally, these two areas heavily influence women, so pay special attention to them. Another point to consider is that most of the housing decisions are made by women. Items such as appliances, cabinets, and floors are likely to be put under more scrutiny than closets and garages, for example. Hopefully when you looked at the property before you bought it, you thought about these items. Cabinets would be a major expense if they need to be replaced and might be a point of negotiation before you buy the unit. You might want to negotiate to have some additional money to have them replaced.

Appliances are quick and easy to replace and the highly visible ones can have a dramatic effect on the overall appearance of the unit. Washers and driers do not cost much money and don't have to be the best shape, as long as they work. If they are older, you will have to think about the reliability of them. Older appliances are more likely to break down, which results in service bills and an inconvenience to your renters. Our rule of thumb is simple. If they are more than five to six years old, replace them. You can stretch that a year or so, but after that they will more than likely to break sooner than you are planning to replace them. When things break, they demand your immediate attention. That means you have to stop doing what you are doing, go shopping for a new one, spend money that you may not be planning on, and wait for them to be delivered. It also means your renters may be inconvenienced, which could be a larger problem than you see initially.

Dishwashers and refrigerators are items that are extremely visible during a walk through and need special consideration. Dishwashers are simple and last a long time. As long as they are not the wrong color, don't have visible scratches, and work, they can probably stay and won't need to be replaced. The following is a statement that you should consider when buying the replacement appliances—if the appliance looks like it belongs in a college dorm, has a door that is going to fall off, is nicked up, has paint peeling off, or has missing or broken shelves or drawers, then it should be replaced. There are a lot of rental units on the market that you will be competing against. Many landlords buy these units and don't put any money into them to replace the appliances; or they buy the least expensive appliances that they can find just to make sure they increase their cash flow. We have seen some nice units with fifteen cubic foot refrigerators. We also go by the age rule. If it is five to six years old, then it should be replaced. You can go a couple of years longer, as long as the appearance is still good. Refrigerators tend to last a while longer than washers do. Be careful on this point though. The first time a refrigerator breaks and all of your renter's food spoils, you will soon understand that the money you saved is not money that should have been saved.

Another point to consider is that a prospective renter will probably ask your current renter how they like it there and sometimes, more importantly, how they like you. You don't want them to tell about the time that all of their food spoiled because of the broken refrigerator. It will probably mean you will need to show the unit again.

If you are showing a vacant unit, make sure everything has been cleaned. Otherwise, it won't show as well. Everyone knows that the appliances will look better after they are cleaned. It will leave a negative impression if your prospective renter sees the last renter's dirt. There is nothing that will have a prospective renter shuffling for the door faster than the thought of putting their food and dishes into an appliance that is soiled, dirty and stained.

As long as we are on the subject of appliances, let's talk about extended warranties. In our experience, we have found that the money spent on those warranties is not worth it and only cuts into our overall profit. Most appliance and electronics manufactures show this as a large profit center. They usually do not have to perform much service against the money taken in for those warranties. Most individuals will lose their warranty information or forget that they purchased it or extended it by the time the appliance breaks. The rule that usually holds true is—if it doesn't break within the first thirty to sixty days, then it should last for a long time. That means you have essentially paid an insurance policy, in the hundreds of dollars, for a two to three year contact on an appliance that has a life expectancy of five to seven years before things start to break down. If you pay the service contracts for that period of time, it will come out to more than the cost of a new appliance. As mentioned earlier, we have found it best to get the five to seven years use out of them and then just replace them. Remember the benefits: 1) if it looks new, it will make a better impression on your perspective tenants, 2) if you don't get that impromptu call that brings your world to a halt, then this stays a part time business, 3) if you don't inconvenience your tenant it will sound better at lease renewal, or when you are renting to your next renter.

All of the locks will need to be changed out after each tenant moves out. We have found that if you have two sets for each unit then it will save money, protect your tenant from the previous tenant, and protect you from the liability of duplicate or unaccounted for keys. Also, the same key should open all of the locks. It is difficult to manage multiple keys for one unit and your tenant will thank you for it too. The problem is multiplied if you own more than one unit. The door knob lock should be a lock that has a flip type lock on the inside and a key on the outside. The dead bolt should be the type that requires a key to open it on both sides. This is done so that if someone breaks the window on the door, if there is one, they cannot simply reach in and open the deadbolt lock and gain entry into the unit. You will need to instruct your tenant to hang the key somewhere close to the door, a few feet away, so if someone does break the window, they still won't be able to get at the key to open the lock. It needs to be nearby, in the event there is a fire and they have to get out quickly. You don't want tenants searching for the key to get out. This should also limit your exposure for liability in the event that someone breaks in and robs your renters or worse yet, hurts the tenant. At least, you have attempted to protect your tenant.

Make sure either you or a professional clean the unit from top to bottom. We have covered the idea of showing a dirty unit and the impression it will have on a prospective renter. Always show only a unit you would be proud to rent yourself.

Replace any torn, cut, damaged or ripped linoleum in the kitchen, bathroom, or any other area. This is another important area that adds or detracts from the overall appearance. If all of the linoleum is the same pattern, or the pattern matches the room, make sure what you replace it with is consistent with that theme. One pattern of linoleum usually won't cost any more than another pattern, so use a pattern that enhances the appearance.

Have the furnace cleaned and checked before your first renter moves in, and then annually during the course of the lease. Ask the furnace technician, during the first cleaning, if it is in good shape. This service is usually performed by a person who is honest and doesn't have any incentive to sell you a new one. If it needs to be replaced due to age or condition, it is better to do it while the unit is empty, or before the first showing.

Some units that you buy may have a fireplace. Fireplaces should be cleaned and checked every year or two, depending on how often they are used throughout the winter season. Also, depending on the type of wood, they may have to be cleaned more often. From a liability standpoint, cleaning the fireplaces will help show that you did your best to protect your tenant from harm.

Fire, smoke, and carbon monoxide detectors are extremely important and should be put in each unit before your first tenant moves in. Carbon monoxide detectors became mandatory in Illinois at the time of this writing. Even if it is not a state law, we would highly recommend that you add one for every floor of the unit. They should be tested annually, and the batteries replaced every year. Fire extinguishers should also be placed in each unit. The tenant will acknowledge an extinguisher is in the unit by signing that line item on the lease. There are a number of items that you will give to your renter that will require an acknowledgement signature. We will cover the checklist later in this chapter.

Keep any receipts pertaining to cleaning, maintenance, or replacement of any items that are related to safety. It is impossible to insulate yourself from lawsuits, but the more you can illustrate that you have done your best to protect your tenant, the better chance you will have in winning, or lowering, the amount of payment made during the suit.

A moment on the "Make It Easy" philosophy

As you have noticed, or probably will throughout this book, the philosophy that we live by is—this can either be a part time or full time business. If this is a part time business, (meaning you have a full time job and this is a way to either reduce your overall work life, or produce a lot of equity on the side), then you want to make sure it doesn't require much work. That means you will spend a bit more money, in the right places to help rent it quicker, get paid on time, and not get those untimely calls that take you away from your full time position at a moments notice.

If you take our advice, you will take care of everything on your full time schedule and simply show up annually to sign a new lease. The rental units can almost run themselves, if you do it the right way. They can also be a full time job on a part time salary, if you do it the wrong way. There is nothing more satisfying than picking up a rental check every month from a smiling tenant, for a property that you have not had to worry about, or put effort into. To add to your satisfaction, periodically check the selling price of houses in the area to determine how much your unit has appreciated.

If you choose to do this process full time, meaning you have a number of units that produce enough money so that you don't have to have a regular full time job, then you can afford to "do more" and save money on some things. You will also have more time to devote to those on demand issues that come up as a result of saving a bit more on the front end.

To make this point very clear, determine what your time is worth and keep in mind:

You can make a little more money by going cheaper *but* you will have to work a lot harder.
        Vs.
You can make a bit less money and hardly work at this process at all

This is a quick list of items for your reference:

Everything in the unit gets replaced or repaired that isn't new, doesn't look new, or the first time an issue requires a service call.
Washer
Dryer
Dishwasher

Refrigerator
Carpet
Change the locks
Install dead bolts
Paint everything
Replace any linoleum that is damaged
Clean everything
Furnace—checked and cleaned
Fireplace—checked and cleaned
Fire/Smoke Detectors—tested and batteries replaced
Fire Extinguisher

It is also important to have receipts for everything. In the unlikely event that one of your tenants does have an issue, or wants to create one, they may decide to take you to court. All you can do is protect yourself by illustrating that you have taken every possible action to assure that the unit is safe and in working condition. We will get more into this later in the legal chapter. There are also tax benefits that you can claim from these repairs.

Take a look at the blinds, light fixtures, fans, and any remote controls. All of these items can look bad and detract from the overall appearance of the unit. Most are not that expensive and can be easily replaced. If you can't afford to do these up front, then prioritize them and replace them when you can.

Renting the Property

After you have prepared the unit to rent, the next step is the process of renting it out and getting the lease signed. There are a few easy steps to this and, once taken, you will be well on your way to officially being in business. The good news is you have completed the hard part and the rest is easy and mostly fun. It can be tricky but, done properly, hardly any work.

Probably the biggest deterrent for most people to get started in acquiring and renting properties are the tenant nightmares that have been direct experiences, or rumors and stories that others tell. These nightmares include problem tenants, evictions, court costs, unpaid rents, damage, and midnight move outs.

The next decision to be made is where a lot of people in this business make the biggest mistake. It revolves around the age-old question of how much to charge for a product. In this case, the difference between charging the correct monthly rental rate and being a few dollars off can mean the difference between occupancy and vacancy. Remember, an occupied unit that rents for a few dollars less will provide a much higher return than a unit that is vacant. Keeping that unit full, and getting paid for it, is the key to making a lot of money.

How much should it rent for?

In traditional businesses of goods and services, you need to charge more than your costs to make a profit. You start by adding up all of your expenses and then take a look at similar products in the marketplace where you plan to sell. At that point, you set your price; project profits, and start advertising. Renting housing units is slightly different from the traditional product sales in that the money is made in several areas—not just on a monthly, straight line calculation of expense vs. income.

Much of your profit in rentals comes from keeping the units full as much as possible, buydown of the loan, and appreciation. If you base your monthly rental solely on your costs, you may find yourself with units that are not being rented. That sounds simplistic but, as stated earlier, a lot of people we know have vacancy rates that are in the 25%–30% range. There are some folks who write books and hold seminars on renting that tell you to plan for that type of vacancy rate. That isn't a way to make money, or reduce your involvement. If you were going to open a business and were told you wouldn't have clients on Tuesdays and Thursdays, your natural assumption would be that you would have to raise your prices to make up the loss of revenue during those times. Since you would have already done your homework and priced your product correctly in line with your competition, raising your rates would compromise your ability to sell your product.

In the rental business, your product is time. By setting your rates to align with your competition and minimizing your vacancy rate, you will be able to keep your rates in line, which will minimize your vacancy rate. Rates and vacancy rates are tightly integrated and go up and down proportionately with each other.

This is an example of why monthly rental rates should not be based on your costs:

If you put down 3% on a unit, and you pay 10% more than you should have, your costs could be hundreds more than the going rates of what similar units are renting for in the same neighborhood. If you add up your costs and they come out hundreds higher, will you be able to rent it for that amount? You can try, but you probably won't get any calls or a signed lease. That leads to high vacancy rates and/or lost rents and you probably won't be in this business for long.

The question of monthly rate will dictate either your success or failure in this business. To look at it another way, it will determine whether this is a business where you will make money, or one that you end up writing off on your taxes as a loss. As stated above, if the monthly rate is too high, it will not rent.

If it is too low, you will feel like you are giving it away. Neither is a position that you want to be in after you have put all that money down and taken the time to prepare the unit for renting. This will be a learning point based on the area you are in and what housing prices are doing from year to year. Things like interest rates, employment, type of area, and other factors play a part in this learning curve. Don't worry, you will learn this quickly and there are some ways to help you while you are figuring it out. Everyone will make a mistake the first couple of years, but it is better to make the mistake of being too low on your monthly rate than too high. At least the unit will be occupied and you will be receiving a check. If the monthly rental charge is too high it will mean you have an empty unit without any incoming money.

The rule: The market sets the price, not your costs (mortgage, assessments, taxes, etc.).

"Your costs have nothing to do with what you charge for monthly rents"

If there is a rule that we have seen ignored more than not, it is this one. This is not your traditional cost of production price vs. selling price business that most of us understand. As stated earlier, your skill, or lack of skill, your extra money, or lack of money, does not have much to do with the monthly rate you charge. That is just an implication as to the amount of money you may make in simplified terms, or a reflection of your monthly cash flows.

The following represent some easy rules that should serve as basic guidelines while you are figuring out the area where your properties are located:

Price it 10%–20% above apartments
  Price it on the low end of the average of other, similar, townhouses in the area
  5%–10% above the low end
  10%–20% below the high end

Here is an example of why it is important to price it right, fill it, and avoid owning an empty unit.

Rent = $1,300/month
Lose one month = $1,300

Rent = $1200/month
Rent it for twelve months

If you get eleven months rent for $1300 it is like getting twelve months for $1200.

11 x $1,300 = $14,300

12 x $1,200 = $14,400

If you could not get $1,300 one month, you might have to reduce the price to rent it, which would put you even more behind.

This would also mean that you are showing the unit multiple times until someone looks at it who is willing to pay a higher price. This leads to more financial exposure, more wasted time, and no guarantee that you will rent it. That isn't a very good trade off. Remember that potential renters are comparing your property and monthly price to several more in the neighborhood or area that may be exactly like your unit. In some cases, price may be the only determining factor.

There is a saying that we like to think of when we are setting our price that best describes our feelings toward not being greedy.

"Pigs get fat.... Hogs get slaughtered"

If you sell a top of the line product for a middle of the road price, it will be easier to sell and the competition won't stand a chance. That doesn't mean you give away your product (low rents), and not make money. It means you will make more with just a little less monthly rent than you would make if you try to get top rate and it sits vacant.

We mentioned earlier that looking in the local newspapers to determine what the range of your monthly rental rate should be, as compared to other rentals around your unit, is an ideal method of determining your price point. There are some tips to understand and use in order to avoid mistakes. Some of these will be more important the first couple of years of renting and will not be necessary once a much better understanding of your local market is gained. Others should be done every time you have a unit that comes up for lease.

> ➢ Do your homework on similar units in the area where your unit is. Since the market sets the price, you will need to be in line with the market. This is another way to say that supply and demand will always determine the price. Look in the newspaper to see what your competition is renting and what they are providing for that price: square footage, appliances, location, number of bedrooms and bathrooms, garage, and basement details.

➢ Call some rental services, look in apartment finding brochures, check several local papers, and call some listings yourself to ask some questions on the units available that you are competing against. Do your research.

➢ Call some apartment buildings to find out what they are renting. You may even want to set appointments up so you can look at other rentals in the area and compare what your prospective tenants are looking at prior to coming to check out your unit. This will enable you to hit the right price point and provide you with the comfort that you are not significantly over or under priced. Some renters know they want a townhouse, while others will compare apartments to a standalone townhouse. Some of the upscale apartments offer garages, which is usually the primary difference between an apartment and a townhouse. If you do encounter someone who is comparing your unit to an apartment, find out if it has a garage and talk to them about the close proximity of their neighbors.

➢ Once you have done your research and are comfortable you have reached a monthly rental price that is competitive with the market, ensure that the following activities are complete before placing an ad for your place:

➢ Buy top of the line appliances. They are more appealing to prospective tenants, require less repair and maintenance, and have a longer period of time before they need to be replaced.

➢ Buy top of the line carpet and padding. Saving money by buying cheap carpet is short sighted when it comes to repair and replacement.

➢ Clean everything. There is nothing that either appeals to a prospective tenant, or is an immediate deal breaker, than the cleanliness of a unit. Do it yourself or bring in a cleaning service, but make sure that the unit is spotless before showing it to your first prospective tenant. Have a friend or family member walk through the unit with you and ask them to be ultra observant to general condition and cleanliness. It is always better to have a new set of eyes look at a unit that you are so familiar with. You may be missing the obvious. (This is the same principal as driving through the streets of your neighborhood everyday but not knowing the street names when you are giving someone directions.)

➢ Paint everything. Repair dings and gouges and paint the unit. This will make the unit appear clean and fresh and is immediately noticeable by the prospective renter.

➢ Air conditioner checked and recharged

➢ Furnace checked and cleaned

➢ Fireplace cleaned. Use a qualified chimney sweep and have them check for any cracks or broken parts.

➢ Fire, Smoke Detector, Carbon Monoxide Detector, and other security systems. Test and replace all batteries and make sure you point this out to those you are showing the unit. This will indicate that you pay attention to the smaller details and provide them with a sense of comfort that you are concerned about your property and about them. If you have had fire extinguishers in the unit for over three years, replace them.

➢ Have receipts for everything. We discussed this earlier, but it is key to protecting your business and personal assets. You will want to have as much legal protection possible, in the event of a lawsuit. This will be covered more in the legal section. Please remember to always check with your lawyer prior to getting into this business. They should help guide you along the way, so that you protect yourself as much as you can in our litigious society.

Once you complete the final walk through, and before showing the unit, ask yourself the question—Is this a property that I would live in myself, or with my family? During the final walk through, if there are areas that make you pause, it is likely another individual will notice the same concern. Take care of it without hesitation, before it costs you a prospective tenant, lost money, lost rent, and frustration.

Properties are similar to meeting people for the first time. The first impression occurs immediately. The potential renter's decision to rent your property will either start off on a positive note and be validated as the walk through continues, or your place will be mentally checked off the list, just as quickly. If there are major areas for the prospective tenant to focus on like wall marks, stains on the carpet, and general disrepair and neglect, you are accelerating your prospective tenants' decision to look elsewhere. They may choose to rent the place they were in forty-five minutes earlier, where the landlord may have paid more attention to the smallest details. A small repair, or cleaning a spot on the carpet, will cost you less than $50.00 and one hour of your time to remedy. An empty unit can cost you more than $1000 a month in rent.

Looking for Renters

Looking for renters can be an easy process, or a tricky process. Some people put signs up, run newspaper ads, post ads in grocery stores, talk to friends and family or, as we have suggested earlier, run newspaper ads. Ads generally reach the largest pool of prospective renters.

A quick reference guide that we use, every time we rent a house, is the local paper. By local, we mean the *really* local paper. If you live in, or near, a major city—you have a lot of papers. There is usually a local paper that focuses on segments of the larger areas. In Chicago, the Tribune and the Sun Times are papers that focus on Chicago and the surrounding suburbs at a macro level. But the Daily Herald breaks the areas down, and actually publishes different papers for each region around Chicago. When looking for rentals, people want a more localized paper. You don't want to waste your time answering calls from people who are fifty miles away and will never rent in your area. This will also serve as a filter. People from your area are more likely to have some understanding of the price of rent, and what you get for that money, than someone in a totally different part of your state.

Never underestimate the network of friends that you have established in a particular area, to help you rent your property. (Greg)—Prior to moving into my primary residence and vacating the townhouse that I was planning to convert into a rental, I made sure my neighbors were well aware of my intentions. I received no less than three leads through this network. People who enjoy an area, and plan to stay, want to be surrounded by family and friends, and will do your selling for you. You can motivate them even more, by providing an incentive such as dinner, or a gift basket. This represents a small percentage of the rental price. I have also maintained my friendships in the old neighborhood, to provide the occasional status on my new tenants. I feel an extra sense of security, based on the periodic information, and can be proactive in dealing with any issues, before they possibly become a large problem that will involve time, effort, and money to eliminate.

We have also used "for rent" signs outside of properties that we intend to rent, for the same reasons. Some people like certain areas and will spend time driving though them to find a place that might be available for rent. This is another great way to increase your pool of prospects, and will probably generate calls you might not have otherwise received. Make sure you are in compliance with any association by-laws on posting signs, or notifying them in writing, before you decide to post signs. Neighbors within the area also notice the sign, and will pass that information on to someone they know, who might be looking for a unit. They will also hype up the community and benefits of living near each other. Phone calls from interested parties will happen soon afterwards.

We have also used rental sites on the Internet and the MLS (multiple listing services), for Realtors. Any Realtor has access to this network and can help you post your ad. The advantage of using MLS is—your property is being exposed to a larger pool of potential renters. The significant disadvantage is—you can expect to pay a significant premium, which could include up to a month's rent, to the realtor, for a placement. In addition, you will be required to enter into an agreement with the Realtor formalizing the agreement. This is not a recommended approach, but an option, especially if the unit has been vacant for a number of months.

Another option is placing the ad on an Internet site catering to Renters with Properties. There are many good sites out there, and you can easily find them through a search engine (like Google or Yahoo), by typing in a phrase like Rental townhouses—(your city name here). The advantage is you are opening up your ad to another group of renters who may be more comfortable conducting commerce on the Internet. We also get calls from professionals who are being relocated by their companies and are doing searches based on proximity to employment.

Keep in mind, your goal is to keep the vacancy rate down to zero, if possible. When qualified people have an understanding of the local rentals call, your work will be kept to a minimum. Rent it quickly and keep it full, and your profits go up.

After you have attracted a pool of renters, finding the right renter becomes your next goal. We have found that the main criteria are based solely on the credit rating of that potential renter. Simply put, if they pay their credit cards, their utilities, and their car payments, then they will probably pay you. If they don't pay those, they won't pay you either. Their credit says a lot about their character, and their general sense of accountability and responsibility. You are not special to them just because you are providing the roof over their head. You are just another bill that needs to be paid every month. We will cover this topic in greater detail later, but for now, let's break it down into the who, how, and the timing of the process.

There are certain profiles of what we call the "typical renter." They range from singles, married and unmarried couples, mothers and fathers with kids, roommates, temporary folks due to job transfers, to retired folks. In other words, your possible client is just about anyone. Any of these people might respond to your ad.

This is a high level overview of the groups and points about them:

Profile of candidates for ideal renters

Divorced mothers/fathers

We have rented to men and women who have recently divorced. In many cases, they cannot afford to buy a house immediately, due to having recently gone through a divorce, so they rent a house for awhile.

Some have children who live with them, and some do not. Both groups have their own reasons to rent. Parents with children don't want their kids feeling different by living in an apartment. There is enough pressure from other kids, because they come from a divorced family, so the person who has primary care wants them to feel as much like they did in "their old house" as they can in "their new house."

Parents also want their kids to have a yard, so they can play in an outside area that is close to the house. Most townhouses have common grassy areas right around the house, so the kids can play and still be around their own house. They won't have to go down the street to a park, or in the center of the apartment complex, to find grass on which to play.

In many cases, parents will rent a house close to their old house, so they can keep the kids in the same school district with their old friends. It could also be that it is a great school district, and the parents do not want to leave it.

Another reason might be that their friends, family or work might be in that area. It is tough to raise children as a single parent, and by moving to a house that is close to places that you frequent, such as employment, recreation, education, necessities (groceries, cleaning, gas, and banking), it will dramatically reduce the amount of travel time required to do the same activities. This is amplified if the kids have a lot of after school functions. People also want to be near their support structure, to provide some relief from the pressure of being a single parent.

Older People/Seniors

We have found that many people, in this group, are looking for a quiet place to live, in a neighborhood setting. Seniors do not want to be in an area where there are a lot of teenagers, singles, or a place that seems to have a party every night. Run down areas, or areas with a high crime rate, are also places from which they steer away. Most just want to feel safe, in a quiet area, so they can relax and not worry about noise, or be disturbed when they are sitting on their balcony, patio or watching TV in their living room.

Seniors are also looking for a home that is well maintained, inside and out. Yard work, painting, outdoor lights, and snow shoveling are chores that they would like to think they gave up years ago. They do not want to do them in their retirement years. Most associations collect monthly association dues from the owner. These dues pay service groups to take care of these chores. In some cases, they also pay for garbage collection and driveway repairs, and will cover anything on the outside of the unit.

Unlike younger people, seniors usually do not put a lot of wear and tear on your unit, as they are more sedentary and don't entertain much. Parties, dinners, and having company over, generally tend to put more wear and tear on your unit, which can lead to pattern wear, carpet stains and premature broken appliances. Because they do not usually have as much traffic through the unit, they are less likely to leave signs of increased hardship in your unit. Seniors tend to make ideal renters.

Seniors will usually stay multiple years in a location. Their lives tend to change less than those of younger people; therefore, they are less likely to move often. We usually keep the monthly rent rate the same, or increase it slightly, to provide incentive for them to stay longer. Turnover causes additional wear and tear on your units, and leaves you exposed, when it comes to keeping the unit full, and getting paid for every day that you own the unit. If not timed correctly, you may miss a day, or more, during the transition period from one tenant to another. The more years you can keep a tenant in your unit, the more money you will make.

Job Transfers

Companies continue to move their people from one location to another, to keep the right people in their jobs. This used to happen a lot more than it does these days, but still happens quite a bit. Most of the time, people will rent for a year or so, until they figure out where they really want to live, and determine if they are comfortable in the new position and location. Initially, they will want to be as close to work as possible so they can get there easily. Also, when they are new to the area, even though they have been with the company for a while, most of their new friends will come from their office.

As mentioned, they will generally only rent for a year or two, until they get to know most of the areas around and can decide where they want to live. In some cases, they might build a new home, and will need to wait until that is finished to move in.

"Yuppies" (Young Urban Professionals)

This is an interesting group of renters because generally, they see themselves differently than any other group. They tend to see themselves as a step above their peers and, as a result, have special requirements that are contradictions to the reasons they rent.

Usually, Yuppies drive nicer cars, own higher quality "things," and expect to live a bit better than the common person. They also tend to be more devoted to paying their bills, and usually have higher levels of education than the average renter. They usually earn slightly more than those around them, but also spend more than most. They don't want to live in an apartment, where they might have to listen to the neighbors next door, or park their car in a public lot every night, where it might get damaged or nicked from the old, run down car in the space beside them.

The contradiction is—they are still renting. One may wonder why these folks rent, since it appears they have enough money to own the unit they are renting. The answer is simple. Due to the amount of money they spend on a day to day basis, in order to support their more expensive lifestyle (luxury cars, etc.), they don't have enough money saved for the required down payment and closing costs to buy a unit. Most of them will also not compromise on their lifestyle, such as living in an apartment for a couple of years while they save, because that isn't part of their thought process. They just don't view themselves as people who might be forced to ever "rough it."

Don't waste time

There is an old saying—Time is Money. We have provided the typical renter profiles, so that you will know what each group is looking for, and what motivates them to rent, as opposed to buying, a unit of their own. We don't want to give you the impression that these are the only groups you should rent to, but rather, these are the prime targets that will make this easier and more profitable. Show it, and rent it, to those who will more than likely rent from you. On that note, we can go to the next step in renting, which is how you handle phone calls that result in advertising your unit.

Pre-qualifying potential renters over the phone

Showing the property to someone who you wouldn't want living in your property, or someone who doesn't want to rent from you, is a waste of valuable time and energy for both you, and the person on the other end of the phone. If the phone call is done correctly, it's like the real estate equivalent of Match. com™. After speaking to them, you will either feel more inclined to show your property, or eliminate them from further consideration. Either way, you have done both parties a favor, by not embarking on a relationship that has no potential.

Develop a questionnaire that encompasses the factors important to you in renting to an individual, and a series of questions that will determine what they are looking for in a home. Your questionnaire could look something like this:

> ➤ Their Current Situation–Why are they renting?
>   When we get calls asking about our units, we always ask why they are renting or looking to rent. People will tell you a lot about their situation and their lifestyle, when they tell you why they are looking to rent your unit. The key to this is to make sure you listen closely for any clues that

may tell you to either rent to them, or not. For example, if they tell you they need to find a place soon, they might be saying they need to get out of their current situation soon. Is that because they haven't been paying the rent on time? Is it because they are breaking up with their partner, or getting a divorce? Or is it as simple an upcoming job transfer and they need to start at the new location in a couple of weeks? Some reasons will tell you that this is someone you shouldn't rent to, and some are just circumstance and have no negative implications. Again, the key is to read between the lines of what they are saying, and ask additional questions when they say anything that might be a warning signal.

➤ What is important to them in a prospective home?
The size of the unit, number of rooms, basement, garage, yard or no yard—these are some things that are usually mentioned as being impor-tant. If they seem to be looking for what you have to offer, talk a little about some of the features of your property. We saved ourselves the time and energy of a "no match" showing, by explaining that the townhouse we were advertising did not have a fenced backyard. This was the main requirement for the gentleman on the other end of the phone, who was looking for a run for his large dog. Our conversation ended quickly with a polite, "That is not what I'm looking for because I do not allow large dogs, and don't have a large run for the dog anyway." We thanked him for his time and wished him good luck in his search. We have also eliminated showings based on: the unit being on the second floor vs. the first floor, fireplace or not, price, and single car garage vs. two car garage. Every fea-ture of your unit may be liked, or disliked, by your prospective renter.

Please remember to be kind to everyone. Basic human relations and respect may lead that individual to recommend your property to someone else, even if they are not interested.

"The bridge you burn today is one you have to cross tomorrow."

➤ Why are they moving?
People move for a variety of reasons, and this information could become important when discussing your unit with prospective renters. Reasons such as: better school district, better view, nicer living space, yard, or close to work location are some of the reasons we have heard. Any of those could be a strong point you could make when trying to

attract renters. Any one of them could also be the difference between signing a lease, or another showing. We mentioned earlier that we have rented to divorced parents, with children, who wanted to stay in the same school district. If those folks didn't know, or you didn't tell them what school district the unit was in, they might have gone somewhere else to rent.

➢ When is their moving date?

When we first started renting, we made this mistake several times, before we learned to ask early in the phone call. Some renters are extremely cautious about making sure they have a place to live. Others wait until the last minute to make the first phone call on available units. They sound the same on the phone, but the move in dates can vary dramatically. If you don't ask this question on the phone, then you might find out the person doesn't want to move in, due to their current lease end date, until three or so months from when your unit is vacant. They won't be able to move in early, and you can't allow your unit to sit vacant without receiving any rent. We have also found that the answer to this question will tell you a lot about what kind of renter they are. The folks, who seem to only give themselves a week to find a new place and move, are usually the ones who have lower credit scores. The opposite is also true. Those who allow themselves more time to move usually have higher credit scores, and seem to prepare more and do their research.

➢ How long do they intend to stay?

Tell callers about the length of the lease you are proposing, and see if that is in line with their objectives. If you're looking for a year and a half commitment, at a minimum, and your prospect plans on moving within the next six months, that doesn't work. Determine this early in the cycle, to avoid an awkward situation where you are sliding the lease agreement over to the prospective renter, after you have run their credit, and they pause after seeing the commitment you are expecting.

➢ Do they have any pets?

Pets are an important part of many people's lives and will be a defining question when it comes to prospective renters. Some landlords allow pets, such as cats or small dogs, while others won't allow pets of any kind. Whether you will allow pets, or not, is a decision you will need to make, when you are deciding how you will run your business. Once you allow a pet in your unit, you are dictating one key difference in renters from that point forward. There are many renters who will not rent a unit that has ever housed a pet, due to allergies and other issues they may have with pet dander. Some landlords think they can simply have the carpet cleaned and it will take care of any residual pet remains—only to get notified from a renter that they have to move out, due to allergies. If you tell them the unit has never contained a pet, when it has, you may end up in a court battle, if you fight the early lease termination. The only way to actually rid the unit of all pet residue is to replace all carpet and carpet padding, clean everything, and paint the entire unit, from floor to ceiling. You may decide to change your policy back to one of "no pets" when it is time to replace the carpet, after you have rented that unit for a while. If allowing pets has not been an inhibitor to renting your unit, then you may want to continue with this policy. If you are pet friendly, you can expect to be able to choose your prospective renter from a larger renter population, since that population includes renters with and without pets. Also, depending on the pet, expect more wear and tear on the unit that will eventually cost you money.

➤ Smokers

It is said that due to the number of smokers, when you light up a cigarette, you offend 50% of the people around you. If that is true, then you will eliminate 50% of your potential renters by allowing someone to smoke in your unit. Once a smoker has lived in your unit, the smell of smoke will be there for a long time, and will be detected the minute you walk in to the unit. As mentioned in the pets section, this is something that is not easy to get rid of, once it is in the carpet and walls. One primary difference between smoke and pet residue is that, unlike pet residue, smoke is something you will smell within seconds of entering the unit. It can stop someone from renting, seconds into the showing. Smoke is harder to get rid of than pet residue because it permeates every porous surface, several layers deep. You can't simply paint over it and make it go away. You will need to use a cleaner on the walls, apply primer, and then paint at least two coats of good paint. Most smokers are used to stepping outside to smoke, and won't have an issue with that in your unit. Additional deposits must be taken on any lease that is written, where smoke remediation may be involved, due to the cost of cleaning up after they move out.

➤ Their credit—good or bad score?

We elaborate extensively on this issue through this book, since it is one of the most important criteria in making you very successful, or a disgruntled statistic, who rents and then dumps the property based on a bad renter experience. Most people think they have a great credit score, or at least will tell you they do, when you ask this question. Let them know that part of your process is to run a credit check, so you have more information about their credit. Ask them what their score is, and if they know of anything that might be considered negative within the credit report. We have found that those who know what their score is, and respond with a credit score number, probably have pretty good credit. Those who respond with an answer such as, "It's pretty good," probably have some issues with their credit. Remind them that issues will show up in the report, and you do not want them to waste their time or yours, or their money, by running the credit check only to find that it contains too many bad marks to rent to them.

If they do have bad credit, they will usually tell you at this point, and the process is effectively over and you continue your search. If you have a score in mind as a minimum, let them know what it is. If they know they don't exceed that score, you may want to discontinue the process at that point, and save everyone from wasting time.

The only people we have ever talked to who are honest about bad credit, is Section 8s.

Section 8 people will usually tell you they have bad credit because they don't make any money, and realize they can't lie about it. Section 8 is a piece of legislation that allows people, who don't make any money, to receive on average $450 a bedroom, from the government, that acts as a subsidy toward housing.

➤ What do they do for employment?

You can tell a lot about a person from what they do for a living. The most important piece of information you may get from this question is an indication of the amount of money they are making. Keep in mind though, annual income is *not* a determining factor in selecting a renter because, they can make a lot of money, but still not pay their bills. It will usually only be an indicator of ballpark earnings and the ability to pay you, on a monthly basis.

➤ Why are they interested in the community your property is located in?

The person who tells you their sister lives down the street is someone you want to have as a tenant, if all of your other criteria are satisfied, and they have good credit. By asking this person a simple question, you have uncovered a compelling factor in an individual being highly motivated to rent your property, and subsequently, be happy to stay in it for a longer period of time. If they tell you that your unit is twenty minutes from their office, then you have yet another reason to elevate your level of interest and due diligence in researching them. There are several reasons, some you may not see yourself, that a renter may be looking at that location over others. Mentally catalog these reasons and mention them, in the future, to prospective renters. When discussing your unit with them, these reasons may differentiate your unit from others. If you have a written checklist completed, use it. This will allow you to keep the information straight on the different, prospective renters, and will keep you consistent in asking all of the questions to satisfy all of your criteria, in every interview.

➢ Ask them why they choose to rent vs. purchase.

One of our tenants indicated that she had purchased a property, along with a family member, who deserted her and left her with payments she could not make. This put her in a foreclosure position. She has been a model tenant who has had some tough breaks in life. As a result of asking a simple question, we found out about something, within her life, that left some bad marks on her credit, that really wasn't her fault. Since then, she rebuilt her credit, is going to school at night, and has stable employment. She has been in one of our units for over two years, without incident or complaint, and we just extended her for another two-year term.

➢ How many kids do they have, ages, and how many bedrooms will then need in a unit?

Most cities have limitations regarding the number of people per bedroom that can occupy a dwelling. Check with your local municipality to obtain this information. We have seen people attempt to rent a two-bedroom unit when there are three boys, one girl, husband and wife. On the lease, make it a point to specify how many people can live in the unit. You want to avoid a situation where multiple families, or people you were not originally aware of, are suddenly calling your place home.

Some of these questions may seem intrusive and difficult to ask. If asked properly, most renters will perceive them as someone taking an interest in their life, instead of someone prying into their personal situation.

If a prospective tenant seems to be meeting your list of rental criteria, before renting to them, you might want to meet with them a few times, in person. This is to validate your first impressions you received, over the phone. Things you might look for when meeting them:

➢ Are they on time?

Again, this can be a reflection of character, accountability and responsibility. This will be the first time you meet the person with whom you are entrusting a large investment. They should understand that and make every effort to be on time.

➢ Watch their body language when showing the property.

You can generally determine, by comments and facial expressions, if your relationship will be very short, or extended. Pay attention to the questions they ask. Some people have a great deal of difficulty asking direct questions. With a little probing, you can generally determine what is truly important.

Questions that are a waste of time to ask

➢ Asking to speak to their current landlord.

You may be violating the fact that your tenant has not given notice, or expressed their interest in leaving. This puts everyone in a very awkward position. The other side of this is, if their current landlord wants them out, and you are that ticket out, then they will say anything to accomplish that goal. This gets them out of their house and off of their problem list, and into your unit and onto your problem list.

➢ Asking for references.

Most people will not provide you with the names of individuals who are going to discredit them, by providing a bad reference. Your prospective tenants will only provide you with references who will speak kindly about them.

➢ Asking them their current income.

We have talked to people who make a lot of money, but spend more. They may have nice cars that are financed, but their credit is terrible. With these people, creditors are calling every month, trying to get paid. Some of the richest people you may know have filed for bankruptcy, due to their spending habits. How they manage their money is important, not how much they make. This can only be seen in a credit report.

➢ Asking them where they work.

Some seek this information for the purpose of using it to apply leverage later; in the event they don't pay. You can't do anything with this information that will get you money, unless you allow missed rents to build up into the several thousands. In most cases, the amount you are trying to collect falls under the jurisdiction of the small claims court.

Showing the property

Encourage the potential renter to drive by the property, to verify they like the house and location. This will save you some time prior to showing the house. If the "curb appeal" and general area don't thrill them, it's unlikely they will be able to overcome any initial exterior disappointment with an interior inspection. Ask them to contact you, after the initial drive by, with their opinion, to let you know if they would like to look inside. If it wasn't a positive experience for them, you won't hear from them again, and you will have saved yourself a showing. If they like it, they will call you after they drive by and want to set up an appointment with you. This will indicate a serious interest.

At times, the potential renter won't like the location (such as a second floor unit), or the door being on the side of the unit instead of the front, or one of many other potential issues. Everyone has needs and wants that are unique to them. People try to find their ideal house as if they were buying it, and not just renting that unit. Most people are more likely to "settle" with less than ideal when they are buying a house, and look for perfection when they are renting a unit.

The next step is to actually show the unit. The prospective tenants have become a bit more "qualified" as future renters, by driving past the unit, and still being interested. The questions you have asked them, based on your criteria, have also indicated a possible, ideal renter. There are different approaches to accomplishing the task of showing the unit. Most landlords approach this step by driving to the unit for each individual showing. As you can imagine, this process is not very efficient, since all but one of the showings will be a wasted trip. You will not show it only to the person who will eventually become your renter.

We have found a middle ground that allows you to show the unit more than once, but not be a burden on you. What we propose, and have found to be highly successful, is to ask your existing tenant to show it for you. This is ultimately a judgment call, based on the type of relationship you have with your tenant, and the reason they are leaving. If you have treated them correctly, then they will happily show and "sell" it for you. We know that the following statement isn't true—but there is a perception that most renters have regarding their deposit. When asked to perform a simple task (such as showing the unit to prospective renters), and they agree to do that task; renters think their landlord might be a bit more generous when it comes to refunding their security deposit. This proves to be a compelling motivation to provide a positive tour and landlord experience stories. This technique will save you a lot of time and expense. We have also used cash/gifts as an incentive, if one of their showings results in a lease signing.

Someone wants to move forward—What to do?

At this point, you can take a deep breath because most of the work has been done. You are much closer to renting your first unit. There are a couple of items that are left on the checklist, but there is very little effort involved and most of it happens within a couple of days. Those days, by the way, are markers of time, and not the amount of time you will need to invest. From this point, your actual time investment should be measured in hours. Much of that will be drive time, to meet them at the unit when you finalize the paperwork and collect your checks.

There is a systematic approach to moving from this point to your next lease signing, a year from now. We have broken each step down and provided an explanation for each. These steps are designed to help you cut down on the time spent, protect yourself from exposure, and provide tracking that you will refer to at later points in the lease process. Each step has also been developed through years of experience, with some mistakes being made along the way. We hope you won't make any of the mistakes (or what we refer to as learning lessons), that we made during our early years in the rental business. The whole point of this book is to condense our experiences into an easy to use methodology, or checklist approach, so that you can realize the same success we have enjoyed over the years—without the trial and error.

You will receive a few checks from the prospective tenant throughout this process. These will be recorded individually, and used as a matter of record keeping and for your protection. This will insure that the person giving you the money knows what is, and is not, refundable. You will also explain to the prospective tenant why you are taking each check, and what money will be used for what purpose.

Fill out credit application

You will need to locate and initiate a relationship with a service that can perform credit checks for you. There are a number of credit agencies that cater to small businesses, such as the rental market landlord, with a small number of units. Many of these businesses will send, email, or fax you the required forms to be signed and returned to them. These forms provide protection for them. They indicate, through your written authorization, that you are going to run credit checks for the purpose of providing rental services. After you set up your account with these folks, you will be given a user name and password, so that you can use the Internet to log on and run these checks from the comfort of your desk or home. This also allows you to run them quickly, so your unit is never "off the market."

The next step in the rental process is to fill out the credit application. You will do this at the same time you take the first and second checks. Filling out the rental application and credit check form should take about five minutes. You don't need much information, other than their social security number, current address, past address over the previous three to five years, any other names they may have used (such as maiden names), and the date of birth.

It is an important step to get a signature on the credit application, which authorizes you to run their credit. There are certain legal actions they can take against you for running their credit, without their permission. As with the other steps we have advised you to take to help you run a smooth and trouble free business, please do not skip this piece of advice. We have had people tell us that they will fax the credit application "later." In the event the prospective renter changes their mind and wants their money back, on either the credit check or the deposit, you will need an original signature to prove that they authorized you to move forward with the credit check. Also, if at a later point they get turned down from another creditor due to "too many credit checks in a specific period of time," they won't be able to come back to you with any legal action. People's credit is very personal, as it should be. You will want to have everything on your end documented, to protect yourself from legal action.

After you run the credit check, there are things you need to be aware of, and look for, which will indicate whether they are going to pay you, or not.

The high level indicator of their credit worthiness is their overall credit rating. This number can range between a low of 450 and a high of 850. At this point, 720 is considered to be premium credit and means that they pay most people, aren't over leveraged, and don't have too many loans or creditors to whom they owe money. When you see numbers below 600, it should be a warning sign that tells you to keep looking for a renter. This isn't to say that if someone is below 600 then you shouldn't rent to them.

Events such as divorce, workman's comp claims, and sudden injuries are some reasons the score might be lower. If you see that kind of score, and it is for one of the reasons listed above, you will also see several missed or late payments with creditors, in a relatively short period of time (within a one to three month timeframe). You might also see some hospital claims or collections from hospitals, or their agencies, or even lawsuits from hospitals.

One item on their report that you will want to take notice of, and steer clear of, is a bankruptcy filing. If you see any information related to a Chapter of any kind, you would want to reject the potential renter, in favor of someone who will pay you on time. We have some friends who have rented to folks with bankruptcy filings. Even with five or six months security deposit, they still got burned. This is a good rule to follow: If they don't pay everyone else, then they probably aren't going to pay you. You can't think you are special and will get paid, simply because you are providing the roof over their head. Save yourself the hassle and headache by not renting to these folks.

You will also want to look for, and steer clear of, any foreclosures, repossessions or collections. These are symptoms of someone who doesn't pay their bills, nor has much respect for folks to whom they owe money.

People with good credit have good credit for a reason. Simply put; they pay their bills and meet the obligations they signed up for, or agreed to. There are enough people out there with good credit who need to rent a nice unit. They will find you and pay you, on time. Rent to those folks and your life and business will be better. You will avoid being the hard luck story of another individual who ventured into the rental market—only to sell the property early after a troublesome tenant caused you more headaches than you needed, or expected.

People with good credit will also come to you if they encounter a problem, and attempt to work something out vs. not taking your calls and avoiding you. They want to meet their obligations and will work hard to keep their word. If they lose their job and can't pay you, they will call you and do what they need to do so you both will come out with a win-win. They are generally honest people who want to do the right thing.

Fill out rental application

The rental application will need to be filled out so that you will have a record of some key information. In our experience, we have found this form to not be extremely important, but it does provide a quick snapshot of their rental history and provides some legal protection. Some applications have places to list: income history, past landlords, credit cards, bank accounts, and automobile information.

You should be able to find some standard rental application forms at your local office supply store, which will usually also comply with your local laws. There are usually several versions that can be used. For the most part, they are all basically the same.

Some people want to have the list of previous landlords, so they can call and check out their payment history and the condition of the units after they move out. We have not placed a call to any previous landlords since we started in this business, because we have not found any value in doing so. The landlord will usually speak highly about the renters and tell you they paid on time every month—even if they didn't.

This response is an effort to avoid legal trouble; in the event you choose not to rent to those prospective renters. Imagine you received a phone call from a landlord who was looking to rent to someone to whom you had rented in the past. If they ask if they were good renters and paid on time, and you answered with any negative information, and this caused them not to rent to those folks, you might be liable for slander or discrimination. You would then have to go to court, on your time and expense, and prove that the statements you made were true. You may have to show that they paid you late, or produce pictures of the damage to the unit that they caused. Many people don't want to take the time or money to defend their rightful position, so they end up settling out of court with a monetary pay off.

Another reason the current landlord might not be honest with you is if he/she just wants to get rid of those folks because they aren't paying them. They would have every reason to get them out of their unit and into yours. He/she wants the unit back and can later say they did pay and he/she doesn't see why they "suddenly" won't pay you.

Another use of the application form is to obtain that signature that authorizes you to check out information; in the event you need to do so. Several times throughout this book, we have stressed the point that you will need to do what you can to protect yourself from those seeking to make some quick money on one of your mistakes, via litigation.

Collect a check for credit application—Check #1

The first check you request will be taken at the time someone says they want to move forward. This will usually manifest itself in one of the following questions that they will ask:

What do we need to do to rent this unit?
Do I need to fill out an application for this unit?
Do you take a deposit for this unit?

Those are good questions and positive indicators that someone likes your unit and wants to take the next step. If they ask to take the application and fill it out later, then they are usually not really interested. Many people feel they need to make you feel good about showing them the unit, and do this by showing interest. They also think they can demonstrate interest by implying they are taking the next step, filling out a credit application, but not actually taking that step.

If they really want to move forward, then paying the thirty five to fifty dollars for the application, and filling it out on the spot, will be something they want to do. If they have looked at several places in the area, like the area, and really like your unit, then they should be able to take the next step. They should also realize that other people will also like it more than the other units on the market. Most of the time, when people find a place that suits all of their needs. they will want to make sure they don't lose it and won't let a small credit check fee get in the way. In addition, if a prospective renter has difficulty with the small application charge, could this be an indicator that they will struggle with the monthly rent?

The check that you will receive will be non-refundable, and will need to be presented to the prospective renter that way. Ask them to write the words "Credit Check—Non-Refundable" in the check memo field, so that it is recorded that way. This is for your protection; in the event their credit is not high enough to meet your minimum standards. In order to run a credit check on someone; you will need to work with a credit agency that charges for this service. The amount they charge varies—based on the number of credit checks per month and the purpose of those credit checks.

As mentioned earlier, you will need to establish a relationship with an agency and open an account with them, as part of your preparation. Credit checks are run online and only take a few minutes. There are different levels of credit checks available, ranging from a simple payment history, to complete background checks. The cost can run as low as $10, and up to $100, for a full background history. For most situations, you can run a simple credit history, which should cost between $15 and $25 if you only run a couple per month.

Most apartments, or other units on the market, will require a credit check, and will charge for obtaining that information. As a result, most renters are used to paying $35 or more when they apply for a rental unit and this should be what you charge. Renters are also aware of what is a reasonable rate to run credit checks. You do not want to establish a negative initial impression that you are trying to gouge them, or pad the amount, so you can make a few extra dollars on the credit checking process. In some cases, when we are almost certain that the credit will come back above normal, we have charged $25.

Occasionally, we have allowed someone to bring a copy of a recent report to us and not charged them to run a new one. This should only be done if the credit report was within the past sixty days. Credit bureaus update credit every sixty days and you want to have the most recent information possible when making this decision. If the report is older than that, there might be new information that could dramatically change the overall score, to a point that is lower than what you are willing to accept. For example, a person could have lost their job ninety days ago and stopped paying their bills, which wouldn't affect their numbers until the next update cycle.

Deposit this check into the bank the same day you take it, and make a copy of the check prior to depositing it. This is a good practice for any paperwork that you need to keep. The check will also have the banking information, legal address, and possibly a phone number that you may need to use later. In the event you encounter an issue where they are asking for this money back and take you to court, you will need to have this copy for the judge.

Check for deposit—Check #2

The second check is for the deposit on the unit. It serves to hold the unit, until it is determined that the prospective tenant is credit worthy, and meets the other criteria that you have established. in finding an ideal candidate. This check is only refundable if they have a bad credit score. Instruct them to write the words "Initial Deposit Check" in the check memo field. The deposit check is non-refundable; in the event the tenant decides they no longer want the unit for any reason. We have had situations where we have run the credit check, called the renter to schedule a time to fill out the paperwork, and have been told that they are no longer interested. They may have gone out looking while we were running the credit and found something that was less money, was closer to their office, was larger than our unit, or had another feature that appealed to them. That is why we take that deposit check.

While we are running the credit, we also let people know that the unit has a deposit on it and probably will not be available for rent. What would happen if you did tell someone inquiring about the unit that it wasn't available, and then the other person backed out? You might have to run that ad again, at your cost. There is also a timing issue (when the ad needs to be ran in the month), and you may have just missed the best time. This is why you take the deposit and explain that, as long as the credit comes back with a good score, then it is non-refundable.

If the credit comes back bad, then the deposit check should be given back to them. The credit check money is not refundable, because that is money you had to pay the credit agency. This is also why you take separate checks for each step. If you take one check, then you will have to deposit that check and then wait for it to clear, before you write them a check back for the difference. It is much cleaner, both from your time, and legally, to just deposit the credit check money and give back the initial deposit check, if their credit is bad.

The amount of this deposit should be in the range of 15%–25% of one month's rent. This amount will also filter out those who are serious about renting your unit and those that are just looking. If they are just looking, they will usually ask for a rental application and credit check form to take with them. They will tell you, promise you, and swear up and down that they want the place and will fill out the paperwork and get it back to you the next day. They will also come up with a lot of excuses as to why they can't give you money on the spot. Do not provide them with any paperwork. Do not, under any circumstances, tell any callers that the unit has been rented. You will never see these folks again. Chances are, they loved the unit, but do not have the money to pay for the rent, or know that their credit will be too low.

Make a copy of the initial deposit check also. The reasons are the same as for the previous check. Put these copies in the master file for this unit so you have all of the history and associated paperwork in one place. You will want to keep a file for each unit, for each year containing all records for that unit. By keeping all of your documentation organized by each property, it will also make it easier for your accountant to do your taxes at the start of each year, or in the event you have to go to court. Remember, this is a business and your job is to keep your units occupied all of the time, with people who will pay you the rent, on time. You can not lose sight of this point as your ultimate objective.

What to do after you have found your renter

You have found and screened the renter. Now you need to finalize everything by collecting some more money, going through some paperwork, and signing the lease. At this point, you are almost done.

After you have verified that they have sufficient credit, take the next step and get the lease signed. A good way to get this done is to meet in a restaurant for lunch, dinner, or drinks. It is a great way to get to know your new renters and further cement the relationship. It makes the paperwork part of this process more fun and relaxed, so they don't get nervous over signing the lease and understanding the rules. It is also one of the many write-offs in this business that lessens the actual cost of going to dinner.

You will need to go through the finer points of the lease including: what to do if something happens, where they can reach you, the association rules, the lease itself, the rider, and what your expectations are regarding when you expect the check to arrive in your mailbox.

The basic lease paperwork can be found at your local office supply store and is usually slightly different, depending on the state. You will need to have your attorney review the lease and create an additional rider back page, to include terms particular to your situation, and what is important to you as a landlord. That rider can include items such as: set carpet cleaning fees after move out, pet issues, late rental payment fee structure, additional association constraints, inspection timelines, first and last months rental payments, end of lease notification parameters, occupant limitations, and next tenant showing requirements. This short list reflects some more common items, but there can be more, depending on your specific situation. Spend time thinking about these points so nothing is left out. Be conscious of not getting into things that the tenant may consider overly complex, restricting, or demanding. Tenants will compare the paperwork you expect to be signed to the paperwork of other properties they have considered. An overly demanding lease document may be the difference between renting from you, and renting from someone else. On the other hand, if it is too lenient, it may not provide the protection you need to run a profitable business. The objective is to set out meaningful terms of the landlord/tenant relationship vs. being to onerous or ridiculous. During the course of the lease, most issues will be resolved based on the strength of the overall relationship, without resorting to the terms. You need to be very clear about your needs when explaining them to your attorney, so they can include the protection and security you need to limit your exposure.

When you are sitting down with your prospective tenant, you will need to explain most points on the rider. It helps to explain *why* it is included. If you have not gone overboard, the points should flow and make logical sense so that you won't receive much, if any, pushback. You will also want them to initial some of the more important points on this piece of paper, as you go through them. One of the points we expect them to initial is the payment due date clause. We want to make sure the tenant clearly understands that the due date for the rent is not a floating date, based on convenience. Also, next to their initials, you should initial each point. In the event something happens later, and you find yourself in court, this illustrates that you explained that particular point to them in detail, and they have acknowledged their understanding of the point.

One point you will need to be clear on, is when the rent is due, in your hand. Our policy is that it is due in our mailbox, on the first day of each month. We consider it late as of that day, instead of the typical five-day grace period. We suggest you be stern on this finer point; you are not a bank that floats non-interest based loans. Explain that you have mortgages to pay and, with clearing time frames and trips to the bank, you have to have the money by the first day of the month. If you allow the grace period of five days, then the check might not clear until the tenth or later, due to hold times. You also need to put a line in the sand because if you own more than one unit, you don't want to make multiple trips to the bank to deposit rental checks. Remember our philosophy, make it easy. Do what you can to keep it a part time job, which makes more than your full time job, or supplements your primary income.

After doing this for as long as we have, we have not had a single renter find this to be a problem. They understand that you aren't a bank and aren't asking that much of them. The side benefit of this is, in many cases; some renters will get it to you much earlier than the first, just to avoid it getting hung up in the mail, which would cost them some late fees. We have had some renters get it to us on the fifteenth of the month. Establish the expectation of on time payments so that getting the rent check to you on time is ingrained, and will not be deviated from, regardless of what is happening in their lives. You could also help them establish a pattern through reminders, for the first two to three months of the rental relationship. Put in a call to them asking how they are enjoying the unit, about any issues they are having, and provide a gentle reminder that the rent is due by the 1st.

The important point to convey is that you won't cash the check prior to the first, regardless of when they send it to you. We even go so far as to tell them they can send us twelve post dated checks, if it makes it easier for them, with our promise that we won't cash any of them a day earlier than they are due. Their biggest concern with this arrangement is that you will cash it early and there won't be money to cover that check. Remember, they are renters, not owners. In many cases, they are living pretty close to check to check.

Another reason you need it there on time is that it takes forty to ninety days to evict someone. If you start the eviction process on the sixth of the month, instead of the second of the month, then you have just cost yourself another week. Once they are late, you will usually start hearing a litany of excuses. They are all believable, but are still excuses, which means you have not been paid. You may fall for one, or two, or more, but this just extends your time on the back end of not getting paid. You put money in the bank, not excuses.

If you adopt our rules and abide by them (meaning you don't do anything differently), you should have a great rental experience. On the other hand, if you break one of them, the happy rental experience will most likely turn into a nightmare. Late payments can quickly turn from days into months of not getting paid for the mortgage that you carry on that unit.

You will also want the lease to expire in what we refer to as "the rental season." In colder climates, this is more important due to the consequences and struggles of moving when there are ten inches of snow on the ground and temperatures are sub-zero. People don't like to move during extreme variations of temperature. It isn't fun and it makes finding moving buddies difficult. People with children also want to wait until they are out of school. In the event you do have a lease that begins out of "season," you will need to time the expiration to coincide with the rental season. Never write a lease for less than a year. Instead, extend the lease to meet the season. If you are renting the unit in February, for example, instead of renting it to the following February, extend the term to June of the following year. Explain to them the benefits of getting more than a year without an increase in their rent, and that it will be much better to move when the temperatures are more favorable, if either of you decide to end the relationship. Sell this one a bit and they will quickly understand that it will work in their favor. Most people don't mind doing this, since they usually haven't even unpacked all of their boxes within the first year anyway.

The benefits to you are obvious. You will get the maximum monthly rent, if you are in prime rental season, and you will increase your pool of prospective renters dramatically. Even one or two months too early or too late can mean a difference of ten to fifteen percent in the monthly rate that you will be stuck with, for the full twelve month lease. You will also be in the same position the following year. That isn't good because it will skew your returns.

You are probably asking the questions; how do I keep the unit in the rental season every year, when it takes time to prepare the unit between tenants? Won't the unit sit vacant for a few weeks during this period?

The answer to both questions is—timing.

If you time things properly, you won't have any issues with either. People like to move out on the weekends. Usually, they like to start on Friday night or Saturday morning. They also like to have a day or two where they have the new place and the old place, at the same time. They will start moving out on Saturday, and take their belongings to the new place the same day. Often, they do this the weekend before the end of the month. Looking at a calendar, you will see that, more times than not, the first of the month does not fall on the weekend, but during the week. If the first falls during the week, they will want to get the new place the prior weekend, so they can start moving things over slowly. This results in a few days in between their departure and the new tenant's arrival. You can use that time to get the unit ready for the next tenant. If you find this isn't workable, write the next lease to fall within the next rental season, and your problem is solved.

Earlier, we mentioned the association rules that the new tenant will have to follow. Make sure you give them a copy of the rules, and that they sign your rider stating that they received a copy. If they break a rule (like cutting down a bush outside or leaving trash containers by the curb for a week), you will be charged to have another bush planted or you'll get a fine warning from the board of the association. Associations do have inspectors. Not only are they attempting to ensure uniformity in the community, but they are also generating a lot of revenue for the association as well. It will be hard for you to go back to them to collect that money, if you haven't given them a copy of the rules. In the event it is something bigger than a bush, you will need to prove, in court, that a copy of the rules was given to them. We take an additional step by going through some of the areas that the association tends to monitor more closely. Leaving garbage cans out more than a couple of days after pick-up, mounting things on the exterior of the property (like satellite dishes), signs, parking in front of the unit during the late evening or during snow removal; these are some of the items that the association watches carefully. It always pays to protect yourself by being as proactive as you can be.

Collect the remainder of the deposit—Check #3

This will usually be done at one of two times. The best time to collect the third check is when you get together to sign the lease after running the credit check, or you can do this when you meet them at the unit the first day, to give them the keys. Either way, you will need to collect the remainder of the deposit, prior to them taking possession of the unit, or giving them the keys. The amount of this check will be the difference between check number two, and the full deposit that you request.

The deposit is usually equal to one month's rent. As a note—the deposit is the deposit and should be made clear, both verbally and on the rider, that it is *not* the final month's rent. This money is collected as an insurance policy, in the event that they leave the unit with damage, unpaid water bills, the need for carpet cleaning, or any other reason that may cost you money, after they are gone. As with the other checks, make a notation in the memo field as to what it is for, make a copy of this check, and put it in the file.

Collect the first month's rent—Check #4

This will be the first check that you collect from your renters to pay for the monthly rent due on that unit. As mentioned before, you can collect this first month's rent check with check #3, or wait until the actual first day of the lease. At whatever point you do this, we always give them the keys when we take the first month's rent, so they have the flexibility to move in when they want. From that point, they are paying for the rent, so they should have the keys. We usually do this a day or two in advance, providing that the timing isn't so tight that you don't have the extra day. The renters like to have the keys and everything taken care of, in advance, so they can just show up on move day with the truck and all of the belongings. If you meet them the day of the move, then it causes a delay that they and their friends have to endure.

You will also need to make a notation in the memo field and make a copy of this check, prior to depositing it into the bank, so you have a record of that first check. The copy and notation will not have to be done on the monthly rent checks, other than the first one. We only do this so there is not any confusion as to what check is paying for what.

Rent Day—1st Day

The first day of the lease is a great day and one that you will always enjoy, no matter how many times you have done it before. This is the day when most of the work is done, and it is time to basically coast, for the term of the lease. You simply collect the checks, and let the appreciation make you money, while waiting for the time you can refinance some of your equity out of the unit. It is a relief, in that you own this unit and someone else is paying you, and the bills, to live there. It takes that "bill," or liability off of your plate, which relieves you of that underlying stress factor. As many times as we have gone through this, it still feels great, each and every time, and reinforces your desire to purchase another property.

During the process of collecting the previous two checks, the first month's rent and the remainder of the deposit, you had the option of collecting them in advance or collecting them on the first rental day. Here are things to do when you meet them at the unit on that first day. Remember that you can meet them a day or two early, to help them out. In many cases, it might also work better with your schedule to meet them early. You will appear as a generous land-lord for giving them access to the unit, rent free, a couple of days early. This is another win-win that they might mention to the next tenants, when they are showing for you later.

We have provided a check list of items that you will need to give your renter. They will initial this checklist, acknowledging that the items have been received. Having this signed list gives you proof that they received those items, in the event that they have to be replaced later. Those replacement costs will come out of their security deposit, after they have left the unit. Having the list will avoid any disputes. This list also serves as a great reminder for you. A year later, you won't be able to remember how many mailbox, garage door remotes, or front door keys you gave them. In the event you have many units, this is imperative because then you will be able to keep straight the items associated with each unit. This list may also assist you in a liability situation. In the event of a fire your ability to prove that you provided a fire extinguisher when they signed the lease will help limit your loss during a lawsuit.

Whether you meet them early, or on the first rental day, you will need to meet them at the unit, before they take possession. This serves to establish the condition of the unit by doing a quick walk through, and also provides an opportunity to go over some points that need to be covered. Take them thorough a quick tutorial of the appliances. Show them how to change the air filter in the furnace. (We always have about two or three extra ones near the furnace). We call them a couple of months after possession to provide them with a friendly reminder that they should change the filter. This will obviously promote better air circulation in the unit for them, which makes it more comfortable. It also delays cleaning or replacing the furnace—small extra steps to delay, or avoid, cost and headaches for you.

-What to sign

They will sign off on the rider, or a checklist, that they have received the following:

- Lease
- Move in checklist
- Condo Rules/Regulations/By-Laws
- Local municipality information (such as water, pets, etc.)
- Door Keys
- Dead Bolt Keys
- Mail Box Keys
- Water Softener Inst. (if applicable)
- Alarm Inst. (if applicable)
- Fire Place Inst. (if applicable)
- Carbon Monoxide Detector (in unit)
- Smoke Detector (in unit)
- Fire Extinguisher (in unit)
- Appliance instructions (keep in unit)
- Village or city ordinances (such as parking restrictions)
- A list of important numbers

The following worksheet can serve as a handy signature check list to make sure you have everything covered. A copy should be given to them and put in the lease file for this unit.

Important Numbers

City/Area Number Work Sheet

Service	Account Number	Phone Number	Done
Cable	_____	_____	___
Electric Company.	_____	_____	___
Gas Company	_____	_____	___
Sewer & Water	_____	_____	___

	Items	**Received**
Your Name	Lease	___/___
Your Address	By-Laws	___/___
Your City, State, Zip	Door Keys	___/___
Home Phone	Dead Bolt Keys	___/___
Office Phone	Mail Box Keys	___/___
Cell Phone	Water Softener Inst.	___/___
	Alarm Inst.	___/___
	Fire Place Inst.	___/___
	CO Detector	___/___
	Smoke Detector	___/___
	Fire Extinguisher	___/___
	Garage Door Opener	___/___

What to give the renter

The records the renter will want to have are listed below. We recommend having two copies of each form, and that the tenant signs both copies. This will eliminate the need for you to have to send anything back to them later. It allows you to wrap everything up in one meeting, which saves time and money.

The lease is one of the more important items they will want to have a copy of, to keep in a safe place. It has your mailing address, dates, phone numbers, and specific rules that need to be followed. Because you will provide two copies, both you and the renter will sign and initial two copies of each form.

The following is a short list of what the renter will hold on to from this meeting:

➢ Copy of lease

➢ Door keys

➢ Mail box keys

➢ Copy of the by-laws

➢ Copy of checklist

We also mentioned that you need to give them, and have them sign, a form that they received a fire extinguisher, Carbon Monoxide (CO), detector, and smoke detector.

Providing CO detectors, smoke detectors, and fire extinguishers illustrates that you have provided detection and alerting systems that should warn them of an issue, and allow them to escape in time. Giving them a working fire extinguisher illustrates that, in the event something catches on fire (such as a kitchen fire), they are equipped to put it out, or at least contain the situation. Fire extinguishers are generally effective in cases of small fires, and are not to be used for larger fires. These items will also help your insurance rates and save you some money. Mount or store your extinguishers where there is the greatest risk of fire—by stoves, furnaces, fireplaces, and dryers. Ensure that you have a CO detector on every floor, especially the bedrooms. These are relatively inexpensive and can be plugged right into any electrical outlet.

Protecting your tenants from injury should always be your number one priority. Nobody wants a major accident in a property, when it might be averted by something as simple as providing a detector, or fire extinguisher. These are also important considerations in terms of protecting yourself from lawsuits, or at least limiting your exposure during a lawsuit. If your tenant wants to sue you, you will have to defend yourself. Your best case scenario is that you have done everything you can do; to illustrate to the court that you tried to protect the tenant from harm during the time they spent with you. Furthermore, if you can show a history of "doing the right thing," in terms of protecting your past tenants, it also will help your case.

It is important to remember the underlying reasons for doing these things. You want to do the right thing, but you also want to limit your exposure in the case of the "get rich quick" tenant who wants to own all of your assets. We cannot say it too many times. Make sure you get their signature, showing that you gave them all of these items—and they were working at the time you signed the lease. Protect yourself.

We mentioned earlier about getting the furnace and air conditioning units cleaned and checked, annually. Servicing the furnace illustrates that you are doing your best to make sure it does not malfunction and end up with a bad burner, or some other problem. If the furnace malfunctions, it could start putting out CO and your tenants could get sick, or die. Reality tells us that these tragedies may happen anyway, but at least you have done your best to limit your potential exposure. Get it done once a year, and make sure you keep all of the receipts, which you may have to produce in court. Remember, this would be a worst case scenario. Of all of the units we have owned over the years, and all of the tenants we have had, we have never had a major accident or litigious situation with a tenant.

In a later chapter, we cover, in more detail, the insurance and exposure topics

During the term of the lease

What a great feeling. You bought the unit, prepared everything, found a renter, collected some money, and signed some paperwork. Right now, you are thinking you are home free and ready to sit back for a year, or two, or three. Providing you have followed our methodology and done this the right way, then you should be able to mainly coast, until you either turn it over, or simply sign the next lease.

Month after month, the rent checks will come in and your only job is to deposit them, so you can pay the bills on each unit. That's it. At this point, you might be thinking about all of the things that can go wrong that you will have to deal with. Don't worry. There shouldn't be much that can go wrong. Making the right decision on the tenant, on the front of the qualification process, will ensure that.

What if something goes wrong?

This is a great time to reinforce one of our key concepts. If something breaks, take care of it immediately, without hesitation. Treat it like you live there, and not like someone else lives there. If you do this, everyone ends up satisfied. In some cases, this may mean making a phone call to have an item fixed by one of your tradesman partners, or it may mean that you drop what you are doing and take care of the problem. Either way, do it now and don't put it off until tomorrow, if at all possible, depending on the issue.

We had a situation one time where a water heater developed a pinhole leak, on a Saturday, two days before Christmas. The call came in from the tenant at about four o'clock that day, an hour before we had to be at dinner. The tenant said it could wait a day or two, and she would make do. We told her that we wouldn't want to get up the next day and not be able to take a shower. We spent the next hour on the phone, until we found two guys in a bar who could fix the water heater. They had been there for a couple of hours, and it was going to cost an extra two hundred dollars over the cost of the normal job to get them out of that bar and over to the unit. We happily paid them, and by 7:00 PM, the water heater was fixed. The tenant was able to get up the next day, Sunday, and go to her Christmas Eve festivities. If it were you, would you want to go over to your relatives' house without having taken a shower? When it came time to turn that unit over, the tenant bragged about how her landlord spent a lot of money taking care of the water heater, so she could take a shower. Needless to say, the people to whom she told that story called within minutes of looking at that unit, and asked to meet so they could sign a lease.

What the tenant will do

During the term of the lease, the tenant has a couple of obligations to fulfill. They have to pay you on time, and let you know if something isn't working. They need to work with you like a partner works with you. If they do, then you will work with them much better and you will both have a better rental experience.

Getting out early

Every now and then, a renter will have something in their life that will cause them to need to get out of the lease early. Remember the credit score conversation? They work hard to keep it in good standing with everyone else and they will work to do the same with you. We remind you of this because, when things change in their lives, people with good credit will come to you and work something out that is good for both parties. People with bad credit will simply leave, or give you a lot of excuses after the fact, and leave you with additional expenses you did not anticipate. That is the reason this is the first rule of the five, earlier in this chapter. Credit means everything—only rent to people with good credit.

What should you do if a tenant calls you up and needs to break the lease early? You will need to take into consideration the time of year, ease of renting again quickly, and any exposure you may have in letting them out early. In most cases, you don't have too much exposure, unless you are in an area that has a definite "rental season." In that case, you will want to have the renter assume part of the exposure and you will assume another part. In this case, the exposure is missed rents that come as a result of you being in an area where people don't want to start a lease, or move, at that time of the year.

The tenant is contractually obligated for the term of the lease. Although you want to do the right thing based on the tenants changing circumstances, you have the signed lease as leverage to minimize your financial exposure. Always determine the reason they are leaving and their true sense of urgency in needing to get out. Then, depending on the circumstances, see if you can work something out so they can stay until you find another renter to take their unit. During this period, request that they show the property, as they will be highly motivated to provide a good positive showing to the people that you qualify.

Here's a cold climate example. Your tenant calls you in November and tells you they are getting a transfer, or they just bought a house and need to be out in January. They could also be getting a divorce, or one of several other reasons. The result is—they need to be out in the beginning of January, but their lease doesn't end until May 31st. You might tell them they will need to pay through January and February, and you will assume the exposure of the other months through the end of May. At that point, you place an ad in the paper at the end of December, with an availability of January 15th. You explain to the tenant that if you get it rented before the end of January, then they would get part of the additional rent money back with their deposit. If not, then they are obligated. If the unit rents in February, then you make a little extra money. If the unit doesn't rent, then you either break even, or start losing money.

Under this agreement, the tenant will also have to pay for the newspaper ad costs during that time. This shouldn't be your responsibility, since under the terms of the original lease you would not have had to run that ad until much later. You can agree to pay for the first week, because you would have to do this at the end of the existing lease. The ad cost is the same as the rent money, in terms of exposure. If the unit rents by the end of January, then they won't have to pay much. If it goes past that point, then you either break even, or lose money. You are obviously motivated to get it rented before your money is involved.

Keep in mind that you have exposure either way, because you would be renting it out of season, and the monthly rent would be lower than your normal rates. This needs to be explained to the tenant, if they push back at all during the negotiations. Keep this to yourself until you need to mention it, to help persuade them that you will be losing money either way. Under the terms of the lease, they are obligated to pay through the end of the lease term. By giving them this out, even though they will pay some extra money, they are still getting out of the obligation a few months ahead, without paying.

Please remember that if you end up finding a renter to rent this unit out of season, you will need to write the lease with additional months so it ends the following year, during the normal season. As mentioned earlier, most people don't have all of their boxes unpacked within the first year and usually don't mind writing that lease for a couple of extra months. Don't be shy about asking for this. as long as you explain the reasons. Slant it so it sounds like it is for them. Why would they want to move where there is snow on the ground next year? This keeps the rent at the same price for some extra months as well.

The tenant could also ask about subletting the unit. This means they would find the new tenant to take over the unit and monthly rent, though the remaining term of the lease. They might have a friend, or know someone who has been in the unit, who would just love to live there. This is a perfectly good working situation, but there are some rules they would need to adhere to. The rules we are referring to are all of the rules you follow when finding a tenant. The primary rule that must be followed is the rule stating that credit is everything, and the credit of the prospective renter needs to be up to your standard. This is called—first right of refusal. Simply, this means you have the right to accept the application of the new renter and it is at your sole decision. Some tenants want to take this path because they think they can rent it faster and save some money. Usually this doesn't work out because they aren't in the business and don't understand good renters vs. bad renters, or the term "rental season." If your lease allows them to go down this path, then you need to redefine what happens after the first defined rental period.

Last Day of the Lease

At a certain point, hopefully not until the end of the lease, you will get the call to notify you that the current tenants are moving out and you need to turn the unit over. Your lease should cover the amount of notice they provide, which should range between thirty and ninety days prior to the lease expiration date. This provides enough time for you to run the ad, sign the new lease, and prepare the property for the new tenant.

When the time comes and they have moved out, you will need to meet them on site to do a walk through. During this time, collect all of the items you gave them when they moved in, based on the lease and move in checklist that you prepared at the beginning of the lease. You will need to bring your lease folder with you, so you know exactly what you gave them. This is where their signature on all of the paperwork will help, if there are any disputes about what you gave them. Don't forget the by-laws, manuals for appliances, fire extinguisher, CO detector, and smoke detectors. You will need all of these items for the next tenant.

As standard practice, we usually change out all of the locks after a tenant moves out. This will help with the liability factor, in the event your new tenant gets robbed or someone breaks into the unit. If you haven't changed out the locks, then the current tenant might sue you and bring your last tenant into court with you. Although you are hopefully collecting the same number of keys you gave to the tenant when the lease started, keys can be cut and you can never really be sure of who is in possession of any extras. Changing the locks out is a simple solution that costs an extra thirty to fifty dollars. It provides some additional protection from the exposure of a lawsuit, in addition to all of the hassle of dealing with the police and insurance company in the event of a break–in that was not a forced entry into your unit. Again, keep copies of the receipts in your property folder for two reasons: evidence that you changed the locks, and a tax write-off. This is one of the items on the checklist that doesn't really matter, in terms of getting back what you gave them. We have also used the same locks in different units and rotated them around from unit to unit. This avoids buying new locks every time, but still provides the protection for your tenants and you. If you do this, you will need to imprint serial numbers on them, for record keeping purposes.

Other items, such as the mailbox key and garage door openers, are items that will cost a lot of money to replace. The post office usually charges between fifty and one hundred dollars to replace the lock on common mailboxes. They will not just replace the key, but rather, must replace the lock, for safety reasons, and the federal laws around the delivery of the mail. Garage door openers may not cost much, but can sometimes be hard to replace, if that opener has been there for ten to fifteen years. Getting the generic openers to work can sometimes be a challenge. Fan remote controls are items that are also sometimes overlooked and can be difficult to replace.

The renters will usually think that you will bring your checkbook with you so you can write them a check for their deposit, on the spot, during the walk through. Your lease, and basic common sense, tells you that you won't be writing them a check at that time. There will be costs that need to be deducted from that security deposit including, but not limited to, carpet cleaning, any unpaid water bills, damage to the unit, missing keys or garage door openers. Let the tenants know that you will, per your lease, mail the remainder of the deposit back to them within thirty days, with an accounting sheet showing any deductions. If there are any damages or items that need to be replaced, mail a copy of the receipts to them with their deposit refund.

During the walk through, you will need to look for some obvious issues. Some of these include the condition of the carpet, walls, appliances, and even the floors. There are some others that you won't be able to see, such as pet stains that will show up during the carpet cleaning. Non-working appliances will also show up when the unit is prepared for the next tenants. Run all appliances during the cleaning and preparation process for the next tenant, to determine if they are still working. You wouldn't believe some of the items people put in their washer and dryers and dishwashers. Pens, paint stained clothing, and even tennis shoes can damage a washer to the point where it will need to be replaced. Even if you have a warrantee on that washing machine, the repair company will know the damage isn't due to normal usage and not honor the warrantee.

Look for damage to counter tops, screen doors, garbage disposal units, cabinets, sinks, and faucets at the same time. These too, can be costly and time consuming to repair, prior to renting it to the next tenant. You don't want to start off with a negative impression with your new tenant because of a non–working appliance, which you missed identifying when the last tenants moved out. This will cost you money if it wasn't deducted from the security deposit from the last tenants before you sent it back to them. You will not always be able to find everything, but do your best to look for anything that might need to be fixed.

"If you don't care about your property, you certainly can't expect someone else to, who doesn't own it ..."

To repeat an earlier point, in your rider, you will need to write a statement reinforcing that the deposit cannot be used as the last month's rent. It is important to keep the purpose of the deposit clear, as it is your only recourse to recover any money that you may need to spend a week or two after they move out. Otherwise, you will be stuck with the bills just mentioned, and will not be able to collect that money. The chance of the old tenant sending you any money (especially if it is more than a couple of hundred of dollars), after they move out, is slim. Don't put yourself in this position of exposure.

"Hoping that you will get paid is not an effective financial strategy"

Turning Over the Property

Remember our "make it easy" philosophy? When it comes time to turn the unit over, we do our best to keep the work down and profits up.

Just as you did when you first bought the unit, you will need to do some of the same tasks. Running the ad, showing the property, preparing the property, and the leasing steps are mostly the same. The two that differ are, showing the property and preparing the property.

Showing the property

The primary difference is that you have the option of either showing it yourself, or having the current tenant show the unit for you. If you decide you want to show it yourself, you can do a quick assessment of cleanliness/general upkeep, so that you have a higher degree of confidence in allowing the tenant to show it the next time around. If there are things that you are concerned with during this showing, you can address them before the next showing. If you have a good relationship with your tenant and the period of the lease term has been relatively issue free, you may want to have your tenant show the property. You might be thinking, "Are you crazy? They can't show that unit like I can show it." That isn't always the case. Consider how powerful testimonials can be. You see them all of the time on television—in commercials and infomercials. Would your opinion of a weight loss product be the same if the representative on the commercial were overweight vs. someone who was fit and in shape? It probably wouldn't have the same impact.

When your renter shows your unit, and tells the prospective tenant how much they love living in that unit in that neighborhood and how great you have treated them, it has a greater impact than you doing the same. It puts the prospective renter in a position of believing the information and not thinking it is a sales pitch. This is especially powerful if you have had any problems during the lease and fixed them immediately. Listening to some people who have talked to our renters can sound like we paid those people. The point is—the prospective renter expects you to say great things about your own property. When renter (who is perceived to not have a vested interest), says those things, they can be more powerful and persuasive. If you have any doubts about what your tenant will say, ask the renter after the showing. Either way, you will be in a better position for the next showing, if you need another one. If they can't wait to write a check to you for the deposit, your answer, as to how the showing went, is obvious. You may consider some kind of gift to your tenant for doing such a great job in showing the unit. By asking the tenant to show the unit, you will cut down on the number of times you need to make a trip to that unit. As we also know, the faster you can rent that unit, the more likely it will be that you get the price you are asking. Remember, vacancies mean loss of money.

This method will also save you the time and hassle of doing it yourself. Your schedule might not line up with the prospective renter's schedule, but, if you don't drop what you are doing and show the unit, you may have missed a good renter and the possibility of eliminating your vacancy.

When showing the place, find out if they are familiar with the area and point out some of the amenities. You're not only selling your property and subdivision, but the surrounding area as well. Make a list of all of the attractions, transportation, educational institutions, and shopping in the area.

Timing is everything

Timing is everything, when it comes to turning over the unit from one tenant to the next.

We mentioned earlier that you need to time everything so that one is out on Tuesday, and another is in on Saturday. In most cases, you won't miss even one day of rent, if you have your timing lined up. In some cases, you may actually end up ahead monetarily. When someone moves out a day or two early, due to where the weekend falls, you won't give them a prorated month. They end up paying you through the end of the month. The new tenant will also give you a full month's rent, so there might be some overlap. The overlap will mean that you will receive more money than the standard month rental, which goes into your pocket.

This timing issue is why we have advised you to make sure you line up your business/trades partners (painters, cleaners, carpet repairers or replacers), and know what type of advance notice they require. Many of them don't require more than a few days to a week, before you are on their schedule. A painter, maid, and professional carpet cleaning service are the three you will need to hire every time you turn the unit over. If you have them perform their services in that order, they won't mess up the other's work. You don't want the painter to step all over the clean, wet, carpet to do their job, because you will have to call your carpet people again.

Occasionally, things may happen that don't allow you to time the departure of one tenant and the arrival of the new tenant so ideally. We are merely painting the picture that you want to strive for, to decrease the amount of time you own the unit but aren't getting paid for it. Think about missing the rent for a week or so, due to the timing of preparing the unit, every year over the course of ten or more years. That will add up and, over that time, will minimize your returns. Time is money, in most businesses. In this business, it isn't just a reference to your time. but rather the amount of time your property remains vacant. Since you are charging for time occupied, any day that goes by, without your property being occupied and paid for, is considered a loss.

Remember the five "Prosper Through Real Estate" rules of renting and don't break them.

1) **Credit is everything**. If they pay everyone else, then they will pay you. If they don't pay anyone else, or are not fulfilling their financial obligations, they will be the same with you.

2) **Location, location, location**. Renters want to look at beautiful things and be in great locations that are peaceful and serene. They want family oriented places or communities with an abundance of children, that will provide new friendships and extended support opportunities. They want areas of recreation, and to be close to day to day necessities like daycare, groceries, cleaning, banking and finance, and schools.

3) **Your costs have nothing to do with what you charge for monthly rents.** Just because you paid too much, didn't put enough down, bought the wrong unit, or structured the loan incorrectly, it doesn't mean you will be able to charge enough to cover your mistakes.

4) **Appearance can make the difference between renting and another showing.** Make the inside of the unit look better than the other available units. Appliances, blinds, carpet, and paint need to look good and function properly.

5) **Fix it now.** Treat your renters like you would want to be treated. If something breaks, fix it now and fix it right.

** * **No Vacancies or Unpaid Time is always the objective*****

Keep it rented at all (most) costs

Lowering the rents to get it rented is usually better than letting it sit vacant. This quick example shows why:

If you get eleven months rent for $1300, it is like getting twelve months for $1200.

11 months x $1,300 monthly rent = $14,300 yearly total

12 months x $1,200 monthly rent = $14,400 yearly total

If you could not get $1,300 one month, you might have to reduce the price to rent it. This would put you even further behind. You will still have to pay the utilities and insurance yourself, which will compound the loss.

Chapter Eleven

A Summary on Renters

Renters will usually fall into two categories: those who are desirable, who you want to attract and retain and those you diplomatically and quickly eliminate in the qualification process. Making a decision between the two, early in the process, is the single most important differentiator between being successful as a real estate investor, losing money and time, and being frustrated to the extent of selling the property at a loss, to eliminate the aggravation of making a poor tenant decision. It will cost both time and money due to court proceedings, damage, repairs, cleaning, liability, and insurance situations. Tenants in either category have certain characteristics that are indicative of both that you need to be aware of, and deal with, appropriately.

Good Tenants vs. Bad Renters

Late pays

This can point to a variety of negative scenarios, all of which should concern and alert you to the risks of renting to this individual. Another reason to carefully analyze the credit report is to specifically look at the number and pattern of the late payments history. Running a credit report, prior to signing the lease will provide that information.

➤ Their expenses exceed their revenue, and they are living month to month by continuously juggling bills and creditors. Individuals in this predicament are one financial crisis (job loss, divorce, health issue, and car accident), away from being in a position of not being able to recover, and defaulting on their lease obligations.

➤ Having the funds necessary to cover expenses on a monthly basis, but not the organizational skills or aptitude to pay on time. The classic procrastinator, last minute, fly-by-the-seat-of-his-pants type of personality who will only follow through on his obligations when the pressure is on. If the credit report is good, give an individual with this type of mentality an incentive. Include a penalty clause in the lease, specifying a penalty of

$ 50.00 for every day their payment is late. Get them to initial that clause in the lease to ensure they fully understand it.

If late payments start occurring during the lease, this pattern could be attributed to a couple of probable scenarios.

➤ Your tenant is unhappy and he is sending you a message. They want to move out, are unhappy with a situation with you that has been either unresolved, or not resolved to their satisfaction. Find out what is going on and fix it, if it is within your capabilities, before the unhappiness escalates and you lose a tenant—or you find the unit empty on one of your periodic drive bys. This is another reason to forge relationships with neighbors of your units. They will feel comfortable in picking up the phone, if they see a moving van at the back of the unit, at midnight.

➤ Something has changed in the tenant's financial or personal situation. Get the facts early and ask the tough questions, in a non-threatening way. They are under a lease and bound by contract for the term. Their obligation is to continue to pay you the agreed rental cost, on the specified day, every month.

Bad credit

The general rule—***"Do not rent to individuals with a score of less than 600."*** The credit report is the single most important criteria in which to assess an individual's financial worthiness and character. Run it, review it, realize what it is telling you, and do not deviate from the rule. The credit report is an important piece of information which is the single biggest criteria in determining your success or failure in the rental business.

Under certain circumstances, you may see a score that is under 600 and it will still be okay to rent to that person. If that person went through a messy divorce shortly before the bad marks started showing up on their credit report, but everything was good before and after that period, then they might be okay to rent your unit. The same applies to someone who has a workman's compensation lawsuit, or has an illness that caused a job loss. Doctors and hospitals are known for turning someone over to a collection agency as soon as they miss their first payment. During divorces, or lawsuits, people usually don't pay the bills until the courts decide who should pay the bill. This process could take months to finalize. Doctors, hospitals, and some other professions don't care about these circumstances and will act quickly to attempt to get their money.

Reference checks

Reference checks are extremely limited in value and, for the most part, we don't even recommend that you do them for the following reasons:

> - If you call the present landlord and he is unhappy with them, they may not provide you with much in the way of details because:

  - → In the litigious times that we live in, a former landlord may be exposing themselves legally if they provide you with information that would be a factor in you not renting to that individual.

  - → If they are unhappy with the tenant, they want them out and will not provide you with information that will deter you from taking the problem off their hands.

> - What is the likelihood that a renter will provide you with a reference with less than glowing accolades? Spend the time you would have taken in making the call to review the credit report instead.

> - Not Reliable
>   Whether a potential renter is reliable, or not, is something you can start to assess in the first meeting. Are they on time for the showing? Do they follow up, as they agreed to, for signed credit authorizations, checks, and general information? Is there is a disturbing pattern that manifests itself early on these relatively simple requests? Can you expect them to follow through with respectably maintaining your property, paying the rent on time, and cooperating during repairs and upkeep?

> - Pays in cash, money order or cashier checks
>   If the prospective renter indicates they want to pay you in cash, cashiers check, or money order early in the process, you need to consider this a red flag. If the individual whom you are considering is considered a default risk for an institution with significant capital reserves, then appreciate the fact that they have done an initial qualification for you. Most people with good credit have checking and savings accounts. They also write checks instead of wasting their time going to the currency exchange to get money orders.

Are these hard and fast rules? They are not. But, consider them as strong guiding principles that have been tested and validated continually, by the authors. Ultimately, you have to consider all of the circumstances and information when evaluating a particular tenant, and make the best decision based on information available. Remember, there is a seemingly unending pool of tenants available who will have interest—if your price is competitive with other units in the area, and your property is in a desirable location where people want to live. Don't be too eager to sign a lease with the first individual who shows interest, especially if you are going through the process with your first property. The allure is powerful to deposit your first rent check and tell everyone you are a real estate investor. Neither of these actions is worth making a poor choice on the first individual who desires to write a month's rent and damage deposit check to you.

Typical Renter Profiles

In the number of years we have been renting, we have found that the majority of the caller's profiles will fall into one of a few areas. Keep in mind that we have a specific footprint for the type of rental unit we purchase. If you are buying units that are bigger, more stand alone, or vacation properties, then your typical renter profile will potentially fall outside of these parameters. With our profile, the caller would fall into one of these categories: Yuppies, baby boomers, immigrants, couples, or divorced parents with one or two children living with them.

We have listed each category and provided some insight as to what is driving them to this type of rental unit. Assessing what category a person falls into, and knowing what generally motivates those individuals, will help you guide the discussion. For example, when speaking to divorced mothers, you want to point out schools or daycares in the area, early in the discussion.

Yuppies

Young urban professionals still comprise the largest group in our defined rental market, with estimates as high as 60%. They rent because they:

➢ Want to remain mobile—having not settled on a profession, area of desired permanence, relationship, or having kids. Renters with kids will bring about a different set of decisions, like school districts and recreational areas geared to kids.

➢ Have priorities that are more oriented toward travel and material possessions (like a flashy vehicle, and clothing). They see themselves "above" an apartment. They also don't want to park their expensive car in a community parking lot, which could get dinged and scratched by the other, lower end, cars. (Their German sport car shouldn't be parked next to the 1982 rusty bolt bucket). We have had Yuppie couples drive up in nice "status cars" to sign leases for our houses. Their car payments total more than the rent we are charging.

➢ Are still accumulating assets for a major purpose, like a house.

> Are paying off student loans and other educational debt, which may be reflected in credit scores.

> Don't want to be burdened with all of the additional responsibilities that come with making the largest and most significant purchase an individual will ever make in their lifetime—a home. Due to their lifestyle of being on the go, they don't want to be responsible for lawn cutting, maintenance of a home, or having to take care of things that break.

> Don't need the room associated with a dwelling larger than a townhouse. It is early in their life, and they haven't accumulated a lot of possessions yet. They will usually use one bedroom for their bed and dresser, and the other bedroom for either an office, or an exercise room.

Baby Boomers

Most baby boomers are looking at retiring in the next ten to twenty years. Some want to sell existing homes and downsize, based on children leaving the nest and reducing the burden of home ownership. These are a few reasons why they want to rent, instead of continuing to own their own home.

> The yard upkeep and maintenance is a big burden that they either don't want to keep up with, or aren't healthy enough to do so, on their own. They want to move in and let someone else take care of everything, so they can just enjoy life.

> Some are on fixed incomes, and their primary source of income is fixed social security. Usually, that means they aren't making much money. They may have some money from the sale of their house, or some pension, but that still doesn't add up to much. They also may not want to use the money from the sale as a down payment on another house, and face another thirty-year mortgage, and the associated insurance payments.

> A desire to live in an area that has more to offer, in terms of entertainment and recreation. The house they have lived in for the last thirty years may not be close to things they want to experience, now that they have time to do them. It also may not be close to their friends or kids.

Immigrants

Immigrants consist of approximately 15% of the total rental market. This percentage will only continue to increase. Immigrants rent for the following reasons:

➢ To stay close to family and friends, and areas of those of similar heritage, because of the comfort, network, and opportunities this proximity provides.

➢ They may not have the large down payments or credit required to purchase a home.

Couples

Couples will also constitute a large number of the inquiries that you will receive. Couples tend to rent for the following reasons:

➢ They are newly married, or together, and saving for a house of their own. In this scenario, try to gauge when they are anticipating having the assets for a place of their own. Determine, as a landlord, what is the minimum period of time you are looking to lease your unit. If you are looking for a commitment of one and a half years, and they are looking at getting out in six months, you have unaligned expectations from the outset, and don't need to go any further in the process.

➢ Couples with children are also drawn to areas, for the welfare of the children. They want do be near specific school districts, daycare, recreational areas, entertainment, family, and friends.

➢ Couples are motivated to seek residence in areas close to work, to eliminate and reduce commutes.

Divorced parents

One of the eventualities of divorce is the division of marital assets. This frequently means the sale of the marital residence, or a buyout of the other party. Regardless of the circumstances, either or both members of the former couple typically find something semi permanent, and a townhouse is frequently the perfect residential solution. You will get inquiries from recently divorced people for the following reasons:

➢ They need a place to live, generally in a short time period. They may have just moved out of their old house and need a place quickly. Only one person will get the marital house, which puts the other person on the street, in immediate need of a residence. Co- habiting with the ex, or soon to be ex, is rarely an option. Many times, they want to be close to their old house for either legal reasons from the divorce, or so it is more convenient to see their kids.

➢ They need time to re-establish financial assets, before considering another purchase. We mentioned earlier, a divorce can be harsh on your credit.

For this reason, their credit may not support getting a mortgage, until they pay their bills for a period of time and rebuild their credit score. This can take a couple of years, and they will need to rent for that period of time. Remember the exception to our credit rule. If their score is low, due to a divorce, then it is okay to rent to them. Be careful, and make sure you know that a divorce is the reason, and not something else.

> They want to stay close to the kids, or have them remain in the same school district, to minimize too much traumatic upheaval. This can be either the parent with the kids, or the one without the kids. The parents usually want the kids to still have a normal life and not feel different from the other kids in their class. Living in an apartment can make kids feel different from their peers with yards and a front door. Living in a townhouse has all of the comforts of a regular house, like the one they use to live in (such as a lawn, garage, and front door), and will be in a community with other houses.

> They don't want the stress of home ownership, after the emotional turmoil of a divorce. Most people, who go through a divorce, do not enjoy the process. Between the lawyers, accountants, judges, and all of the meetings, they just want to walk in the door and keep everything simple for awhile. They want to think about as little as possible for the next couple of years. This is another side benefit of buying the right unit that looks at something nice, and not the back of some big store. It is peaceful and calming.

Make your final decision on qualitative information such as the credit report and your instincts when assessing individuals from any of these renter groups as potential renters. You should also factor in the time you have spent with them after interacting with the individual(s) a couple of times. We typically attempt to get together with them at least two times in person, and a couple of phone calls, prior to signing a lease. We find it important to validate our initial impression of an individual and make the final decision based on the various interactions we have had, and the tangible data on the qualitative reports. Being able to compare them to a number of individuals provides you with the opportunity of making the selection from the best of the bunch.

Chapter Twelve

Handling Calls

Handle issues like you live there and they are directly affecting you. This is something we preach over and over again, and should never be taken lightly. It is too easy to put something off because you are not, or think you are not, directly affected. What most landlords don't realize is that it is directly affecting them, in terms of lease renewals and putting a new renter in the unit. Any call or trouble with the unit, that isn't handled quickly, is a poor reflection on the overall living experience someone will have there.

The first step is to make sure the renter can find the right phone number quickly and knows who to call, for what issue. Provide your renter with a list of emergency numbers at move in, especially if they are from out of the area such as:

➤ Your home, cell, work numbers, and any other you feel comfortable giving them (like your vacation house, if applicable, etc.). If you leave for any extended period of time, let them know, and provide them with a way of getting in touch with you.

➤ Association customer care numbers and emergency numbers for after hours

➤ Utility—Gas

➤ Utility—Electrical

➤ Utility—Water

➤ Hospital

➤ Fire

➤ Police—Non-emergency numbers

After the move in, there are other community numbers you can provide. This is a gracious gesture and will make their adjustment into a new and stressful situation easier. This will also minimize the number of calls you receive and help build the relationship. They could include:

➢ Waste
➢ Cable
➢ Telephone
➢ Area Postal Depot

What if something breaks and needs to be taken care of?

Handle it as quickly as possible because:

➢ Not handling it will cause the problem to get worse, which leads to more of a repair effort and cost
➢ Aggravating and frustrating your renter makes them more likely to disrespect your property and not maintain it
➢ You, the landlord, won't have anxiety and stress worrying about the problem

If everything is new, you shouldn't be overly burdened with appliance repair issues. We are proactive with our renters. When we buy furnace filters for our primary residence, we pick up a few extras for our renters. Drop them off when you are collecting the rent. Not only is this a nice gesture for your renters, it reinforces the point that you want them to replace the filter. This could also decrease the need to do a major clean, or repair, to your furnace. This is the same concept as changing the oil in your car. By keeping an eye on the property, you might save yourself a major repair. In addition, you are slightly reducing your renter's utility costs, which yield more money they can use to pay the monthly rent. Don't be shy in pointing this out.

We have heard the GOLDEN RULE from our mothers on countless occasions—treat others like you would want to be treated. As with any relationship, there are going to be times when you need each other. It is much easier to ask a friend for a favor vs. someone with whom you have a strained relationship.

For those renters who we have not had any problems with, who have paid their rent on time, and kept the place relatively clean; we have given them a bottle of wine on the anniversary of the lease, or at Christmas. We have helped them out with a personal issue, congratulated them on a birthday, or significant event. You generally get back what you put in to any relationship. It's amazing what kind of dividends a simple gesture of kindness can generate.

You want a good renter to stay, so you feel comfortable about wanting to renew their lease, and your renter feels equally good about committing to paying your mortgage for another lease period. They will brag about it when THEY show the house to the next renter. There is no better situation for you than to have a reliable, responsible, low maintenance renter in your property, for five years.

Realistically, it is going to cost you around $500 to $1,000 to clean and paint your unit, before showing it to a new prospective renter, and you may also have lost rental payments. Minimize the possibility of these costs and the time to find qualified new renters. There are countless ways that you can reward positive behavior. We are not advocating that you spend an inordinate amount of time being gracious to your renters, but a little well timed kindness goes a long way, when you may need it the most.

To repeat once again, the key is to attend quickly to issues or concerns. Ask questions until you fully understand the nature of the difficulty, to determine if the problem is making the property unlivable, or creating a situation that is extremely uncomfortable for them. If so, respond as quickly as you can to right the situation. These are the times when you will be assessed as a landlord. When it is time for the lease renewal, the renter's memories of how you handled situations will resurface. Those memories may impact if they complete the term, or get out early. This is the same situation as the interaction you have with your insurance carrier. All of the companies out there are extremely competent at collecting premiums, but the true test of what they think of you as a customer comes when you need them in a claims situation. Landlord/tenant situations are no different. The renter is your customer, paying your mortgage, and enabling you to gain all of the other benefits (like appreciation and tax benefits), associated with home ownership. Don't lose sight of this symbiotic relationship and continue to nurture it.

Problems with appliances are likely to be the majority of the calls you receive. You can count on most of your major appliances running pretty well for the first seven years or so, without a great deal of maintenance. Be conscious of this time frame, when minor repair costs and aggravation are no longer worth the time and expense of continual repair. Always assess the projected repair cost vs. the potential gains of maintenance free operation of a new unit. A $300 repair fee on a washer that is six years old will not provide you the same return as spending $500 for a new unit, that you can count on for another seven plus years. However, any decision like this must be calculated with the reality of how long you intend to keep the property.

Don't put off a repair—even if the renter says it is okay. Some renters don't want to sound as though they are complaining, or just find it difficult to ask for things. Make the assessment and put yourself in the place of the renter, with the thought—what would make me happy in this situation, if I lived here?

"Treat them like you would want to be treated"

Chapter Thirteen

Working with the Tradesmen

Handle issues that arise in your unit like you own it, because you do. An ignored, relatively minor repair will lead to a problem that will only get worse, more expensive, and compound the frustration and dissatisfaction of your renter. It is critical to have a list of qualified trade people you can access quickly. It is wise to develop a relationship with them. Then, they will respond in a timely manner, do the work, and you won't need to have it redone six months into the future. You don't want to be searching for a qualified plumber when the basement of one of your homes is filled with water.

Assess the nature of the problem personally, if possible. That doesn't necessarily mean you have to run over to the unit every time your renter calls to tell you the air conditioning isn't cooling like it should. Gather the facts and make the calls if it's an area that you need some assistance understanding. This will allow you to personally gauge the problem, so that you can determine whether you can repair it yourself, or need to enlist the services of someone more qualified. You will then be able to precisely explain the nature of the problem, what your repair expectations are, and negotiate the price of the repairs. It will also enhance your credibility with your renter as someone who cares and will take action, when needed. This action will pay dividends when it comes time to request a favor of the renter (like doing a minor repair on their own), or make it easier for them to accept the fact that you are raising the rent during a lease renewal. You will also need them to have the property in a condition to show it, or rave about you as a landlord to a prospective renter, should conditions dictate that they need to move. It would be an unrealistic expectation for a renter to care about a property they do not own, if the owner demonstrates they don't care about it.

On the following page, we list the trades people you'll need to hire. It is a good idea to have one primary contact and, at least one back-up contact, for each trade. Regardless of the relationship, the primary trades people in your network are not waiting to respond to your crisis, and will likely be occupied with another paid engagement. Having more than one trade person can also

138

allow you to validate, or compare, prices that you receive from them. You can make sure the range of price is reasonable. Ensure that your tradesmen are accessible after hours and have some kind of pager, or cell number, you can use to reach them. Because non- business hour work rates are higher, be sure the renter truly needs the repairs completed at that time, and the claim is serious enough to warrant your paying those premium rates.

You should have a network that involves every type of major trade: painter, electrician, plumber, landscaper, and general trades person, even if you have skills in some of those particular areas. We have developed such a group and feel comfortable knowing that these individuals will deal promptly to our requests, and their work will be done well, without the likelihood that we will have to call them back five months after the work was completed. This will cause frustration and cost time and money for you and your renters, which could have been avoided had you had the right person do the work in the first place. You do not want to be searching for a qualified trades person in time of need, such as an emergency repair that needs to be completed during off-hours. This situation will minimize your negotiation leverage.

Expect to pay premium dollar, without the assurance of quality work, if you are fishing through the yellow pages as the basement of one of your properties is filled with water, and your renter is calling you every five minutes at 10:00 PM. According to Murphy, this call will inevitably happen on a Sunday evening, on the day before you were planning to take a vacation, to compound your poor planning. In a situation like this, your benefit is being able to access an individual, in your trusted network, whose work you have certified and trust to be completed at a fair price. The end result is work that is done quickly— before damage and renter dissatisfaction mount. Never select a tradesman without getting a few quotes first, unless it is someone with whom you have done business several times in the past. It is important to understand: the going rate for the job, amount of time required to do the work, what you can expect from a parts and material/labor breakdown, and the type of warranty for the work completed. After each discussion with a prospective tradesman, you will become more informed about the process. Utilize your network of friends and business associates to provide you with recommendations on tradesmen who have performed work for them, to their satisfaction. Consider this as another level of qualification, and an opportunity to fill your pipeline with potential tradesmen from which to choose.

Try to pay them in cash

Most trades people run their own companies and appreciate when their clients deal with them in cash transactions. Some of them even provide additional discounts, if you are willing to pay them in cash, instead of checks or credit cards. The key to this is to ask them if this is something that will help them. Many of them also treat these transactions differently on their books, because it may be more favorable.

You will still need a receipt, regardless of how you pay for the service. Receipts provide the recourse you need, to ask the trades person to back up any service they perform. At the end of the year, you will also need the receipt for your tax deductions. It shows that you spent that money on your unit. In the event of a litigation situation, receipts can also serve as evidence.

Line Up Your Resources In Advance

The following list should provide a guideline on the type of trade partners you will need. There are more that you could use, but that would depend on a few factors, including your level of involvement, and the type of units you are renting.

Carpet

> New carpet dealer

> Repairman for pulls/snags or stains on carpet

> Cleaner to clean carpet between tenants

Painter

Carpenter

Chimney Sweep

Windows

HVAC—Heating and Cooling

Water Heater

Plumber

Electrician

Landscaper—includes yard work and concrete/paving stones

Appliance/Furniture/Cabinet repair

Furnace—Duct/Vent Cleaner

Chapter Fourteen

Accounting For The Profit

Taxes

As with any business, accounting for the tax end of this business is an important aspect in maximizing your returns. We have mentioned several times, throughout this book, that the need for receipts is crucially important for minimizing exposure and will be used for accumulating write-offs.

As with most businesses, the idea is to show as little profit as you can, while still making money. That said, making sure you have as many deductions as possible will be key, when it comes time to filing your taxes. Most of the preparations you do with any unit are considered tax deductions. Even painting, cleaning, mileage to and from the unit and the lease forms are potentially deductible. In this area, we can only provide some guidance and not hard stated rules. In many cases, these rules will vary from state to state, and from tax bracket, to tax bracket. We urge you to consult with your accountant when your taxes are being prepared. We also urge you to talk to your tax advisor prior to purchasing your first unit, so you know how to structure the purchase to maximize your benefits.

We will provide a short list of items that are usually deductible, in the normal course of running your rental business. Usually the rule is—if you spent money to purchase, prepare, rent, maintain, re-rent or sell the unit, then it is deductible.

Deductions

Deductions can come in almost any form. They range from things you spend money on, to things that you don't spend money on, but are still a cost (like mileage). Remember, if you have to put money out on the unit then it is probably deductible. The list below provides some of the more common, but sometimes overlooked, items that can be tax deductions.

Anything that goes into that unit:

➢ Appliances

➢ Painting

- ➤ Advertising
- ➤ Appraisal fees
- ➤ Entertainment with renters
- ➤ Interest
- ➤ Repairs
- ➤ Any work done from contractors or repair people
- ➤ Interest
- ➤ Mortgage Principal Payment
- ➤ Association dues
- ➤ Closing Costs
- ➤ Attorney fees
- ➤ Lender fees
- ➤ Depreciation
- ➤ Carpet
- ➤ Trips to house
- ➤ Dinner/Lunch when you have initial meeting, lease signing

Income

Income is defined as the money you receive in monthly rent. You will need to show this as income every year on your taxes. In the IRS' eyes, this is used to offset your expenses, which ultimately figures into your overall gain or loss. You might want to keep copies of each check; in the event you get audited. Your lease will also show the amount of monthly income and the dates you received that income. The only exception would be in the event of an eviction, which would cause the dates and income to differ from the original lease dates. Court papers and other documents you would create and receive during that process can explain that.

Long Term Gain/Loss

There are a couple of ways of dealing with the long-term gains/loses. This depends on how you set it up on the front end, and the amount of money you make annually in your full time job.

Depending on your tax bracket, and the IRS rules that are in place that year, you will either take the gains/loses in that year or you will accumulate them until either you sell the unit, or you make less money throughout the course of the year. As your income increases, you move up in your tax bracket and the number of deductions decrease, which means you won't see them as direct deductions on your tax filing. With regard to this business, those deductions will not go away, but rather, start to accumulate. You will end up getting those deductions when you sell the unit, as they figure in to the overall gain/loss number of that unit.

There are different ways of showing involvement in your properties also. These can be shown as either active or passive involvement. You will need to make this decision on the front end also, and will determine the level of deduction owed to you, and how aggressive you can be with your accounting. Discuss the impact of using either method with your accountant, prior to making your determination.

There are other deductions that will calculate into the annual, or final accounting, such as: depreciation, purchase price and sale price. Your gain or loss number can be estimated on the front end, with your accountant's help.

Due to the complexity of this issue, we strongly advise you to seek further information from a qualified tax advisor in your area. We also suggest you use their services annually to prepare your tax returns, due to the rules changing from time to time.

Chapter Fifteen

The Legal Section

The legal aspects are similar to the accounting portions of running this business. You will need to have a good real estate attorney from the beginning, and make sure you use their services throughout your first couple of rentals. A call to that person from time to time, to ask for advice, can be a charge free interaction, depending on the relationship and the amount of units you own.

You will also want to make sure you maintain this relationship throughout your time in the rental business. During this time, you will probably buy more units, and eventually sell these units. You may also require the services of an attorney, in the event of a tenant issue. Although these issues should be minimal, by following the processes prescribed in this book, they may still occur. Attorneys can be found through ads in local papers, or yellow pages, or through realtors. When making your selection, qualify them—like you would any other trades. See several to determine:

➢ Years of experience

➢ Rate structure

➢ Services they provide

➢ Type of impression you get; personable, trustworthy, reliable, competent

➢ Advice they give you in personalizing a generic rental agreement

➢ If they are investors as well, and own property

➢ Responsiveness and desire to have you as a client

Most initial consultations are free, so take advantage of an opportunity to get educated. While setting up the appointment, indicate that you are a real estate investor and are looking at establishing a relationship with a good attorney. See how enthusiastic they are in arranging an appointment and working with you. If you get the impression, while setting up the appointment and during the first consultation, that they are not overly interested to retain you as a client, they likely won't be responsive when you really need them. There are plenty of attorneys to choose from. Find a good one for you. Although you will rarely use them, if/when litigation situations arise; they can be costly and stressful. This would not be the ideal time to be searching for an attorney.

The Lease and Rider

Your attorney will help you modify the stock lease that you picked up from the office supply store, to meet your individual needs and help you create your rider page. They are on your payroll and are paid to protect you; as best they can, from the exposures of the rental business. Many real estate attorneys have rental properties as a form of retirement income, so they are familiar with the good and bad side of renting. If they don't own units themselves, then they certainly have clients that own multiple units. They might be a source for networking, or drawing from their experiences. Use them to gather as much information as possible, to help your business run smoother.

Your attorney can reiterate the need for receipts, CO detectors, smoke detectors, and other safety related items (such as annual furnace cleaning). That person will also be able to help you define a more complete list, tailored to your specific circumstances, and the case precedence in your area. This important point has been stressed many times in this book—and they will echo that sentiment.

Standard Lease

We mentioned that you will be able to buy a standard lease at your local office supply store, which should be somewhat tailored to your local area. These need to be customized to your individual situation. Some items on the lease form may not be important to you, while other items may need to be restated to fit your needs. There are points on the lease that will not apply. You will need to cross out those items, each time you sign up a new renter. Your attorney will walk through the first lease, and explain what each section states, and the potential liability of both parties. To this very point, that is the reason the rider will require corrected, or added language—to create a document specific to your area and needs.

Rider contains "other rules" specific to you

The rider should contain language that is specific to your situation, area, and needs. This is a sample list of some of the subjects you may want to cover in a rider:

> ➤ Late payment fee, specifying what day of the month the rent is due, and the daily penalty for late payment
>
> ➤ Carpet cleaning fee

➤ Renters should abide by the terms of the homeowners' association by-laws

➤ Pets

➤ Security deposit, when it will be repaid and under what conditions

➤ Showing parameters for the renter, prior to the termination of the lease

➤ Notice of inspection

➤ Grounds requirements

➤ Appliances owned by you, what is expected in terms of general maintenance and penalties for misuse and neglect

➤ Occupancy limits—who can live in the home (On more than one occasion, we have heard where a homeowner failed to specify this clause in a rider, and found themselves with a situation where more than one family took up residence)

➤ Disturbance issues—"The good neighbor clause"

➤ Clause that specifies damages from furniture (like a waterbed)

Your attorney will spend some time with you, asking questions and sharing some of their experiences. All of that information should be captured, using the rider. As with the lease, you will want the renter to initial some specific items on this document and then sign the bottom. We always make sure we get the renter to read, and acknowledge, the clause-specifying penalty for late pay. Make this point early in the relationship so there is no misunderstanding of your expectations. You won't be in business long if you are not vigilant about collecting all of the rent, on time, every month. Don't set a precedent with your renters about being lenient in collecting the rent. You can develop a situation where five days becomes two weeks, and continual requests are not respected, or acknowledged.

Discrimination

It is illegal to discriminate based on race, sex, or age—and the rental business is no exception to that rule. Throughout this book, we have tried to reinforce that the main criteria should always be based on credit. There have been many people in this business, who have chosen to rent to a less qualified renter, simply because the more qualified renter is in a group that they do not like. Many of those folks have found themselves in a lot of trouble, because of this practice.

The rule is that *everyone*, no matter what color, sex, or age, can have good credit and be a great renter. The better the credit, the better the renter they will be—regardless of the race, age, or sex of that individual.

It doesn't take much for a disgruntled renter to make a phone call to a government agency to complain about you. Shortly after that point, you may get caught in a sting, aimed to vet out the legitimacy of that complaint. Either way it comes out, you will have some attention that you don't need, or want, and may end up in a lawsuit. If you do your best to be fair to every potential renter, and stick to the methodology we have profiled in this book, you will minimize your exposure, and the headaches involved in dealing with a discrimination case. Don't set yourself up for a litigation situation. If you choose not to rent to someone, base it on the research you have completed. For those you disqualify as a result of a bad credit score, retain a copy in your records. In the event of future litigation, you will be glad you did.

This is another area that you will want to discuss with your attorney. That person will have many stories of other clients who have received that unwanted attention, and paid a heavy price.

Obligations

CO detectors, smoke detectors, fire extinguishers, furnace cleaning, and many other points that we have mentioned are all aimed at lessoning your exposure, in the unlikely event of a lawsuit. Keeping receipts is the way you illustrate that you have done the things to keep your renters safe, and provide a safe living environment. Doing the right thing and having proof that you did your best is wise.

As long as you are providing a safe environment and treating your renters right, they are less likely to want to cause you problems, and sue you over that issue. When all is said and done, you can't stop someone from suing you, if they want to try to make some quick cash, or feel as though they have a legitimate reason. They may see you as a "rich landlord" and know that the money will come out of the insurance company's pocket, and not your's. If you have to go before the court, all you can do is protect yourself, by having the proper documentation with you. Discuss this point, in depth, with your attorney.

Liabilities

By default, you do have a fair amount of liability when it comes to someone getting hurt. That is a fact you can't avoid. People fall, people get burned, people get sick, and in general, people can hurt themselves.

Whether it is falling in the tub, falling on some ice in the driveway, or falling down the stairs, things will happen that are totally out of your control. As mentioned, all the court wants to know is that you did your best to protect them from harm. Keep records and be able to show them, and it should reduce your exposure. This is yet another important point that you should discuss with your attorney.

Going to court

Going to court is never fun, for any reason. It involves your time and money to defend yourself. This is counter to the "make it easy" philosophy—owning a no hassle business that makes lots of money. This is an area where the idea is to do *more* than you should, because you never know if you are going to have to go to court. The idea of being proactive means you will do more work than you have to, which is the opposite of making everything easy. Like an insurance policy, it is a waste of money—until you need to use it. Receipts, signatures, and records are additional effort that you won't need to do, but will save you a lot of money, if you have to go to court.

This point is worth repeating one more time. Keep receipts, and do the right thing.

If you do go to court for any reason (a lawsuit or an eviction), everything needs to be documented. Generally, the courts look at landlords as being culpable, and will usually favor the renter. If you can show/prove that you did your best, and the renter was blatantly wrong, then you stand a better chance of having the case thrown out of court. Without receipts, it is your word against the renter's, and at that point, they have the distinct advantage.

Make sure you have the furnace cleaned annually, and keep the receipt. Change the battery in the smoke detector, and get a signature from your renter that you did so. Test the battery in the presence of your renter. The same goes for the CO detector. Make sure you give them a copy of the by-laws, and get the signature that shows they received that copy. This may seem redundant and a bit overly cautious, but if you have to go to court, you will think it was the best advice ever. Protect yourself.

Insurance

You will need to take out an insurance policy on each unit covering everything the association policy doesn't cover. The association will normally cover the shell of the unit, meaning everything up to the drywall. The drywall, flooring, electrical, windows, appliances, and blinds are your responsibility. In the event of a fire, the association will have the shell rebuilt, so they can get the neighborhood back to the way it looked prior to the fire. Your responsibility is to finish the unit.

You will also want to take out an umbrella policy, over and above the policy that you take out on the unit. These are different policies that serve different duties. Let's say you have a base policy on the unit of $500,000, and something happens. If the total claim is one million dollars, then you pay the second five hundred thousand out of your own pocket. If you have an umbrella policy, it will pay the second part of that claim, and your personal assets are more secure. Your insurance agent should be able to set up the correct policies to help protect you and your personal assets.

Here's a good thing. You need one base policy for each unit, but only one umbrella policy for all of the units. The umbrella policy is taken out on your primary homeowner's policy, at a slight increase to your normal rate. Make sure you discuss this with your insurance agent, so that you arrive at an adequate, overall number that provides the protection you need.

The renter should also take out a policy to cover their belongings. That is up to them, and you can't force them to have a policy. There are some exceptions to this rule. One exception is a waterbed. You can write a line into your rider that forces them to insure the damage incurred, in the event of a leak in the waterbed. Before you sign the least, you will want to ask if they own one, and inform them of this rule, if they want to keep it in your unit.

Local Renter's rights

In some cities, there are city mandated "renter's rights" that you will have to be aware of, and know how they affect your lease. Usually, they take most of the "teeth" out of your lease. They are designed to make sure that the landlord doesn't write language into the lease that takes away all of the rights from the renter, and allows the landlord to do whatever they want. Some of it makes sense, and some slants everything to the renter's side.

Check with your attorney to see if the city that your unit is in uses this. If it does, then they can inform you on how to write your lease and rider, and what rights you have left.

Chapter Sixteen

Associations and Management Firms

Associations

Associations are in place to insure that all of the units are maintained at a similar and reasonable level. They do this by collecting a monthly dollar amount from each owner in the community, and applying that to things such as: landscaping, snow plowing, painting, garbage pickup, and other common maintenance items. The amount varies from development to development, and is based on the projected costs, calculated by the original developers, and tailored slightly by the current board. There is also a reserve amount built in to that amount, to cover long term issues or unplanned items.

In many associations, the reserves that build up over the years are a large dollar amount. Many board members have pondered the question of what to do with all of that extra money. If you have ever been part of an association board, you have seen this first hand.

The question is whether to lower the monthly amount, due to the excess money not being required for expenses and common projects like roofing or siding; or just leave it alone, and let it continue to build. If you lower the monthly amount, you will not get any complaints and it will pass by the homeowners without discussion. If something comes up and there is a need to raise money, it will be difficult to do so. People are willing to pay less, but are obviously resistant to paying more. If you don't have the money, and need it, then you could have a special assessment, which needs to be discussed and passed. Special assessments are also not popular for anyone selling their house, or looking to do that soon. Would you want to buy a house if you knew that you would have to write a check for five thousand dollars one month after that purchase? That would probably motivate you to look at buying a different house. On the other hand, would you write a check for the five thousand dollars if you knew that you were selling your house, and wouldn't be there to enjoy the benefits of that money? As a rule, special assessments are never popular.

Earlier, we mentioned that part of the association fee equation is the projected cost that the builder calculated, as the amount of money required to complete ongoing maintenance projects, while putting some aside for future projects. There are a few factors that come into play in that formula. Some builders think if they show higher association dues when they are selling the houses, it will turn away potential buyers and take longer to sell out the development. They are correct. As a result, they try to keep these as low as possible, and accomplish this by taking out some of the items usually covered by the association. Snow plowing, garbage pickup, and some exterior items, are a few items that might not be included. This leaves the liability of those items on the home owner. The builder will sell some more houses faster, but be careful, because down the road, you may be responsible for the shortage that causes a special assessment. We have seen things like balconies called a special assessment, because the builder included the coverage of the framing, but not the paint and upkeep. This means that about fifteen years later, they all need to be torn down and replaced. This also means that the current board had to increase the monthly fees, so they could include some painting in the future.

It is important to leave an association guide for your renter; in addition to emergency numbers for the association customer care departments. Instruct them to call you in most situations, and not the association emergency number, as you want to determine whether the issue is your own (the owner), theirs' (the renter), or the associations'.

Emergencies are typically defined as, "not being able to live in the home until the next business day." Emergencies that constitute a call to you, and/or the association would include:

➢ Leaks from drains, faucets, toilets or any other plumbing

➢ Air conditioning pipes, leaking or freezing

➢ A total stoppage of the plumbing, after plunging has been tried

➢ The discovery of frozen drains or pipes that could rupture

➢ Complete loss of electrical power, for the entire home

➢ Non–functioning sump pump that is, or could result in, basement flooding

➢ Complete loss of heat during the winter, after checking the electrical switch and breakers

The association typically takes care of what is referred to as common elements, which typically involve some of the following:

> Siding, which includes gutters and downspouts
> Concrete drives, walks, stairs, foundations
> Landscaping
> Roofs
> Balconies—typically structure
> Driveways
> Grass cutting
> Light fixtures
> Snow removal
> Garbage pickup

Not all associations provide all of the above services. These are determined by the board, and mainly based on the amount of money collected monthly. Overall, it is a pretty simple formula. Just like most things in life, the more money they collect from you on a monthly basis (in the form of your assessments), the more services they are able to provide.

This should be something you look at carefully, during your analysis of your costs. Since the association is providing some of the services that you might have to deal with yourself, at retail cost and on your own time, it sometimes makes sense to pay a bit more in your dues. The association can probably purchase said item or service for less than you could, for a single house. They will also keep the records and manage the process for you, which will relieve you of those tasks. Remember that make it easy and you will do better and make more money.

There are other things that the association boards will do to help you, other than just repair and maintenance. One primary function of the board is to insure that the standards of the neighborhood are maintained. This means they want all of the properties to look the same, and ensure that you, as a resident, do not infringe on your neighbor's rights, or the enjoyment of his or her property. This includes making sure that your neighbor doesn't park his cement truck, or thirty foot stretch limo, in his driveway, on the weekends. It also insures that your neighbor doesn't pull all of his trees out of his lawn, or paint his house an outrageous color.

The idea of keeping things uniform is so that the property values continue to go up, and a few houses aren't responsible for pulling down your value, due to some personal preferences. This also includes sheds, porches, and additions that can make a property look out of place and, in some cases, ugly.

Management Firms

Management firms are companies that are set up to take care of the duties and responsibilities that we have covered prior to this point—renting and maintaining the property, and the relationship with the renter. They will handle all, or part, of the process—from running the ad, to re-renting the unit, and everything in between. They will also deal with any repair calls that need attention.

The principle of this book is to provide you with a step-by-step methodology that allows you to be able to run this business yourself, and not rely on anyone else, while still working at your full time job. In certain situations, you may want to use a firm to take care of some of this for you. Those situations are, in our mind, limited to a few.

You might want to use a management firm if you want to make more money with some money you have parked in a money market, or aren't satisfied with your returns in the market, and don't have the time to handle the process yourself. You will still need to find the unit and buy it, but from that point, you can turn it over and let someone else manage all or part of the process for you.

You might also own some units, but for one reason or another, need to relocate to another area. It also might not make sense for you to sell these units. This would be another case where it might make sense to use a management firm, in some capacity. As mentioned earlier, this is not the kind of business that you want to try to run from another state. Renting and taking care of any issues that might arise would preclude you, because of distance.

Management firms require some form of payment for their services. Depending on what you want them to do, they might just take one month's rent for finding renters, and doing the paperwork, to rent your unit. If you want them to do more, then the cost goes up from there, and will vary from firm to firm, depending on the services they provide.

There are a couple of other "hidden" things that you need to know about these firms, that can sometimes cost you a bit more money than doing it yourself. Most management firms have companies that they deal with on a regular basis, that do work for them. This can be a good thing. Those companies usually respond quicker, because it is a "regular" client and they can count on getting work from that firm, from month to month. This can also be a bad thing, because sometimes they get kickbacks, or it might be someone's brother, relative or friend who ends up doing the work. The bill can also be slightly inflated so the management company can take part of the margin, knowing there isn't anyone that will be checking or getting other bids, for the same work. You can always put an approval process in place. This requires them to have the work approved by you, prior to having it done. You can also ask for competitive bids, prior to having the work done. These are two safeguards against out of control repair costs. These actions still don't guarantee you won't be overcharged. This falls under the category of paying for convenience. If you can do it yourself and select all of the contractors, then you will save money, in the long run. If you are in a situation where you have chosen not to do this, then you will need to rely, or trust, someone else to handle this part of the process and accept the fact that you are losing profit, in exchange for having another party look after these issues.

This is a quick refresher checklist to help you decide when to use management firms:

When to use them

➢ If you have money, but don't have time to manage all, or part of the process

➢ If you are relocating and it doesn't make sense to sell the units

What they charge

➢ Usually a fee equal to one month's rent, per lease period

What they do for what you pay them

➢ Find renters

➢ Field the calls

➢ Line up tradesmen and oversee the repairs

Pros and cons of doing it yourself vs. using them

➢ Pros—Time saving

➢ Cons—lack of control, don't have the same interest as you do, inflated markups from the tradesmen they have agreements with, not as diligent in qualifying potential renters

Depending on your situation, it might make sense for you to use a management firm or save the money and do it yourself. Just like anything else, if you throw some money at the problem, then you will save some time.

Chapter Seventeen

Getting started today

Remember the rules

Credit is everything

People with good credit have it for a reason. They typically are financially responsible and pay off their debt. Bad credit results from a pattern of late and non-payments. If they aren't paying others, it is likely that you will also have difficulty collecting your rent. Avoid these difficulties from the outset by properly qualifying your prospective renters. Better to have a property vacant for a longer period of time, than move someone in who doesn't fit the criteria we have provided in the book, and ultimately have to go through an eviction. An eviction is a costly and stressful waste of your time, and money.

Location, Location, Location

It is commonly referred to as "curb appeal." Simply put, this speaks to how one feels when they look at the property. Is it appealing, or do you feel like you are glad it is someone else's home? What does the property back up to? Is it a large retail store and are you looking at the loading docks? Or it is a golf course, lake or nature preserve? Is there traffic, or is it quiet?

Proximity to large businesses draws people into the area so they can be close to their employer. We don't know many people who enjoy a lengthy commute or getting up at 5 AM to beat traffic. In profiling areas to purchase property, keep in mind why the area would be considered desirable to live in:

➢ Businesses that provide employment opportunities

➢ Recreational opportunities, water parks, forest preserves, bike and hiking trails

➢ Transportation, such as rail stations

➢ Retail outlets, groceries, clothing

➢ Restaurants and entertainment

➢ Good schools

People are always looking for convenience and access to goods and services that they need on a weekly, or biweekly, basis which include:

➢ Groceries

➢ Dry Cleaners

➢ Gas

➢ General retail

"Your costs have nothing to do with what you charge for monthly rents"

Add up all of your costs and give these to your accountant. He will use this information for tax purposes. They shouldn't be used to set your monthly rental rate. Use the information in the ad papers to determine what your competition is charging for similar units in your area. Do they have great locations, or do they back up to a train station? This might help your rate a bit, but it won't skew it to the point where your tiny down payment, bad interest rate, or an overpaid purchase price can be overcome.

The market sets the price—not your monthly bills on that unit.

"Appearance can make the difference between renting and another showing"

Does the unit look like it is well maintained, or are the shutters hanging down on the windows? Do the appliances look new and are they sized right for the unit, or are they old and remind you of living in a college dorm? Is the carpet faded and worn? The prospective renter might be there for thirty minutes looking at your unit. You want them to feel good in the first three minutes. Prepare the units as if you are going to be living there for the next five years.

Fix it now.

Always think about the time when the next prospective renter is talking to the current renter. Will they say nice things about how quickly you made the problem go away? What if you lived there? Would you fix the problem as soon as possible, or would you wait until it was convenient? Would you like to live there for a few days without water, a dishwasher or a refrigerator? Treat renters like you would want to be treated.

Keep it rented.

Vacancy costs money and you are in the business to get paid for time. Many people don't understand that even though they are renting out a unit, what they are actually getting paid for is the amount of time the renter spends in that unit. A day, a week, or month without a renter means you don't have income for that amount of time. Keeping that unit occupied means you get paid, and in turn, you can pay your bills against that unit.

We have used big business bulletin boards, newspapers, word of mouth, and yard signs to advertise our properties. If you're feeling particularly bold, pick up the phone and speak to a Human Resources (HR) representative in a local company. Let him/her know that you have a place available. Extend the offer of a "thank you lunch," if they can recommend an employee that is seeking housing. The HR representative might be able to assist both you, and an employee thinking of relocating, with one of their most significant decisions—housing. Your advantage is that you have found another source for prospective renters. If HR is relocating an employee, rather than hiring someone locally, they probably fit your desirable renter criteria. Also inquire about the possibility of doing corporate housing directly through the company. A lot of larger companies actually have corporate housing for employees or long term consults, and there is always the possibility of signing longer agreements, from three to five years.

Delay only costs appreciation.

Every day that you delay getting started is another day that someone else gained from the appreciation of that unit. Appreciation is usually viewed as an annual number, but occurs on a daily basis. The longer it takes you to make the decision to move forward, the less money you make.

Once you make the decision this is something you want to do, start immediately.

"Don't let your retirement catch up with you"

Chapter Eighteen

Final Thoughts

Do you realize that 90% of people who purchase books do not read past the first couple of chapters? If you have read all of our material to this point, we congratulate you. You likely have the determination, dedication, and perseverance to "Prosper Through Real Estate." We have provided a series of checklists that provide a step-by-step process for you to follow our proven and successful methodology, which has led to the creation of this book.

We have also designed a web site to provide our readers with ongoing education and relevant information. It is our intent to ensure that your education continues, and that you network with other real investors and experts through the site. Come and visit us at www.prosperthroughrealestate.com. On our site you will find:

➢ Our mission statement

➢ Biographies of the authors

➢ Information to know your authors, their combined experience in real estate and investments, their goals and objectives.

➢ Online courses and material

➢ Course materials available for download and instructional sessions available for registration.

➢ A place to ask question of the authors and regular columnists, via email and periodic chat sessions. Questions and answers will be featured on the site for the benefit of other members and viewers.

➢ Features and contributions from other real estate experts. Obtain information from leading real estate experts in a wide variety of topics to benefit you, the investor. We will feature regular columnists along with guest contributors and keep you aware of features and information through email alerts. In addition, we will feature stories and tips from our members.

➢ A download section containing the latest forms, checklists, and other materials. These tools will provide you with the knowledge necessary to "Prosper through Real Estate"

➢ Events and seminar information. We will provide you dates and logistical information on events and seminars near you.

➢ Discussion forums with other member investors. We have also provided you with the opportunity to post comments on the site and network with others members in the real estate investment community. Real people, just like you, all looking to "Prosper Through Real Estate."

➢ Member success stories. We will feature quotes and stories from other readers and members who have taken the initiative to follow our guidance and methodologies to become successful investors, and are now prospering and supplementing their primary income stream, thus becoming less dependent on it. Learn and be inspired from fellow members and hear their stories.

"It's not what you make … its not what you keep … its what you do with what you keep"

Open up an account solely for the purpose of buying investment properties. Determine what you can funnel into that account on a weekly, biweekly, or monthly basis. If you can allocate a portion of your earnings into this account automatically, through a direct deposit, while still being able to cover your monthly costs and expenses, it is amazing how quickly this money accumulates. Look for non-traditional places from which to pull money to use for this purpose.

Have a game plan in mind when you have located the type of townhouse you are looking for, at a price where you can get started. Factor in about-15%–25%of the cost for the down payment and miscellaneous expenses like closing costs, attorney fees, and insurance. Establish a financial target to work towards. This financial goal will channel your energies and focus. After your first property, repeat the process. Hopefully you will be in a cash positive situation and be able to add another monthly income stream into the account, along with your primary income. Other ways of adding to your "Real Estate Account" are through tax returns, on mortgage interest audits, and refinancing.

We hope that you have acquired the knowledge and inspiration you need to follow through, and take the plunge into investing. Both of us were tentative about purchasing our first property, especially after hearing all of the recycled horror stories about nightmare renters, and the subsequent trials and tribulations associated with them. By following the methodology we have detailed in this book, and finding great renters, we were both surprised at the lack of issues and problems. There is a feeling of utter elation when we pick up the rent check every month from a happy renter. Knowing that the equity and appreciation have increased even since the last month is inspiring.

Once a year, when we visit our accountants, this feeling is reinforced due to the tax benefits we receive. In addition, there is a great deal of comfort in knowing that we have a very liquid asset that can be sold relatively quickly, should life deal you an unexpected calamity like a major career set back, or a health crisis. Very few other investments afford you that kind of flexibility.

"It's not what you make" ...

"It's not what you keep"....

"It's what you do with what you keep"

Good luck on your journey. We hope you **"Prosper through Real Estate."** We will see you at the top.

Appendix

Real Estate Terms

During the entire process of finding, negotiating, buying, financing, renting, and re-renting, you will hear and need to understand many potentially new terms. Just like any new venture, whether baseball, shopping, babies, business or other countries, each comes with their own set of terms. Knowing those terms will help you converse with others involved in those ventures. The following terms are all part of the real estate language.

You will probably never use, or need to know, most of the following terms. We wanted to list as many as possible, in the event they come up in the future. There are, however a number of them that you will want to become familiar with, and hear most of the time. We have put "**" next to them.

** 1031 Exchange

A 1031 Tax Deferral permits taxpayers to reinvest the proceeds from the sale of property held for investment or business purposes into another investment or business property, and defer capital gains tax that would otherwise be due on the initial sale.

Abstract (of title)

A summary of the public records relating to the title of a particular piece of land. An attorney or title insurance company reviews an abstract of title to determine whether there are any title defects, which must be cleared before a buyer can purchase a clear, marketable, and insurable title.

Acceleration clause

A provision in a mortgage that gives the lender the right to demand payment of the entire principal balance, if a monthly payment is missed.

Acceptance

An offeree's consent to enter into a contract and be bound by the terms of the offer.

Additional principal payment

A payment by a borrower of more than the scheduled principal amount due, in order to reduce the remaining balance on the loan.

Adjustable-rate mortgage (ARM)

A mortgage that permits the lender to adjust the mortgage's interest rate periodically, on the basis of changes in a specified index. Interest rates may move up or down, as market conditions change.

Adjusted basis of loan

The original cost of a property, plus the value of any capital expenditures for improvements to the property, minus any depreciation taken.

Adjustment date for mortgage

The date on which the interest rate changes for an adjustable-rate mortgage (ARM).

Affordability analysis (cost vs. expense analysis)

A detailed analysis of your ability to afford the purchase of a home. An affordability analysis takes into consideration your income, liabilities, and available funds, along with the type of mortgage you plan to use, the area where you want to purchase a home, and the closing costs that you might expect to pay.

Amenity

A feature of real property that enhances its attractiveness and increases the occupant's or user's satisfaction, although the feature is not essential to the property's use. Natural amenities include a pleasant or desirable location near water, scenic views of the surrounding area, etc. Human-made amenities include swimming pools, tennis courts, community buildings, and other recreational facilities.

** Amortization

The gradual repayment of a mortgage loan by installments.

Amortization schedule (loan buydown schedule)

A timetable for payment of a mortgage loan. An amortization schedule shows the amount of each payment applied to interest and principal, and shows the remaining balance after each payment is made.

Amortization term (note/mortgage term)

The amount of time required to amortize the mortgage loan. The amortization term is expressed as a number of months. For example, for a 30-year fixed-rate mortgage, the amortization term is 360 months.

** Annual percentage rate (APR)

The cost of a loan, stated in yearly terms, including interest, insurance, and the origination fee (points), expressed as a percentage. Often applied to mortgages, credit cards, and automobile financing.

Annuity

An amount paid yearly, or at other regular intervals, often on a guaranteed dollar basis.

Application (loan)

A form used to apply for a mortgage loan and to record pertinent information concerning a prospective mortgagor and the proposed security. Lenders use the information on the loan application to evaluate whether or not they can give the loan, and if so, the amount of money they can lend.

** Appraisal

A written analysis of the estimated value of a property prepared by a qualified appraiser. Contrast with home inspection.

** Appraised value

The appraised value is the dollar amount that the property is worth, based on comparison of other properties of similar size, location, and functionality in the area. When you are either purchasing the property or doing a refinance, an appraisal will be done to determine its market value. The bank wants to make sure that they will not be "upside down" in the event that you default on the loan and they have to foreclose on that property.

Appraiser

A person qualified by education, training, and experience to estimate the value of real property and personal property. This person will compare sale amounts of other similar properties in the area to assess the market value of your property.

** Appreciation

An increase in the value of a property due to changes in market conditions or other causes.

** Assessed value

The valuation placed on property by a public tax assessor, for purposes of taxation. This is usually not a reflection of the real value of your property.

** Assessment

The process of placing a value on property for the strict purpose of taxation. May also refer to a levy against property for a special purpose, such as a sewer assessment.

Assessor

A public official who establishes the value of a property for taxation purposes.

Asset

Anything of monetary value that is owned by a person. Assets include real property, personal property, and enforceable claims against others (including bank accounts, stocks, mutual funds, etc.).

Assignment

The transfer of a mortgage from one person to another.

Assumable mortgage

A mortgage that can be taken over ("assumed"), by the buyer when a home is sold.

Assumption

The transfer of the seller's existing mortgage to the buyer. See assumable mortgage.

Assumption clause

A provision in an assumable mortgage that allows a buyer to assume responsibility for the mortgage from the seller. The loan does not need to be paid in full by the original borrower upon sale or transfer of the property.

Assumption fee

The fee paid to a lender (usually by the purchaser of real property), resulting from the assumption of an existing mortgage.

Attorney-in-fact

One who holds a power of attorney from another to execute documents on behalf of the grantor of the power.

Balloon mortgage

A mortgage that has level monthly payments that will amortize it over a stated term, but that provides for a lump sum payment to be due at the end of an earlier specified term. The principal and interest on the loan are amortized over a longer period than the actual term of the mortgage.

Balloon payment

The final lump sum payment that is made at the maturity date of a balloon mortgage.

Bankrupt

A person, firm, or corporation that, through a court proceeding is relieved from the payment of all debts, after the surrender of all assets to a court-appointed trustee.

Bankruptcy

A proceeding in a federal court in which a debtor who owes more than his or her assets, can relieve the debts by transferring his or her assets to a trustee.

Before-tax income

Income before taxes are deducted.

Beneficiary

The person designated to receive the income from a trust, estate, or a deed of trust.

Bequeath

To transfer personal property through a will upon death of holder.

Bill of sale

A written document that transfers title to personal property.

Binder Contract or "offer to purchase"

A preliminary agreement to buy real estate that is secured by the payment of earnest money. A binder secures the right to purchase real estate upon agreed terms for a limited period of time. If the buyer changes his or her mind, or is unable to purchase, the earnest money is forfeited unless the binder expressly provides that it is to be refunded.

Biweekly payment mortgage

A mortgage that requires payments to reduce the debt every two weeks (instead of the standard monthly payment schedule). The 26 (or possibly 27), biweekly payments are each equal to one-half of the monthly payment that would be required if the loan were a standard 30-year fixed-rate mortgage, and they are usually drafted from the borrower's bank account. The result for the borrower is a substantial savings in interest.

Blanket insurance policy

A single policy that covers more than one piece of property (or more than one person).

Blanket mortgage

The mortgage that is secured by a cooperative project, as opposed to the share loans on individual units within the project.

Bona fide

In good faith, without fraud or without intent to fraud.

Breach

A violation of any legal obligation or commitment.

Bridge loan

A form of second trust that is collateralized by the borrower's present home (which is usually for sale), in a manner that allows the proceeds to be used for closing on a new house before the present home is sold. Sometimes used as builders loan.

Broker

A person who, for a commission or a fee, brings parties together and assists in negotiating contracts between them. Many times this will be used in reference to a mortgage.

Building code

Local regulations that control the design, construction, and materials used in construction. Building codes are based on safety and health standards.

Buydown account

An account in which funds are held so that they can be applied as part of the monthly mortgage payment as each payment comes due, during the period that an interest rate buydown plan is in effect.

Buydown mortgage

A temporary buydown is a mortgage on which an initial lump sum payment is made by any party to reduce a borrower's monthly payments, during the first few years of a mortgage. A permanent buydown reduces the interest rate over the entire life of a mortgage.

Cap

A provision of an adjustable-rate mortgage (ARM), that limits how much the interest rate or mortgage payments may increase or decrease. See lifetime payment cap, lifetime rate cap, periodic payment cap, and periodic rate cap.

Capital

The net worth of a business represented by the amount by which its assets exceed liabilities.
Money used to create income, either as an investment in a business or an income property. The accumulated wealth of a person or business. The money or property comprising the wealth owned or used by a person or business enterprise.

Capital expenditure

The cost of an improvement made to extend the useful life of a property or to add to its value.

** Cash-out refinance

A refinance transaction in which the amount of money received from the new loan exceeds the total of the money needed to repay the existing first mortgage, closing costs, points, and the amount required to satisfy any outstanding subordinate mortgage liens. In other words, a refinance transaction in which the borrower receives additional cash that can be used for any purpose.

Certificate of deposit

A document written by a bank or other financial institution that is evidence of a deposit, with the issuer's promise to return the deposit plus earnings at a specified interest rate within a specified time period.

Certificate of deposit index

An index that is used to determine interest rate changes for certain adjustable-rate mortgage (ARM), plans. It represents the weekly average of secondary market interest rates on six-month negotiable certificates of deposit. See adjustable-rate mortgage.

Certificate of title

A certificate issued by a title company or a written opinion rendered by an attorney, that the seller has good marketable and insurable title to the property offered for sale. A certificate of title offers no protection against any hidden defects in the title that an examination of the records could not reveal. The issuer of a certificate of title is liable only for damages due to negligence. The protection offered to a homeowner under a certificate of title is not as great as that offered in a title insurance policy.

Chain of title

The history of all of the documents that transfer title to a parcel of real property, starting with the earliest existing document and ending with the most recent. This history will be investigated and guaranteed by the title company.

Change frequency

The frequency (in months), of payment and/or interest rate changes in an adjustable-rate mortgage (ARM).

Clear title

A title that is free of liens or legal questions as to ownership of the property.

** Closing

A meeting at which the buyer signing the mortgage documents and paying closing costs finalizes a sale of a property.

** Closing costs

The expenses that buyers and sellers normally incur while transferring the ownership of a piece of real estate. These costs are in addition to price of the property and are prepaid on the closing day. This is a list:

Buyer's Expenses usually include:

- ➢ Documentary stamps on notes
- ➢ Title insurance

- ➢ Survey charge
- ➢ Appraisal and inspection
- ➢ Recording deed and mortgage
- ➢ Escrow fees
- ➢ Attorney's fee

Seller's Expenses usually include:

- ➢ Escrow fees
- ➢ Recording mortgage
- ➢ Documentary stamps on deed
- ➢ Real estate commission
- ➢ Survey charge
- ➢ Attorney's fee

Closing day

The day on which the formalities of a real estate sale are concluded. The certificate of title, abstract, and deed are generally prepared for the closing by an attorney and charged to the buyer. The buyer signs the mortgage and closing costs are paid. The final closing merely confirms the original agreement reached in the agreement of sale.

** Closing statement

See HUD-1 statement.

Cloud (on title)

An outstanding claim or encumbrance which adversely affects the marketability of title.

Coinsurance

A sharing of insurance risk between the insurer and the insured. Coinsurance depends on the relationship between the amount of the policy and a specified percentage of the actual value of the property insured at the time of the loss.

Coinsurance clause

A provision in a hazard insurance policy that states the amount of coverage that must be maintained—as a percentage of the total value of the property—for the insured to collect the full amount of a loss.

Collateral

An asset (such as a car or a home), that guarantees the repayment of a loan. The borrower risks losing the asset if the loan is not repaid according to the terms of the loan contract.

Collection

The efforts used to bring a delinquent mortgage current and to file the necessary notices to proceed with foreclosure when necessary.

Commission

Money paid to a real estate agent or broker by the seller as compensation for finding a buyer and completing the sale. Usually it's a percentage of the sale price: five to six percent on houses.

Commitment letter

A formal offer by a lender stating the terms under which it agrees to lend money to a home buyer. Also known as a "loan commitment letter."

Common area assessments

Levies against individual unit owners in a condominium or planned unit development (PUD) project for additional capital to defray homeowners' association costs and expenses and to repair, replace, maintain, improve or operate the common areas of the project.

** Common areas

Those portions of a building, land, and amenities owned (or managed), by a planned unit development (PUD) or condominium project's homeowners' association (or a cooperative project's cooperative corporation), that are used by all of the unit owners, who share in the common expenses of their operation and maintenance. Common areas include swimming pools, tennis courts and other recreational facilities, as well as common corridors of buildings, parking areas, means of ingress and egress, etc.

Common law

An unwritten body of law based on general custom in England and used to an extent in the United States.

Community Land Trust Mortgage Option

An alternative financing option that enables low- and moderate-income home buyers to purchase housing that has been improved by a nonprofit Community Land Trust and to lease the land on which the property stands.

Community property

In some western and southwestern states, a form of ownership under which property acquired during a marriage is presumed to be owned jointly, unless acquired as separate property of either spouse.

Comparables (Comps)

An abbreviation for "comparable properties;" used for comparative purposes in the appraisal process. Comparables are properties like the property under consideration; they have reasonably the same size, location and amenities and have recently been sold. Comparables help the appraiser determine the approximate fair market value of the subject property.

Compound interest

Interest paid on the original principal balance and on the accrued and unpaid interest.

Condominium

A real estate project in which each unit owner has title to a unit in a building, an undivided interest in the common areas of the project, and sometimes the exclusive use of certain limited common areas.

Condominium conversion

Changing the ownership of an existing building (usually a rental project), to the condominium form of ownership.

Construction loan

A short-term, interim loan for financing the cost of construction. The lender makes payments to the builder at periodic intervals as the work progresses.

Contingency

A condition that must be met before a contract is legally binding. For example, home purchasers often include a contingency that specifies that the contract is not binding until the purchaser obtains a satisfactory home inspection report from a qualified home inspector.

** Contract

An oral or written agreement to do or not to do a certain thing. A contract consists of an offer, an acceptance, and an exchange of consideration, which typically consists of an earnest money deposit, but may consist of an exchange of almost anything of value.

** Conventional mortgage

A mortgage loan not insured by HUD or guaranteed by the Veterans' Administration. It is subject to conditions established by the lending institution and state statutes. The mortgage rates may vary with different institutions and between states. (States have various interest limits.)

Convertibility clause

A provision in some adjustable-rate mortgages (ARMs), that allows the borrower to change the ARM to a fixed-rate mortgage at specified timeframes after loan origination.

Convertible ARM

An adjustable-rate mortgage (ARM), that can be converted to a fixed-rate mortgage under specified conditions.

Cooperative (co-op)

A type of multiple ownership in which the residents of a multiunit housing complex own shares in the cooperative corporation that owns the property, giving each resident the right to occupy a specific apartment or unit.

Cooperative corporation

A business trust entity that holds title to a cooperative project and grants occupancy rights to particular apartments or units to shareholders through proprietary leases or similar arrangements.

Cooperative mortgages

Mortgages related to a cooperative project. This usually refers to the multifamily mortgage covering the entire project but occasionally describes the share loans on the individual units.

Cooperative project

A residential or mixed-use building wherein a corporation or trust holds title to the property and sells shares of stock representing the value of a single apartment unit to individuals who, in turn, receive a proprietary lease as evidence of title.

Corporate relocation

Arrangements under which an employer moves an employee to another area as part of the employer's normal course of business or under which it transfers a substantial part or all of its operations and employees to another area because it is relocating its headquarters or expanding its office capacity.

Cost of funds index (COFI)

An index that is used to determine interest rate changes for certain adjustable-rate mortgage (ARM), plans. It represents the weighted-average cost of savings, borrowings and advances of the 11th District members of the Federal Home Loan Bank of San Francisco. See adjustable-rate mortgage (ARM).

Covenant

A clause in a mortgage that obligates or restricts the borrower and that, if violated can result in foreclosure.

Credit

An agreement in which a borrower receives something of value in exchange for a promise to repay the lender at a later date.

Credit history

A record of an individual's open and fully repaid debts. A credit history helps a lender to determine whether a potential borrower has a history of repaying debts in a timely manner.

Credit life insurance

A type of insurance often bought by mortgagors because it will pay off the mortgage debt if the mortgagor dies while the policy is in force.

Creditor

A person to whom money is owed such as a bank or mortgage company.

Credit report

A report of an individual's credit history prepared by a credit bureau and used by a lender in determining a loan applicant's creditworthiness.

Credit reporting agency (or bureau)

An organization that prepares reports that are used by lenders to determine a potential borrower's credit history. The agency obtains data for these reports from a credit repository as well as from other sources.

Credit repository

An organization that gathers, records, updates, and stores financial and public records information about the payment records of individuals who are being considered for credit.

Debt

An amount owed to another. See installment loan and revolving liability.

Deed

A formal written instrument by which title to real property is transferred from one owner to another. The deed should contain an accurate description of the property being conveyed, should be signed and witnessed according to the laws of the state where the property is located and should be delivered to the purchaser at closing day. There are two parties to a deed: the grantor (seller), and the grantee (buyer).

Deed-in-lieu

A deed given by a mortgagor to the mortgagee to satisfy a debt and avoid foreclosure. Also called a "voluntary conveyance."

Deed of trust

The document used in some states instead of a mortgage; title is conveyed to a trustee.

Default

Failure to make mortgage payments as set forth in the mortgage or deed of trust. It is the responsibility of the buyer—the mortgager—to remember the due date and send the payment prior to the due date, not after. Generally, if the payment is not received by thirty days after the due date, the mortgage is in default. In the event of default, the mortgage may give the lender the right to accelerate payments, take possession and receive rents and start foreclosure. Defaults may also come about by failure to observe other conditions in the mortgage or deed of trust.

Delinquency

Failure to make mortgage payments when mortgage payments are due.

Deposit

A sum of money given to bind the sale of real estate, or a sum of money given to ensure payment or an advance of funds in the processing of a loan. See earnest money deposit.

Depreciation

Decline in the value of a house due to wear and tear, adverse changes in the neighborhood or any other reason.

Documentary stamps/Doc Stamps

A state tax, in the forms of stamps, required on deeds and mortgages when a real estate title passes from one owner to another. The amount of stamps required varies with each state.

** Down payment

The amount of money the purchaser pays to the seller upon the signing of the agreement of sale. The agreement of sale will refer to the down payment amount and will acknowledge receipt of the down payment. Down payment is the difference between the sales price and maximum mortgage amount. The down payment may not be refundable if the purchaser fails to buy the property without good cause. If the purchaser wants the down payment to be refundable, he or she should insert a clause in the agreement of sale specifying the conditions under which the deposit will be refunded. If the seller cannot deliver good title, the agreement of sale usually requires the seller to return the down payment and to pay interest and expenses incurred by the purchaser.

Earnest money/Earnest Money Deposit/EMD

The deposit money given to the seller or his agent by the potential buyer upon the signing of the offer to purchase to show that he or she is serious about buying the house. If the sale goes through, the earnest money is applied against the down payment. If the sale does not go through, the earnest money will be forfeited or lost unless the binder or offer to purchase expressly provides that it is refundable.

Easement rights

A right-of-way granted to a person or company authorizing access to or over the owner's land. An electric company obtaining a right-of-way across private property is a common example.

Eminent domain

The right of a government to take private property for public use upon payment of its fair market value. Eminent domain is the basis for condemnation proceedings.

Encroachment

An obstruction, building or part of a building that intrudes beyond a legal boundary onto neighboring private or public land, or a building extending beyond the building line.

Encumbrance

A legal right or interest in land that affects a good or clear title and diminishes the land's value. It can take numerous forms, such as zoning ordinances, easement rights, claims, mortgages, liens, charges, a pending legal action, unpaid taxes or restrictive covenants. An encumbrance does not legally prevent transfer of the property to another. A title search is all that is usually done to reveal the existence of such encumbrances, and it is up to the buyer to determine whether to purchase with the encumbrance, or to find a way to remove it.

Endorser

A person who signs ownership interest over to another party. Contrast with co-maker.

Equal Credit Opportunity Act (ECOA)

A federal law that requires lenders and other creditors to make credit equally available without discrimination based on race, color, religion, national origin, age, sex, marital status, or receipt of income from public assistance programs..

** Equity

The value of a homeowner's unencumbered interest in real estate. Equity is computed by subtracting from the property's fair market value the total of the unpaid mortgage balance and any outstanding liens or other debts against the property. A homeowner's equity increases as he pays off his mortgage or as the property appreciates in value. When the mortgage and all other debts against the property are paid in full, the homeowner has 100 percent equity in the property.

** Equity Availability Calculation

Available equity = Appraised value–25% - payoff of existing note. The 25% is left in the property as your "down payment" which most lenders will require on non-owner occupied properties. These properties are considered investment, which carries a higher risk to the lender. That risk is calculated into the APR of your mortgage.

Equity Calculation

Equity = Appraised value–loan payoff.

Equity Growth

This is the buydown of the note and appreciation of the unit, compared to the appraised value of your unit.

** Escrow

Funds paid by one party to another (the escrow agent), to hold until the occurrence of a specified event, after which the funds are released to a designated individual. In FHA mortgage transactions, an escrow account usually refers to the funds a borrower pays the lender at the time of the periodic mortgage payments. The money is held in a trust fund provided by the lender for the buyer. Such funds should be adequate to cover yearly anticipated expenditures for mortgage insurance premiums, taxes, hazard insurance premiums and special assessments.

Estate

The ownership interest of an individual in real property. The sum total of all the real property and personal property owned by an individual at time of death.

Eviction

A process by which the creditor goes through a court process and legally has the occupant removed. This process can take as little as 30 days but usually will take 60+ days. This is a costly process that you want to avoid if possible.

Examination of title

The report on the title of a property from the public records or an abstract of the title.

Exclusive listing

A written contract that gives a licensed real estate agent the exclusive right to sell a property for a specified time, but reserving the owner's right to sell the property alone without the payment of a commission.

Executor

A person named in a will to administer an estate. The court will appoint an administrator if no executor is named. "Executrix" is the feminine form.

Fair Credit Reporting Act

A consumer protection law that regulates the disclosure of consumer credit reports by consumer/credit reporting agencies and establishes procedures for correcting mistakes on one's credit record.

Fair market value

The highest price that a buyer, willing but not compelled to buy, would pay and the lowest a seller, willing but not compelled to sell, would accept.

Federal National Mortgage Association (referred to as "Fannie Mae")

Fannie Mae owns, manages, and has available for sale, single-family detached homes, two- to four-unit properties, condominiums, and townhouses in a variety of neighborhoods. The number, type, and sales price may vary substantially.

Foreclose

This refers to a legal action that the bank, or creditor, takes in the event of non-payment. As with any loan you may take on property, cars or anything else, you would normally put something of value up as collateral. That means if you can not meet your payment obligations the creditor has the right to "take" what ever it is that you have given up as collateral. In the case of a mortgage on a piece of property, it is usually the property itself that is used as collateral. The creditor would then go through the process of evicting the occupants of the unit and, through the courts, transfer ownership to themselves.

Federal Housing Administration (FHA)

An agency of the U.S. Department of Housing and Urban Development (HUD). Its main activity is the insuring of residential mortgage loans made by private lenders. The FHA sets standards for construction and underwriting but does not lend money or plan or construct housing.

Fee simple estate

An unconditional, unlimited estate of inheritance that represents the greatest estate and most extensive interest in land that can be enjoyed. It is of perpetual duration. When the real estate is in a condominium project, the unit owner is the exclusive owner only of the air space within his or her portion of the building (the unit), and is an owner in common with respect to the land and other common portions of the property.

FHA coinsured mortgage

A mortgage (under FHA Section 244), for which the Federal Housing Administration (FHA), and the originating lender share the risk of loss in the event of the mortgagor's default.

FHA mortgage

A mortgage that is insured by the Federal Housing Administration (FHA). Also known as a government mortgage.

Finder's fee

A fee or commission paid to a mortgage broker for finding a mortgage loan for a prospective borrower.

First mortgage

A mortgage that is the primary lien against a property.

Fixed installment

The monthly payment due on a mortgage loan. The fixed installment includes payment of both principal and interest.

** Fixed-rate mortgage (FRM)

A mortgage in which the interest rate does not change during the entire term of the loan.

Fixture

Personal property that becomes real property when attached in a permanent manner to real estate.

Flood insurance

Insurance that compensates for physical property damage resulting from flooding. It is required for properties located in federally designated flood areas.

Forfeiture

The loss of money, property, rights or privileges due to a breach of legal obligation.

401(k)/403(b)

An employer-sponsored investment plan that allows individuals to set aside tax-deferred income for retirement or emergency purposes. 401(k) plans are provided by employers that are private corporations. 403(b) plans are provided by employers that are not for profit organizations.

401(k)/403(b) loan

Some administrators of 401(k)/403(b) plans allow for loans against the monies you have accumulated in these plans—monies that must be repaid to avoid serious penalty charges.

Fully amortized ARM

An adjustable-rate mortgage (ARM), with a monthly payment that is sufficient to amortize the remaining balance, at the interest accrual rate, over the amortization term.

General warranty deed

A deed which also warrants that if the title is defective or has a "cloud" on it (such as mortgage claims, tax liens, title claims, judgments, or mechanic's liens against it), the grantee may hold the grantor liable.

Government mortgage

A mortgage that is insured by the Federal Housing Administration (FHA), or guaranteed by the Department of Veterans Affairs (VA), or the Rural Housing Service (RHS). Contrast with conventional mortgage.

Government National Mortgage Association

A government-owned corporation within the U.S. Department of Housing and Urban Development (HUD). Created by Congress on Sept. 1, 1968, GNMA assumed responsibility for the special assistance loan program formerly administered by Fannie Mae. Popularly known as Ginnie Mae.

Growing-equity mortgage (GEM)

A fixed-rate mortgage that provides scheduled payment increases over an established period of time, with the increased amount of the monthly payment applied directly toward reducing the remaining balance of the mortgage.

Guarantee mortgage

A mortgage that is guaranteed by a third party.

Hazard insurance

Protects against damages caused to property by fire, windstorms and other common hazards.

Home Equity Conversion Mortgage (HECM)

A special type of mortgage that enables older home owners to convert the equity they have in their homes into cash, using a variety of payment options to address their specific financial needs. Unlike traditional home equity loans, a borrower does not qualify on the basis of income but on the value of his or her home. In addition, the loan does not have to be repaid until the borrower no longer occupies the property. Sometimes called a reverse mortgage.

Home equity line of credit

A mortgage loan, which is usually in a subordinate position, that allows the borrower to obtain multiple advances of the loan proceeds at his or her own discretion, up to an amount that represents a specified percentage of the borrower's equity in a property.

** Home inspection

A thorough inspection that evaluates the structural and mechanical condition of a property. A satisfactory home inspection is often included as a contingency by the purchaser. Contrast with appraisal.

** Homeowners' association

A nonprofit association that manages the common areas of a planned unit development (PUD), or condominium project. In a condominium project, it has no ownership interest in the common elements. In a PUD project, it holds title to the common elements.

Homeowner's insurance

An insurance policy that combines personal liability insurance and hazard insurance coverage for a dwelling and its contents.

Homeowner's warranty (HOW)

A type of insurance that covers repairs to specified parts of a house for a specific period of time. It is provided by the builder or property seller as a condition of the sale.

HUD

U.S. Department of Housing and Urban Development. The Office of Housing/ Federal Housing Administration within HUD insures home mortgage loans made by lenders and sets minimum standards for such homes.

** HUD-1 statement

A document that provides an itemized listing of the funds that are payable at closing. Items that appear on the statement include real estate commissions, loan fees, points, and initial escrow amounts. Each item on the statement is represented by a separate number within a standardized numbering system. The totals at the bottom of the HUD-1 statement define the seller's net proceeds and the buyer's net payment at closing. The blank form for the statement is published by the Department of Housing and Urban Development (HUD). The HUD-1 statement is also known as the "closing statement" or "settlement sheet."

Income property

Real estate developed or improved to produce income.

Index

A number used to compute the interest rate for an adjustable-rate mortgage (ARM). The index is generally a published number or percentage, such as the average interest rate or yield on Treasury bills. A margin is added to the index to determine the interest rate that will be charged on the ARM. This interest rate is subject to any caps that are associated with the mortgage.

In-file credit report

An objective account, normally computer-generated, of credit and legal information obtained from a credit repository.

Inflation

An increase in the amount of money or credit available in relation to the amount of goods or services available, which causes an increase in the general price level of goods and services. Over time, inflation reduces the purchasing power of a dollar, making it worth less.

Initial Investment—This is the money you put out for the down payment, closing costs, and get ready costs (like appliances, carpet, painting, maid service, furnace maintenance, lighting, etc.). It might also include rental costs such as money you put out for advertising and attorney fees and ongoing costs.

Installment

The regular periodic payment that a borrower agrees to make to a lender.

Installment loan

Borrowed money that is repaid in equal payments, known as installments. A furniture loan is often paid for as an installment loan.

Insurable title

A property title that a title insurance company agrees to insure against defects and disputes.

Insurance

A contract that provides compensation for specific losses in exchange for a periodic payment. An individual contract is known as an insurance policy, and the periodic payment is known as an insurance premium.

Insurance binder

A document that states that insurance is temporarily in effect. Because the coverage will expire by a specified date, a permanent policy must be obtained before the expiration date.

Insured mortgage

A mortgage that is protected by the Federal Housing Administration (FHA), or by private mortgage insurance (MI). If the borrower defaults on the loan, the insurer must pay the lender the lesser of the loss incurred or the insured amount.

** Interest

The fee charged for borrowing money.

Interest accrual rate

The percentage rate at which interest accrues on the mortgage. In most cases, it is also the rate used to calculate the monthly payments, although it is not used for an adjustable-rate mortgage (ARM), with payment change limitations.

** Interest rate

The rate of interest in effect for the monthly payment due.

Interest rate buydown plan

An arrangement wherein the property seller (or any other party), deposits money to an account so that it can be released each month to reduce the mortgagor's monthly payments during the early years of a mortgage. During the specified period, the mortgagor's effective interest rate is "bought down" below the actual interest rate.

Interest rate ceiling

For an adjustable-rate mortgage (ARM), the maximum interest rate, as specified in the mortgage note.

Interest rate floor

For an adjustable-rate mortgage (ARM), the minimum interest rate, as specified in the mortgage note.

Investment property

A property that is not occupied by the owner.

IRA (Individual Retirement Account)

A retirement account that allows individuals to make tax-deferred contributions to a personal retirement fund. Individuals can place IRA funds in bank accounts or in other forms of investment such as stocks, bonds or mutual funds.

Judgment

A decision made by a court of law. In judgments that require the repayment of a debt, the court may place a lien against the debtor's real property as collateral for the judgment's creditor.

Judgment lien

A lien on the property of a debtor resulting from the decree of a court.

Judicial foreclosure

A type of foreclosure proceeding used in some states that is handled as a civil lawsuit and conducted entirely under the auspices of a court.

Jumbo loan

A loan that exceeds Fannie Mae's mortgage amount limits. Also called a nonconforming loan.

Late charge

The penalty a borrower must pay when a payment is made a stated number of days (usually 15), after the due date.

Lease

A written agreement between the property owner and a tenant that stipulates the conditions under which the tenant may possess the real estate for a specified period of time and rent.

Lease-purchase mortgage loan

An alternative financing option that allows low- and moderate-income home buyers to lease a home from a nonprofit organization with an option to buy. Each month's rent payment consists of principal, interest, taxes, and insurance (PITI), payments on the first mortgage plus an extra amount that is earmarked for deposit to a savings account in which money for a downpayment will accumulate.

** Legal description

A property description recognized by law that is sufficient to locate and identify the property without oral testimony.

Liabilities

A person's financial obligations. Liabilities include long-term and short-term debt, as well as any other amounts that are owed to others.

Liability insurance

Insurance coverage that offers protection against claims alleging that a property owner's negligence or inappropriate action resulted in bodily injury or property damage to another party.

Lien

A claim by one person on the property of another as security for money owed. Such claims may include obligations not met or satisfied, judgments, unpaid taxes, materials or labor.

Line of credit

An agreement by a commercial bank or other financial institution to extend credit up to a certain amount for a certain time to a specified borrower. See home equity line of credit.

Liquid asset

A cash asset or an asset that is easily converted into cash.

Loan

A sum of borrowed money (principal), that is generally repaid with interest.

** Loan commitment

See commitment letter.

Loan origination

The process by which a mortgage lender brings into existence a mortgage secured by real property.

Loan Payoffs

This represents the amount of outstanding balance you owe and if you were going to either pay the loan off or refinance this would be the amount to be paid. This is also referenced in terms of what the loan is worth at a given point for sale purposes.

Loan-to-value (LTV) percentage

The relationship between the principal balance of the mortgage and the appraised value (or sales price if it is lower), of the property. For example, a $100,000 home with an $80,000 mortgage has a LTV percentage of 80 percent.

Lock-in

A written agreement in which the lender guarantees a specified interest rate if a mortgage goes to closing within a set period of time. The lock-in also usually specifies the number of points to be paid at closing

Margin

For an adjustable-rate mortgage (ARM), the amount that is added to the index to establish the interest rate on each adjustment date, subject to any limitations on the interest rate change.

Marketable title

A title free and clear of objectionable liens, clouds or other title defects. A marketable title enables an owner to sell his or her property freely to others and allows others to accept without objection.

Maturity

The date on which the principal balance of a loan, bond or other financial instrument becomes due and payable.

Maximum financing

A mortgage amount that is within 5 percent of the highest loan-to-value (LTV), percentage allowed for a specific product. Thus, maximum financing on a fixed-rate mortgage would be 90 percent or higher, because 95 percent is the maximum allowable LTV percentage for that product.

Merged credit report

A credit report that contains information from three credit repositories. When the report is created, the information is compared for duplicate entries. Any duplicates are combined to provide a summary of a your credit.

Modification

The act of changing any of the terms of the mortgage.

Money market account

A savings account that provides bank depositors with many of the advantages of a money market fund. Certain regulatory restrictions apply to the withdrawal of funds from a money market account.

Money market fund

A mutual fund that allows individuals to participate in managed investments in short-term debt securities, such as certificates of deposit and Treasury bills.

Monthly fixed installment

That portion of the total monthly payment that is applied toward principal and interest. When a mortgage negatively amortizes, the monthly fixed installment does not include any amount for principal reduction.

Monthly payment mortgage

A mortgage that requires payments to reduce the debt once a month.

Mortgage

A lien or claim against real property given by the buyer to the lender as security for money borrowed. Under government-insured or loan-guarantee provisions, the payments may include escrow amounts covering taxes, hazard insurance, water charges, and special assessments. Mortgages generally run from 10 to 30 years, during which the loan is to be paid off.

Mortgage banker

A company that originates mortgages exclusively for resale in the secondary mortgage market.

Mortgage broker

An individual or company that brings borrowers and lenders together for the purpose of loan origination. Mortgage brokers typically require a fee or a commission for their services.

Mortgagee

The lender in a mortgage agreement.

** Mortgage insurance

A contract that insures the lender against loss caused by a mortgagor's default on a government mortgage or conventional mortgage. Mortgage insurance can be issued by a private company or by a government agency such as the Federal Housing Administration (FHA). Depending on the type of mortgage insurance, the insurance may cover a percentage of or virtually all of the mortgage loan. See private mortgage insurance.

Mortgage insurance premium (MIP)

The amount paid by a mortgagor for mortgage insurance, either to a government agency such as the Federal Housing Administration (FHA), or to a private mortgage insurance (MI), company.

Mortgage life insurance

A type of term life insurance often bought by mortgagors. The amount of coverage decreases as the principal balance declines. In the event that the borrower dies while the policy is in force, the debt is automatically satisfied by insurance proceeds.

** Mortgage commitment

A written notice from the bank or other lending institution saying it will advance mortgage funds in a specified amount to enable a buyer to purchase a house.

Mortgage note

A written agreement to repay a loan. The agreement is secured by a mortgage, serves as proof of indebtedness, and states the manner in which it shall be paid. The note states the actual amount of the debt that the mortgage secures and renders the borrower personally responsible for repayment.

Mortgage (open-end)

A mortgage with a provision that permits borrowing additional money in the future without refinancing the loan or paying additional financing charges. Open-end provisions often limit such borrowing to no more than what would raise the balance to the original loan figure.

Mortgagor

The borrower in a mortgage agreement.

Multidwelling units

Properties that provide separate housing units for more than one family, although they secure only a single mortgage.

Multifamily mortgage

A residential mortgage on a dwelling that is designed to house more than four families, such as a high-rise apartment complex.

Multifamily properties

Fannie Mae provides financing for multifamily (buildings with five or more units), rental properties through a nationwide network of mortgage lenders.

Negative amortization

A gradual increase in mortgage debt that occurs when the monthly payment is not large enough to cover the entire principal and interest due. The amount of the shortfall is added to the remaining balance to create "negative" amortization.

Net cash flow

The income that remains for an investment property after the monthly operating income is reduced by the monthly housing expense, which includes principal, interest, taxes, and insurance (PITI), for the mortgage, homeowners' association dues, leasehold payments, and subordinate financing payments.

Net worth

The value of all of a person's assets, including cash, minus all liabilities.

No cash-out refinance

A refinance transaction in which the new mortgage amount is limited to the sum of the remaining balance of the existing first mortgage, closing costs (including prepaid items), points, the amount required to satisfy any mortgage liens that are more than one year old (if the borrower chooses to satisfy them), and other funds for the borrower's use (as long as the amount does not exceed 1 percent of the principal amount of the new mortgage).

Nonliquid asset

An asset that cannot easily be converted into cash.

Note

A legal document that obligates a borrower to repay a mortgage loan at a stated interest rate during a specified period of time.

Note rate

The interest rate stated on a mortgage note.

Notice of default

A formal written notice to a borrower that a default has occurred and that legal action may be taken.

Original principal balance

The total amount of principal owed on a mortgage before any payments are made.

** Origination fee

A fee paid to a lender for processing a loan application. The origination fee is stated in the form of points. One point is 1 percent of the mortgage amount.

Owner financing

A property purchase transaction in which the property seller provides all or part of the financing.

Partial payment

A payment that is not sufficient to cover the scheduled monthly payment on a mortgage loan.

Personal property
Any property that is not real property.

PITI reserves
A cash amount that a borrower must have on hand after making a down payment and paying all closing costs for the purchase of a home. The principal, interest, taxes, and insurance (PITI) reserves must equal the amount that the borrower would have to pay for PITI for a predefined number of months.

Plat
A map or chart, drawn by a surveyor, of a lot, subdivision or community; it shows boundary lines, buildings, improvements on the land and easements.

** Points
Sometimes called "discount points." A point is one percent of the amount of the mortgage loan. For example, if a loan is for $25,000, one point is $250. Points are charged by a lender to raise the yield on the loan at a time when money is tight, interest rates are high, and there is a legal limit to the interest rate that can be charged on a mortgage. Buyers are prohibited from paying points on HUD or Veterans' Administration guaranteed loans (sellers can pay, however). On a conventional mortgage, points may be paid by either the buyer or seller or split between them.

Power of attorney
A legal document that authorizes another person to act on one's behalf. A power of attorney can grant complete authority or can be limited to certain acts and/or certain periods of time.

Prearranged refinancing agreement
A formal or informal arrangement between a lender and a borrower wherein the lender agrees to offer special terms (such as a reduction in the costs), for a future refinancing of a mortgage being originated as an inducement for the borrower to enter into the original mortgage transaction.

Pre-foreclosure sale
A procedure in which the investor allows a mortgagor to avoid foreclosure by selling the property for less than the amount that is owed to the investor.

Prepayment

Payment of mortgage loan, or part of it, before due date. Mortgage agreements often restrict the right of prepayment either by limiting the amount that can be prepaid in any one year or charging a penalty for prepayment. The Federal Housing Administration does not permit such restrictions in FHA-insured mortgages.

Prepayment penalty

A fee that may be charged to a borrower who pays off a loan before it is due.

Pre-qualification

The process of determining how much money a prospective homebuyer will be eligible to borrow before he or she applies for a loan.

Prime rate

The interest rate that banks charge to their preferred customers. Changes in the prime rate influence changes in other rates, including mortgage interest rates.

** Principal

The basic element of the loan as distinguished from interest and mortgage insurance premium. In other words, principal is the amount upon which interest is paid.

** Principal balance

The outstanding balance of principal on a mortgage. The principal balance does not include interest or any other charges. See remaining balance.

Principal, interest, taxes and insurance (PITI)

The four components of a monthly mortgage payment. Principal refers to the part of the monthly payment that reduces the remaining balance of the mortgage. Interest is the fee charged for borrowing money. Taxes and insurance refer to the amounts that are paid into an escrow account each month for property taxes and mortgage and hazard insurance.

** Private mortgage insurance (PMI)

Mortgage insurance that is provided by a private mortgage insurance company to protect lenders against loss if a borrower defaults. Most lenders generally require MI for a loan with a loan-to-value (LTV) percentage in excess of 80 percent.

Promissory note

A written promise to repay a specified amount over a specified period of time.

Public auction

A meeting in an announced public location to sell property to repay a mortgage that is in default.

PUD (Planned Unit Development)

A project or subdivision that includes common property that is owned and maintained by a homeowners' association for the benefit and use of the individual PUD unit owners.

Purchase and sale agreement

A written contract signed by the buyer and seller stating the terms and conditions under which a property will be sold.

** Qualifying ratios

Calculations that are used in determining whether a borrower can qualify for a mortgage. They consist of two separate calculations: a housing expense as a percent of income ratio and total debt obligations as a percent of income ratio.

Quitclaim deed

A deed that transfers whatever interest the maker of the deed may have in the particular parcel of land. A quitclaim deed is often given to clear the title when the grantor's interest in a property is questionable. By accepting such a deed the buyer assumes all the risks. Such a deed makes no warranties as to the title, but simply transfers to the buyer whatever interest the grantor has.

Radon

A radioactive gas found in some homes that in sufficient concentrations can cause health problems.

Rate lock-in

A guarantee the interest rate will remain the same for a specified period of time. Whether the loan's interest rate index rises or falls during that period, the borrower pays the rate that was current at the time of the lock-in agreement.

Real estate agent

A person licensed to negotiate and transact the sale of real estate on behalf of the property owner.

** Real Estate Settlement Procedures Act (RESPA)

A consumer protection law that requires lenders to give borrowers advance notice of closing costs.

Real property

Land and appurtenances, including anything of a permanent nature such as structures, trees, minerals, and the interest, benefits and inherent rights thereof.

REALTOR®

A real estate broker or an associate who holds active membership in a local real estate board that is affiliated with the NATIONAL ASSOCIATION of REALTORS®.

Recission

The cancellation or annulment of a transaction or contract by the operation of a law or by mutual consent. Borrowers usually have the option to cancel a refinance transaction within three business days after it has closed.

Recorder

The public official who keeps records of transactions that affect real property in the area. Sometimes known as a "Registrar of Deeds" or "County Clerk."

Recording

The noting in the registrar's office of the details of a properly executed legal document, such as a deed, a mortgage note, a satisfaction of mortgage or an extension of mortgage, thereby making it a part of the public record.

Refinancing

The process of the same person paying off one loan with the proceeds from another loan.

Rehabilitation mortgage

A mortgage created to cover the costs of repairing, improving and sometimes acquiring an existing property.

Remaining balance

The amount of principal that has not yet been repaid. See principal balance.

Remaining term

The original amortization term minus the number of payments that have been applied.

Rent loss insurance

Insurance that protects a landlord against loss of rent or rental value due to fire or other casualty that renders the leased premises unavailable for use and as a result of which the tenant is excused from paying rent.

Rent with option to buy

See lease-purchase mortgage loan.

Repayment plan

An arrangement made to repay delinquent installments or advances. Lenders' formal repayment plans are called "relief provisions."

Replacement reserve fund

A fund set aside for replacement of common property in a condominium, PUD, or cooperative project—particularly that which has a short life expectancy, such as carpeting, furniture, etc.

Revolving liability

A credit arrangement, such as a credit card, that allows a customer to borrow against a preapproved line of credit when purchasing goods and services. The borrower is billed for the amount that is actually borrowed plus any interest due.

Right of first refusal

A provision in an agreement that requires the owner of a property to give another party the first opportunity to purchase or lease the property before he or she offers it for sale or lease to others.

Right of ingress or egress

The right to enter or leave designated premises.

Right of survivorship

In joint tenancy, the right of survivors to acquire the interest of a deceased joint tenant.

Rural Housing Service (RHS)

An agency within the Department of Agriculture, which operates principally under the Consolidated Farm and Rural Development Act of 1921 and Title V of the Housing Act of 1949. This agency provides financing to farmers and other qualified borrowers buying property in rural areas who are unable to obtain loans elsewhere. Funds are borrowed from the U.S. Treasury.

** Sale-leaseback

A technique in which a seller deeds property to a buyer for a consideration, and the buyer simultaneously leases the property back to the seller.

Second mortgage

A mortgage that has a lien position subordinate to the first mortgage.

Secondary mortgage market

The buying and selling of existing mortgages.

Secured loan

A loan that is backed by collateral.

Security

The property that will be pledged as collateral for a loan.

Seller take-back

An agreement in which the owner of a property provides financing, often in combination with an assumable mortgage. See owner financing.

Servicer

An organization that collects principal and interest payments from borrowers and manages borrowers' escrow accounts. The servicer often services mortgages that have been purchased by an investor in the secondary mortgage market.

Servicing

The collection of mortgage payments from borrowers and related responsibilities of a loan servicer.

Single-family properties

One- to four-unit properties including detached homes, townhomes, condominiums, and cooperatives.

Special assessments

A special tax imposed on property, individual lots, or all property in the immediate area, for road construction, sidewalks, or other shared common area items..

Step-rate mortgage

A mortgage that allows for the interest rate to increase according to a specified schedule (i.e., seven years), resulting in increased payments as well. At the end of the specified period, the rate and payments will remain constant for the remainder of the loan.

Subdivision

A housing development that is created by dividing a tract of land into individual lots for sale or lease.

Subject to

Title to property may be transferred from seller to buyer "subject to" the original financing remaining in effect. A form of a wraparound mortgage.

Subordinate financing

Any mortgage or other lien that has a priority that is lower than that of the first mortgage.

Survey

A drawing or map showing the precise legal boundaries of a property, the location of improvements, easements, rights of way, encroachments and other physical features.

Sweat equity

Contribution to the construction or rehabilitation of a property in the form of labor or services rather than cash.

The tax-free payout

When refinancing, there aren't any tax implications on that money.

Tenancy by the entirety

A type of joint tenancy of property that provides right of survivorship and is available only to a husband and wife. Contrast with tenancy in common.

Tenancy in common

A type of joint tenancy in a property without right of survivorship. Contrast with tenancy by the entirety and with joint tenancy.

Third-party origination

A process by which a lender uses another party to completely or partially originate, process, underwrite, close, fund or package the mortgages it plans to deliver to the secondary mortgage market. See mortgage broker.

Title

As generally used, the rights of ownership and possession of particular property. In real-estate usage, title may refer to the instruments or documents by which a right of ownership is established (title documents), or it may refer to the ownership interest one has in the real estate.

Title Insurance

Protects lenders or homeowners against loss of their interest in property due to legal defects in the title. Title insurance may be issued to a "mortgagee's title policy." Insurance benefits will be paid only to the "name insured" in the title policy, so it is important that an owner purchase an "owner's title policy," if he or she desires the protection of title insurance.

Title search or examination

A check of the title records, generally at the local courthouse, to make sure the buyer is purchasing a house from the legal owner and there are no liens, over-due special assessments, or other claims or outstanding restrictive covenants filed in the record, which would adversely affect the marketability or value of the title.

Total expense ratio

Total obligations as a percentage of gross monthly income. The total expense ratio includes monthly housing expenses plus other monthly debts.

Trade equity

Equity that results from a property purchaser giving his or her existing property (or an asset other than real estate), as trade as all or part of the down payment for the property that is being purchased.

Transfer of ownership

Any means by which the ownership of a property changes hands. Lenders consider all of the following situations to be a transfer of ownership: the purchase of a property "subject to" the mortgage, the assumption of the mortgage debt by the property purchaser, and any exchange of possession of the property under a land sales contract or any other land trust device. In cases in which an inter vivos revocable trust is the borrower, lenders also consider any transfer of a beneficial interest in the trust to be a transfer of ownership.

Transfer tax

State or local tax payable when title passes from one owner to another.

Treasury index

An index that is used to determine interest rate changes for certain adjustable-rate mortgage (ARM) plans. It is based on the results of auctions that the U.S. Treasury holds for its Treasury bills and securities or is derived from the U.S. Treasury's daily yield curve, which is based on the closing market bid yields on actively traded Treasury securities in the over-the-counter market. See adjustable-rate mortgage (ARM).

Truth-in-Lending

A federal law that requires lenders to fully disclose, in writing, the terms and conditions of a mortgage, including the annual percentage rate (APR) and other charges.

Two-step mortgage

An adjustable-rate mortgage (ARM) that has one interest rate for the first five or seven years of its mortgage term and a different interest rate for the remainder of the amortization term.

Two- to four-family property

A property that consists of a structure that provides living space (dwelling units), for two to four families, although ownership of the structure is evidenced by a single deed.

Trustee

A fiduciary who holds or controls property for the benefit of another.

Underwriting

The process of evaluating a loan application to determine the risk involved for the lender. Underwriting involves an analysis of the borrower's creditworthiness and the quality of the property itself.

Unsecured loan

A loan that is not backed by collateral.

Upside Down

This is a term that refers to the difference of what the property is worth versus the amount of the loan on that property. When the bank is upside down it means that the amount of the loan is greater than the appraised value of the property.

VA mortgage

A mortgage that is guaranteed by the Department of Veterans Affairs (VA). Also known as a government mortgage.

What-if analysis

An affordability analysis that is based on a what-if scenario. A what-if analysis is useful if you do not have complete data or if you want to explore the effect of various changes to your income, liabilities, or available funds or to the qualifying ratios or down payment expenses that are used in the analysis.

What-if scenario

A change in the amounts that is used as the basis of an affordability analysis. A what-if scenario can include changes to monthly income, debts, or down payment funds or to the qualifying ratios or down payment expenses that are used in the analysis. You can use a what-if scenario to explore different ways to improve your ability to afford a house.

Wraparound mortgage

Seller keeps original mortgage. Buyer makes payments to seller, who forwards a portion to the lender holding the original mortgage.

Sample Information

Sample Ad:

"Your City"

Townhouse—2 Bedroom, 2.5 bath, finished basement, 2 car garage, new appliances, lawn care and snow removal provided. Across from park. 10 minutes from train. $1250—call 555.555.1234. Available Jan 1.

"Your City"

Townhouse—2 Bedroom, 1 bath, new appliances, new carpet, fireplace, 1 car garage, backs to golf course. $1150. Available Immed. 555.555.1234.

Checklist Section

Someone wants to move forward—What do I do?

-Check for credit application—Check #1
Usually $35–$50
Non-refundable

-Check for deposit—Check #2
Usually 15%–20% of one month's rent to hold rental
Tell callers that you have a deposit, but take their number
If the credit does not pass, you can call them back

-Fill out credit application

-Run credit

-Credit bureaus
Find a credit bureau that deals with individuals
Set up an account with them
    Where they pull credit from

Things to look for that are not good
    Scores under 600
    Bankruptcies
    Foreclosures
    Repossessions
    Late payments
    Collections

People with good credit have it for a reason
    They won't burn you
    If something happens they will come to you and want to work it out
    They won't destroy your property
    They are usually honest

-Make copies of checks prior to depositing them
Put these in the files
Keep a file on each house on each rental year
Keep all receipts in the associated file

What to do after you have found your renter

-Sign the Lease
Meet at a restaurant
Make it fun
Another write-off

-Go over the rules
Have it there by the 1st
> You can't put excuses in the bank
> It takes 45–60 days minimum to evict someone.
> You have to start on the 2nd of the month to insure you won't get burned
> Tell them about the by-laws

-Collect the remainder of the deposit—Check #3

Rent Day—1st Day

-What to sign
Lease
Rider
Fire/Smoke detector
Condo rules/regulations
Garage door opener
Mail box keys
Local municipality information (water, pets, etc.)

-What to give the renter
Door keys
Mail box keys
Copy of the by-laws

-Collect the first month's rent—Check #4

During the term of the lease

-What to do and when to do it
Deposit the rent checks
Take care of anything that comes up ASAP!!!

-What the tenant will do
Pay the rent on time

-Getting out early
Tenant buys a house
Tenant gets a divorce
Tenant get transferred

-What money to expect
Possible arrangements
    Re-Rent
        Your right-of-refusal
        Pay for one week of ad time
        Tenant pays for ad time past first week
    Buy out the lease
        Expensive, depending on time left on lease
    Take your chances
        Usually 1–3 months up front and keep deposit
        Lots of exposure
        Could come out ahead

Last Day of the Lease

-The deposit is not the last month payment

-Outstanding Water Bills

-The Walk Through
What to look for
    Carpet
    Appliances
    Walls
    Floors

-What to collect
Keys
    Doors
    Mail box
Garage Door Opener
By-Laws
Rules and Regs.
Instruction Manuals for Appliances

-Mail back the remainder of the deposit within 30 days
Provide accounting worksheet
Include copies of any receipts of damage repairs

Keep copies
Deductions
    Carpet Cleaning
    Damage
        Holes in walls
        Stains/damage to carpet
        Broken fans
        Broken Glass
        Counter Tops
        Doors
        Damage to appliances
    Missing keys, garage door openers, remotes …

Turning Over the Property

-Showing the property

Let the renter show it
    They will brag about the way you have treated them
    New renter will not feel as though they are being sold
    Less work

-Timing is everything

Move them out and move them in
Have everyone lined up
        Painting
        Carpet
        Maid

** * No Vacancies or Unpaid Time***

Pre-Qualification Phone Questionnaire

Where did they hear about the unit?

_____

Their current situation–Why are they renting?

_____

What is important to them in a prospective home?

_____

Why are they moving?

_____

When is their moving date?

_____

How long do they intend on staying?

_____

Do they have any pets?

_____

Do they smoke?

_____

Do they have good credit? What is the score?

_____

What do they do for employment?

_____

Why are they interested in the community your property is located in?

_____

Why did they choose to rent vs. purchase?

_____

How many kids do they have, ages and how many bedrooms will be needed?

_____

Sample Rental/Credit Application

PLEASE PRINT

Address applying for_____ at $_____ per month.

Applicant Name_____
    Phone_____

Date of Birth_____   Social Security Number_____
Applicant Name_____   Phone_____
Date of Birth_____   Social Security Number_____

Number of Dependents_____   Number of other Occupants_____

Name_____   M/F_____Date of Birth_____

Name_____   M/F_____Date of Birth_____

Name_____   M/F_____Date of Birth_____

Name_____   M/F_____Date of Birth_____

Pets-How Many_____   What Kind_____

Applicant
-Current
Address_____   City/State/Zip_____

Month and Year Moved In_____   Reason for Leaving_____

Owner/Landlord_____   Phone_____

-Co-Applicant Current
Address_____   City/State/Zip_____

Month and Year Moved In_____   Reason for Leaving_____

Owner/Landlord_____   Phone_____

APPLICANT
-Employer Name/Address_____

Your Status: Full Time___Part Time___Student___Retired___Unemployed___

Date(s) Employed_____   Position_____
Supervisor_____   Phone_____

Salary or Hourly Wage_____ Total Hours Worked Per Week_____

CO-APPLICANT
-Employer Name/Address_____

Your Status: Full Time___Part Time___Student___Retired___Unemployed___
Date(s) Employed_____ Position_____

Supervisor_____ Phone_____

Salary or Hourly Wage_____ Total Hours Worked Per Week_____

Applicant Drivers License Number_____   State_____

Co-Applicant Drivers License Number_____   State_____
Vehicle Make and

Model_____ Year_____Plate_____State_____

Second Vehicle_____ Year_____Plate_____State_____

Have you ever: Filed for bankruptcy?   Yes_____ No_____
Been evicted from tenancy?   Yes_____ No_____
Willfully or intentionally refused to
    pay rent when due?   Yes_____ No_____
Been convicted of a Sex Crime?   Yes_____ No_____
Been convicted of a felony?   Yes_____ No_____
Are there any judgments against you?   Yes_____ No_____

The above information is true and correct, and I hereby authorize employer and references listed on this application to release information to _____ along with permission to obtain a credit or criminal background check as necessary for the processing of this rental application.

Applicants Signature_____ Date_____

Co-Applicants Signature_____ Date_____

WATERBED ADDENDUM

This addendum is made this _____ day of _____, 20____, and is added to and amends that certain agreement by and between_____ as Tenant(s) and_____as Landlord(s), which agreement is dated _____ day of _____, 20____.

It is the tenant's intention to keep a waterbed in the residence named in the attached Lease/Rental Agreement.

This shall be a conditional privilege granted to the tenant in exchange for guaranteeing that the rules in this waterbed addendum are strictly followed. The Owner/Agent reserves the right to revoke this privilege if the tenant violates any of the agreements herein.

The permission is granted to keep a waterbed under the following terms and conditions:

1) Tenant agrees to keep a waterbed located on the _____ floor of the dwelling.

2) Tenant agrees to be responsible for any defects or damages concerning the premises in relation to the waterbed during or as a result of having the waterbed in the dwelling.

3) Tenant agrees to obtain liability insurance to include coverage concerning the waterbed.

4) Tenant agrees to post $_____additional security deposit which will be returned after tenant vacates, providing the premises are returned as agreed.

5) In the event the Tenant gets rid of the waterbed, it is agreed that it will not be replaced with another waterbed without the owner/agent's expressed written permission. It is also agreed that removal will be done in a proper professional manner, not to cause any hardship on the dwelling or landlord.

Owner/Agent_____   Tenant_____
                                         Date_____

                                         Tenant_____
                                         Date_____

Move Out Related Charges

Below is a list of estimated charges of assorted items or jobs that may sometimes be required, after a residence is vacated. All charges are including labor and any parts or materials required. Tenants are not responsible for normal wear and tear, although excessive wear and tear and neglect may incur charges.

CLEANING

Clean refrigerator 50.00
Replace stove drip-bowls 28.00
Clean stove hood 30.00
Clean kitchen floor 50.00
Clean toilet and sink (per bath) 20.00
Clean carpets (per room) 75.00
Window cleaning(per unit) 11.00
Clean fireplace 35.00

Clean stovetop 30.00
Clean oven 50.00
Clean kitchen cabinets 45.00
Clean tub/shower and surround 30.00 (ea.)
Clean bathroom.cabinets and floor 25.00
Vacuum throughout dwelling 40.00
Clean greasy parking spaces 25.00 (ea.)

FLOORING

Remove carpet stains 80.00
Repair carpet 150.00
Refinish hardwood floor 380.00
Replace bathroom linoleum 385.00
Replace floor tile 75.00

Deodorize carpet 80.00
Repair hardwood floor 95.00
Repair linoleum 85.00
Replace kitchen linoleum 385.00
Replace ceramic tile 150.00

WALLS

Remove mildew and treat surface 25.00
Repair hole in wall 55.00
Repaint (per wall/ceiling) 20.00

Cover crayon/marker/pen marks 35.00
Remove wallpaper 145.00

DOORS

Repair hole in hollow core door 55.00
Replace door (inside) 155.00
Replace sliding glass door 475.00

Repair forced door damage 75.00
Replace door (outside) 285.00
Replace sliding door screen 55.00

ELECTRICAL

Replace light bulb 2.50
Replace light fixture 55.00
Replace electrical cover plate 1.50

Replace light fixture globe 12.00
Replace electrical outlet/switch 5.00

PLUMBING

Replace kitchen faucet 95.00
Replace shower head 24.00
Replace toilet seat 12.00
Replace garbage disposer 125.00
Clear sewer/cesspool line 85.00

Replace bathroom faucet 85.00
Replace toilet tank lid 25.00
Replace toilet 165.00
Snake Toilet 25.00

WINDOWS & TREATMENTS

Replace window pane 75.00
Replace window shade 15.00

Replace Venetian blind 75.00
Replace window screen 20.00

LOCKS

Replace key 5.00
Replace passage door lock 18.00

Replace door lock 37.00
Replace deadbolt lock 18.00

GENERAL REPAIRS

Replace refrigerator shelf 25.00
Repair ceramic tile 150.00
Replace cutting board 40.00
Replace mirror 45.00
Replace towel bar 22.00
Re-grout bath/shower tiles 165.00
Replace thermostat 75.00
Remove junk and debris 250.00
Replace doorbell unit 50.00

Replace stove/oven knob 16.00
Replace countertop 275.00
Replace kit/bth cabinet knobs 10.00
Replace medicine cabinet 85.00
Replace tub/shower enclosure 195.00
Repair porcelain 135.00
Replace fire extinguisher 35.00
Replace doorbell button 5.00
Replace Garage door (each) 525.00

ANNUAL RENT INCREASE REMINDER

Date: _____

Dear _____,

Address:_____

_____

Your rent is due to increase as agreed in your lease. As of _____ your new rent amount will be $_____ per month. Early payment discounts as agreed will remain in effect.

Important Information for New Residence

Welcome! We wish you health and happiness in your new home. Listed below please find helpful information relating to your new residence.

Management : _____   Oil Co: _____

Police : _____   Water Co. : _____

Ambulance : _____   Telephone : _____

Fire Dept. : _____   Cable TV : _____

Electric Co: _____   Landscaper : _____

Gas Co : _____   Sanitation Dept. _____

Other Helpful Numbers

Plumber : _____   Sewer/Cesspool : _____

Carpet Cleaner: _____   Cleaning Service : _____

Household Safety Information

Location of Fire Extinguisher(s) : _____

Location of Smoke Detector(s) : _____

Location of Circuit Breaker Panel _____

Location of Water Shut Off Valve _____

Location of Oil Tank _____

Days of Garbage Pick-up _____

Days of Recycle _____

TENANT'S NOTICE TO VACATE

To: _____ Date: _____

Please take notice of our intention to vacate our residence located at

_____ on or before _____.

The reason we are moving is :_____

We understand that our deposit will be refunded as agreed, less past due unpaid charges, if any, after we have moved out completely and returned possession of the premises to the management, as long as we leave the residence in clean and undamaged condition.

We understand that our Lease/Rental Agreement states that we have agreed to a _____ day written notice to vacate. We understand that we are responsible for paying rent through the end of the term agreed to in the Lease/Rental Agreement or until another tenant is approved by the management and has taken occupancy, whichever happens first. As we have agreed in our Lease/Rental Agreement, we will make the premises accessible to show to prospective tenants or purchasers at any and all reasonable times, whether we are present or not.

Please Return Deposits to our new address at:_____

_____

We would like to request a reference from you.   _____

Thank you, but we do not need a reference.   _____

Tenant: _____

Tenant: _____

LETTER TO TENANT
MOVE-OUT REMINDER

Dear Tenant,

Thank you for giving us advanced notice that you are moving. Now that you are moving out, your lease/rental agreement requires that you leave your unit in a clean and undamaged condition. We have every intention of returning all of your security deposit, as long as you have fulfilled your agreement with us.

Specifically, you should:

- ☐ **Cooperate with the showing of the residence for sale or re-rental, keeping it in presentable condition.**
- ☐ **Begin to put out all unwanted items for trash or special pick-up. (Avoid piles of debris in front of your home on moving day.)**
- ☐ **Remove all food, debris, and other personal belongings.**
- ☐ **Clean (and defrost if necessary) refrigerator.**
- ☐ **Clean stovetop, oven and any other appliances.**
- ☐ **Replace any burned out light bulbs.**
- ☐ **Clean all floors and/or carpeting.**
- ☐ **Be sure grounds and lawn are trim and clean, free of weeds, leaves, etc.**
- ☐ **Report any and all damage in writing.**
- ☐ **Upon leaving, please be sure to fully secure the rental by locking all windows and doors.**
  The designated place to leave all keys to your unit is _____.

After you have vacated the rental, it will be inspected for compliance with your lease/rental agreement and the expense of cleaning or repairing damage, if any, will be charged against your security deposit. You will be notified of any charges.

Good luck in your new home.

Sincerely,

Sample Lease Agreement (IL)

THIS LEASE AGREEMENT (hereinafter referred to as the "Agreement") made and entered into this _____ day of _____, 20____, by and between _____ (hereinafter referred to as "Landlord") and _____ (hereinafter referred to as "Tenant").

WITNESSETH:

WHEREAS, Landlord is the fee owner of certain real property being, lying and situated in _____ County, Illinois, such real property having a street address of _____ (hereinafter referred to as the "Premises").

WHEREAS, Landlord desires to lease the Premises to Tenant upon the terms and conditions as contained herein; and

WHEREAS, Tenant desires to lease the Premises from Landlord on the terms and conditions as contained herein;

NOW, THEREFORE, for and in consideration of the covenants and obligations contained herein and other good and valuable consideration, the receipt and sufficiency of which is hereby acknowledged, the parties hereto hereby agree as follows:

1. **TERM.** Landlord leases to Tenant and Tenant leases from Landlord the above described Premises together with any and all appurtenances thereto, for a term of _____ [specify number of months or years], such term beginning on _____, and ending at 11:59 PM on _____.

2. **RENT.** The total rent for the term hereof is the sum of _____ DOLLARS ($_____) payable on the _____ day of each month of the term, in equal installments of _____ DOLLARS ($_____), first and last installments to be paid upon the due execution of this Agreement, the second installment to be paid on _____. All such payments shall be made to Landlord at Landlord's address as set forth in the preamble to this Agreement on or before the due date and without demand.

3. **SECURITY DEPOSIT**. Upon the due execution of this Agreement, Tenant shall deposit with Landlord the sum of _____
DOLLARS ($_____) receipt of which is hereby acknowledged by Landlord, as security for any damage caused to the Premises during the term hereof.

Interest on Security Deposit. In accordance with Illinois law (765 ILCS 715/1, 715/2), and subject to the exception set forth in this Paragraph, such deposit shall be returned to Tenant, without interest, and less any set off for damages to the Premises upon the termination of this Agreement. Landlord will only pay interest to Tenant if the Premises is an apartment in a building with 25 or more units, provided the security deposit is held by Landlord for more than six (6) months. The interest rate is to be the same rate as given by the largest bank in Illinois on minimum passbook savings accounts as of December 31 of the year before the commencement date of this Agreement. Landlord shall pay Tenant the accrued interest annually by cash or credit towards rent due, except when Tenant is in default under the Agreement.

Timing of Return of Security Deposit. If Landlord withholds some or all of Tenant's Security Deposit, Landlord will notify Tenant within thirty (30) days after the end of the lease Term, and Landlord will include an itemized list of damages and the actual or estimated cost of repairs. Otherwise, if no part of the security deposit is withheld, Landlord will return Tenant's security deposit to Tenant within forty-five (45) days after the end of Tenant's lease Term.

4. **USE OF PREMISES**. The Premises shall be used and occupied by Tenant and Tenant's immediate family, consisting of _____
_____ _____, exclusively, as a private single family dwelling, and no part of the Premises shall be used at any time during the term of this Agreement by Tenant for the purpose of carrying on any business, profession, or trade of any kind, or for any purpose other than as a private single family dwelling. Tenant shall not allow any other person, other than Tenant's immediate family or transient relatives and friends who are guests of Tenant, to use or occupy the Premises without first obtaining Landlord's written consent to such use. Tenant shall comply with any and all laws, ordinances, rules and orders of any and all governmental or quasi-governmental authorities affecting the cleanliness, use, occupancy and preservation of the Premises.

5. **CONDITION OF PREMISES.** Tenant stipulates, represents and warrants that Tenant has examined the Premises, and that they are at the time of this Lease in good order, repair, and in a safe, clean and tenantable condition.

6. **ASSIGNMENT AND SUB-LETTING.** Tenant shall not assign this Agreement, or sub-let or grant any license to use the Premises or any part thereof without the prior written consent of Landlord. A consent by Landlord to one such assignment, sub-letting or license shall not be deemed to be a consent to any subsequent assignment, sub-letting or license. An assignment, sub-letting or license without the prior written consent of Landlord or an assignment or sub-letting by operation of law shall be absolutely null and void and shall, at Landlord's option, terminate this Agreement.

7. **ALTERATIONS AND IMPROVEMENTS.** Tenant shall make no alterations to the buildings or improvements on the Premises or construct any building or make any other improvements on the Premises without the prior written consent of Landlord. Any and all alterations, changes, and/or improvements built, constructed or placed on the Premises by Tenant shall, unless otherwise provided by written agreement between Landlord and Tenant, be and become the property of Landlord and remain on the Premises at the expiration or earlier termination of this Agreement.

8. **NON-DELIVERY OF POSSESSION.** In the event Landlord cannot deliver possession of the Premises to Tenant upon the commencement of the Lease term, through no fault of Landlord or its agents, then Landlord or its agents shall have no liability, but the rental herein provided shall abate until possession is given. Landlord or its agents shall have thirty (30) days in which to give possession, and if possession is tendered within such time, Tenant agrees to accept the demised Premises and pay the rental herein provided from that date. In the event possession cannot be delivered within such time, through no fault of Landlord or its agents, then this Agreement and all rights hereunder shall terminate.

9. **HAZARDOUS MATERIALS.** Tenant shall not keep on the Premises any item of a dangerous, flammable or explosive character that might unreasonably increase the danger of fire or explosion on the Premises or that might be considered hazardous or extra hazardous by any responsible insurance company.

10. **UTILITIES.** Tenant shall be responsible for arranging for and paying for all utility services required on the Premises.

11. **MAINTENANCE AND REPAIR; RULES.** Tenant will, at its sole expense, keep and maintain the Premises and appurtenances in good and sanitary

condition and repair during the term of this Agreement and any renewal thereof. Without limiting the generality of the foregoing, Tenant shall:

(a) Not obstruct the driveways, sidewalks, courts, entry ways, stairs and/or halls, which shall be used for the purposes of ingress and egress only;

(b) Keep all windows, glass, window coverings, doors, locks, and hardware in good, clean order and repair;

(c) Not obstruct or cover the windows or doors;

(d) Not leave windows or doors in an open position during any inclement weather;

(e) Not hang any laundry, clothing, sheets, etc. from any window, rail, porch or balcony nor air or dry any of same within any yard area or space;

(f) Not cause or permit any locks or hooks to be placed upon any door or window without the prior written consent of Landlord;

(g) Keep all air conditioning filters clean and free from dirt;

(h) Keep all lavatories, sinks, toilets, and all other water and plumbing apparatus in good order and repair and shall use same only for the purposes for which they were constructed. Tenant shall not allow any sweepings, rubbish, sand, rags, ashes or other substances to be thrown or deposited therein. Any damage to any such apparatus and the cost of clearing stopped plumbing resulting from misuse shall be borne by Tenant;

(i) And Tenant's family and guests shall at all times maintain order in the Premises and at all places on the Premises, and shall not make or permit any loud or improper noises, or otherwise disturb other residents;

(j) Keep all radios, television sets, stereos, phonographs, etc., turned down to a level of sound that does not annoy or interfere with other residents;

(k) Deposit all trash, garbage, rubbish or refuse in the locations provided therefor and shall not allow any trash, garbage, rubbish or refuse to be deposited or permitted to stand on the exterior of any building or within the common elements;

(l) Abide by and be bound by any and all rules and regulations affecting the Premises or the common area appurtenant thereto which may be adopted or promulgated by the Condominium or Homeowners' Association having control over them.

12. **DAMAGE TO PREMISES**. In the event the Premises are destroyed or rendered wholly uninhabitable by fire, storm, earthquake, or other casualty not caused by the negligence of Tenant, this Agreement shall terminate from

such time except for the purpose of enforcing rights that may have then accrued hereunder. The rental provided for herein shall then be accounted for by and between Landlord and Tenant up to the time of such injury or destruction of the Premises, Tenant paying rentals up to such date and Landlord refunding rentals collected beyond such date. Should a portion of the Premises thereby be rendered uninhabitable, the Landlord shall have the option of either repairing such injured or damaged portion or terminating this Lease. In the event that Landlord exercises its right to repair such uninhabitable portion, the rental shall abate in the proportion that the injured parts bears to the whole Premises, and such part so injured shall be restored by Landlord as speedily as practicable, after which the full rent shall recommence and the Agreement continue according to its terms.

13. **INSPECTION OF PREMISES**. Landlord and Landlord's agents shall have the right at all reasonable times during the term of this Agreement and any renewal thereof to enter the Premises for the purpose of inspecting the Premises and all buildings and improvements thereon. And for the purposes of making any repairs, additions or alterations as may be deemed appropriate by Landlord for the preservation of the Premises or the building. Landlord and its agents shall further have the right to exhibit the Premises and to display the usual "for sale", "for rent" or "vacancy" signs on the Premises at any time within forty-five (45) days before the expiration of this Lease. The right of entry shall likewise exist for the purpose of removing placards, signs, fixtures, alterations or additions, that do not conform to this Agreement or to any restrictions, rules or regulations affecting the Premises.

14. **SUBORDINATION OF LEASE**. This Agreement and Tenant's interest hereunder are and shall be subordinate, junior and inferior to any and all mortgages, liens or encumbrances now or hereafter placed on the Premises by Landlord, all advances made under any such mortgages, liens or encumbrances (including, but not limited to, future advances), the interest payable on such mortgages, liens or encumbrances and any and all renewals, extensions or modifications of such mortgages, liens or encumbrances.

15. **TENANT'S HOLD OVER**. If Tenant remains in possession of the Premises with the consent of Landlord after the natural expiration of this Agreement, a new tenancy from month-to-month shall be created between Landlord and Tenant which shall be subject to all of the terms and conditions hereof except that rent shall then be due and owing at _____
DOLLARS ($_____) per month and except that such tenancy shall be terminable upon thirty (30) days written notice served by either party.

16. **SURRENDER OF PREMISES.** Upon the expiration of the term hereof, Tenant shall surrender the Premises in as good a state and condition as they were at the commencement of this Agreement, reasonable use and wear and tear thereof and damages by the elements excepted.

17. **ANIMALS.** Tenant shall be entitled to keep no more than _____ (____) domestic dogs, cats or birds; however, at such time as Tenant shall actually keep any such animal on the Premises, Tenant shall pay to Landlord a pet deposit of _____
DOLLARS ($_____), _____
DOLLARS ($_____) of which shall be non-refundable and shall be used upon the termination or expiration of this Agreement for the purposes of cleaning the carpets of the building.

18. **QUIET ENJOYMENT.** Tenant, upon payment of all of the sums referred to herein as being payable by Tenant and Tenant's performance of all Tenant's agreements contained herein and Tenant's observance of all rules and regulations, shall and may peacefully and quietly have, hold and enjoy said Premises for the term hereof.

19. **INDEMNIFICATION.** Landlord shall not be liable for any damage or injury of or to the Tenant, Tenant's family, guests, invitees, agents or employees or to any person entering the Premises or the building of which the Premises are a part or to goods or equipment, or in the structure or equipment of the structure of which the Premises are a part, and Tenant hereby agrees to indemnify, defend and hold Landlord harmless from any and all claims or assertions of every kind and nature.

20. **DEFAULT.** If Tenant fails to comply with any of the material provisions of this Agreement, other than the covenant to pay rent, or of any present rules and regulations or any that may be hereafter prescribed by Landlord, or materially fails to comply with any duties imposed on Tenant by statute, within seven (7) days after delivery of written notice by Landlord specifying the non-compliance and indicating the intention of Landlord to terminate the Lease by reason thereof, Landlord may terminate this Agreement. If Tenant fails to pay rent when due and the default continues for seven (7) days thereafter, Landlord may, at Landlord's option, declare the entire balance of rent payable hereunder to be immediately due and payable and may exercise any and all rights and remedies available to Landlord at law or in equity or may immediately terminate this Agreement.

21. **LATE CHARGE.** In the event that any payment required to be paid by Tenant hereunder is not made within three (3) days of when due, Tenant shall pay to

Landlord, in addition to such payment or other charges due hereunder, a "late fee" in the amount of _____
DOLLARS ($_____).

22. **ABANDONMENT.** If at any time during the term of this Agreement Tenant abandons the Premises or any part thereof, Landlord may, at Landlord's option, obtain possession of the Premises in the manner provided by law, and without becoming liable to Tenant for damages or for any payment of any kind whatever. Landlord may, at Landlord's discretion, as agent for Tenant, relet the Premises, or any part thereof, for the whole or any part thereof, for the whole or any part of the then unexpired term, and may receive and collect all rent payable by virtue of such reletting, and, at Landlord's option, hold Tenant liable for any difference between the rent that would have been payable under this Agreement during the balance of the unexpired term, if this Agreement had continued in force, and the net rent for such period realized by Landlord by means of such reletting. If Landlord's right of reentry is exercised following abandonment of the Premises by Tenant, then Landlord shall consider any personal property belonging to Tenant and left on the Premises to also have been abandoned, in which case Landlord may dispose of all such personal property in any manner Landlord shall deem proper and Landlord is hereby relieved of all liability for doing so.

23. **ATTORNEYS' FEES.** Should it become necessary for Landlord to employ an attorney to enforce any of the conditions or covenants hereof, including the collection of rentals or gaining possession of the Premises, Tenant agrees to pay all expenses so incurred, including a reasonable attorneys' fee.

24. **RECORDING OF AGREEMENT.** Tenant shall not record this Agreement on the Public Records of any public office. In the event that Tenant shall record this Agreement, this Agreement shall, at Landlord's option, terminate immediately and Landlord shall be entitled to all rights and remedies that it has at law or in equity.

25. **GOVERNING LAW.** This Agreement shall be governed, construed and interpreted by, through and under the Laws of the State of Illinois.

26. **SEVERABILITY.** If any provision of this Agreement or the application thereof shall, for any reason and to any extent, be invalid or unenforceable, neither the remainder of this Agreement nor the application of the provision to other persons, entities or circumstances shall be affected thereby, but instead shall be enforced to the maximum extent permitted by law.

27. **BINDING EFFECT.** The covenants, obligations and conditions herein contained shall be binding on and inure to the benefit of the heirs, legal representatives, and assigns of the parties hereto.

28. **DESCRIPTIVE HEADINGS.** The descriptive headings used herein are for convenience of reference only and they are not intended to have any effect whatsoever in determining the rights or obligations of the Landlord or Tenant.

29. **CONSTRUCTION.** The pronouns used herein shall include, where appropriate, either gender or both, singular and plural.

30. **NON-WAIVER.** No indulgence, waiver, election or non-election by Landlord under this Agreement shall affect Tenant's duties and liabilities hereunder.

31. **MODIFICATION.** The parties hereby agree that this document contains the entire agreement between the parties and this Agreement shall not be modified, changed, altered or amended in any way except through a written amendment signed by all of the parties hereto.

32. **NOTICE.** Any notice required or permitted under this Lease or under state law shall be deemed sufficiently given or served if sent by United States certified mail, return receipt requested, addressed as follows:

If to Landlord to:

_____

[*Landlord*]

_____

_____

[*Landlord's Address*]

If to Tenant to:

_____

[*Tenant*]

_____

_____

[*Tenant's Address*]

Landlord and Tenant shall each have the right from time to time to change the place notice is to be given under this paragraph by written notice thereof to the other party. In addition, Landlord may provide notice to Tenant by posting notice upon the front door of the Premises.

33. ADDITIONAL PROVISIONS; DISCLOSURES.

_____

_____

_____

_____

_____

[Landlord should note above any disclosures about the premises that may be required under Federal or Illinois law, such as known lead-based paint hazards in the Premises. The Landlord should also disclose any flood hazards.]

As to Landlord this _____ **day of** _____, 20_____.

LANDLORD:

Sign: _____ Print: _____

Date: _____

As to Tenant, this _____ **day of** _____, 20_____.

TENANT ("Tenant"):

Sign: _____ Print: _____
Date: _____

TENANT:

Sign: _____ Print: _____

Date: _____

TENANT:

Sign: _____ Print: _____

Date: _____

TENANT:

Sign: _____ Print: _____
Date: _____

RESIDENTIAL LEASE RIDER: "Property Address"

THIS RIDER IS ATTACHED HERETO AS PART OF THE RESIDENTIAL LEASE DATED ___/___/_____ "same date as lease" BETWEEN _____ "renter's name"_____, AS LESSEE, AND _____ "owner's name"_____ AS LESSOR, FOR THE PROPERTY KNOWN AS _____ "property address"_____, City, State Zip code.

1. Lessee hereby agrees to make available in orderly fashion this home for showing for sale or rent to prospective buyers or renters 90 days prior to the termination of this Lease.

2. A security deposit of $_____ will be held at the termination of this Lease until the property has been inspected for damage and missing fixtures or appliances, normal wear and tear excepted. Any bills incurred by Lessee for which Lessor may be held liable may be deducted from said deposit.

3. The final month's rent is due and payable on the first of the month. The security deposit shall be in no way be applied toward the final month's rent.

4. If the rent is not received by Lessor before the first day of the month, an additional $XX late charge shall be due plus a $XX per day charge beyond the first until the rent is paid.

5. Lessee shall allow an inspection of the premises by Lessor upon a 6-hour notice.

6. Lessee agrees to maintain lawn and premises in a condition comparable to other homes in the neighborhood.

7. The following appliances: washer and dryer, ceiling fan in living room, refrigerator, stove, dishwasher, are owned by Lessor. Lessor shall be responsible for the maintenance of these items unless damage is caused to these items by misuse or neglect of Lessee. In the event of misuse or neglect by Lessee, Lessee shall be responsible for the payment of said repairs.

8. It is understood and agreed that only Lessee and their children shall occupy the premises.

9. It is understood and agreed that at the expiration of the Lease Lessee will be charged $XXX for the cleaning of all carpeted areas of the premises. Lessee agrees that this will be deducted from deposit refunded at termination of Lease.

10. It is understood and agreed that Lessee will not take any action which will result in a disturbance to the neighborhood or a call to the police department to remedy any public nuisance on or about the property. In addition, Lessee agrees to abide by the terms of the covenants, conditions and restrictions and any rules established by The "Name of Association" Homeowner's Association. In the event Lessee violates any of the above, at Lessor's option, this shall be reason to cause termination of this lease within ten (10) days after such event.

_____   _____
LESSEE   DATE

_____   _____
LESSEE   DATE

_____   _____
LESSOR   DATE

_____   _____
LESSOR   DATE

Co-Signer Agreement

Date: _____/_____/_____

For value received I _____ (Co-Signer's Name) hereby guaran-
tee the payment of the rent and the performance of the covenants by the lessee
in the attached lease between _____ (lessor/
owner) and _____ (lessee/renter) regarding the property
commonly known as _____
(rental property address). Dated ___/____/_____ covenanted and agreed, in
manner and form as in said lease provided.

Witness my hand and seal this _____ day of _____ 200X.

Co-Signer Signature:

Move-in Check List

Important Numbers

City/Area Number Work Sheet

Service	Account Number	Phone Number	Done
Cable	_____	_____	____
Electric Company.	_____	_____	____
Gas Company	_____	_____	____
Sewer & Water	_____	_____	____

	Items	Received
Your Name	Lease	____/_____
Your Address	By-Laws	____/_____
Your City, State, Zip	Door Keys	____/_____
Home Phone	Dead Bolt Keys	____/_____
Office Phone	Mail Box Keys	____/_____
Cell Phone	Water Softener Inst.	____/_____
	Alarm Inst.	____/_____
	Fire Place Inst.	____/_____
	CO Detector	____/_____
	Smoke Detector	____/_____
	Fire Extinguisher	____/_____
	Garage Door Opener	____/_____

978-0-595-45942-1
0-595-45942-0